FAVORITE RECIPES OF
CALIFORNIA
WINEMAKERS

IN APPRECIATION

Our sincere thanks are extended to the over 200 individuals
who have contributed to this cook book...California
winemakers, their wives and families, their colleagues
and companions, who have shared with us their love of cooking.
They are the authors of this book, which is dedicated to a
simple truth known for thousands of years in
countless countries: that good food is even better with wine.

The assistance of Home Advisory Service of Wine Institute is
gratefully acknowledged. We are particularly pleased by receipt of
favorite recipes and wine choices from staff members of the
Department of Viticulture and Enology and the Department of Food
Science and Technology of University of California where research
and teaching of viticulture (grape growing) and enology (science
of wine making) were established by the State legislature in
1880. The work of the University has contributed greatly to the
high quality of California wines. We express thanks for participation
by staff members of the Department of Viticulture and Enology of
Fresno State College, which started viticulture classes in 1929
and added enology courses in 1949.

WINE ADVISORY BOARD

D. C. TURRENTINE, Manager

FAVORITE RECIPES OF
CALIFORNIA WINEMAKERS

Compiled by
WINE ADVISORY BOARD
SAN FRANCISCO, CALIFORNIA

EDITOR   **ARTIST**   **FOOD CONSULTANTS**

Lee Hecker   Judy Hibel   Marjorie Lumm   Dorothy Canet

Sandra Hancock   Janet Laird

AN ESSANDESS SPECIAL EDITION   NEW YORK · 1968

THE LORE AND LURE OF WINE COOKERY

The use of wine in cooking is surely the happiest—and probably one of the oldest—of mankind's culinary discoveries: almost as old as wine itself.

Homer tells us the earliest civilized Greeks used wine for cooking as well as for quaffing. Later, under the Romans, wine was ever more at home on the range, improving pot roasts, stews, vegetables, sauces. As the basic drink throughout this ancient world, wine was even supplied regularly to slaves, to keep them in good health.

So entwined is the vine in western cultures, spreading northward from the Mediterranean, that by the 18th century we read quite naturally in the early English cook books of lamb marinated in white wine, pears done in Port, wine soup, Sherry-flavored puddings, Isaac Walton's own fish poached in wine, relishes and sauces containing wine and wine vinegar, swan or beef or hare with Claret, and such goodies. Wine flowed freely into the cooking pots of Europe, and its use was important also to many of our own nation's great. George and Martha Washington took pride in the wine cookery and wine service of their household. Thomas Jefferson selected carefully the wine-cooked dishes (as well as wines) for state dinners at the White House. So universal a custom must be soundly based on a more enjoyable cuisine.

Thus cooking with wine cannot be set off as a specialized field of cookery. It is too old a practice, too international, too intrinsic; it is merely the best way to cook. And no collection of wine cookery recipes could ever begin to cover all the marvels of taste created every day from simple dishes when the cook experiments. One of the beauties of wine cookery is that adding wine can only improve a dish. Itself a food, wine inevitably blends with the flavors of other foods. So use whatever wine you have on hand; and try wine in more kinds of dishes. This book shows some of the wide variety possible.

LEE HECKER, Editor

Published by *Essandess Special Editions*, a division of Simon & Schuster Inc.,
630 Fifth Avenue, New York, N.Y. 10020 and on the same day in
Canada by Simon & Schuster of Canada, Ltd., Richmond Hill, Ontario.

Printed in U.S.A.

Library of Congress catalog card number: 63-21635

CONTENTS

Five Wine Classes	Best-Known Types
APPETIZER WINES To enjoy before dinner or as a refreshment anytime	SHERRY VERMOUTH *(vur-mooth)* FLAVORED WINES
RED DINNER WINES	BURGUNDY *Similar Types:* Pinot Noir *(pea-no no-ahr)* Gamay *(ga-may)* Red Pinot *(red pea-no)* CLARET *Similar Types:* Cabernet *(kab-er-nay)* Zinfandel *(zin-fan-dell)* Grignolino *(green-yo-leen-oh)* ROSÉ *(roh-zay)* "VINO" TYPES *(vee-no)* CHIANTI (Red) *(kee-ahn-tee)*
WHITE DINNER WINES	SAUTERNE *(so-tairn)* *Similar Types:* Semillon *(say-mee-yonh)* Sauvignon Blanc *(so-vee-nyonh blanh)* RHINE WINE *Similar Types:* Riesling *(reez-ling)* Traminer *(trah-meen-er)* Sylvaner *(sil-vah-ner)* CHABLIS *(shah-blee)* *Similar Types:* Pinot Blanc *(pea-no blanh)* Pinot Chardonnay *(pea-no shar-doh-nay)* White Pinot *(white pea-no)*
DESSERT WINES To enjoy after dinner or as a refreshment anytime	PORT TOKAY *(toh-kay)* MUSCATEL *(muss-kah-tell)* ANGELICA *(an-jell-ee-cah)* CREAM (SWEET) SHERRY
SPARKLING WINES	CHAMPAGNE *(sham-pain)* (White or Pink) Brut (very dry) *(brewt)* Sec (semi-dry) *(sehk)* Doux (sweet) *(doo)* SPARKLING BURGUNDY

The more popular distinct types are shown above in ALL CAPITAL LETTERS.

WINES AND WINE USES

Type Characteristics			Favorite Uses *
SHERRY: Rich, nutlike flavor; from dry to sweet, pale to dark amber. Sweet or Cream Sherry is more dessert or refreshment wine.	**VERMOUTH:** Spicy, aromatic, herbal flavor. Dry is pale amber or almost colorless, light-bodied. Sweet is darker, medium-bodied.	**FLAVORED WINES:** Smooth, clear, with natural pure flavors added.	*Serve chilled, without food or with* **HORS d'OEUVRE OR SNACKS** Popular in 2½ to 4-ounce servings either straight or "on-the-rocks." Flavored wines are also served as tall mixed drinks.
BURGUNDY: Dry, robust; traditionally fuller-bodied and deeper in color than Claret. Pinot Noir, Red Pinot and Gamay are "varietal" Burgundies, named for their grape varieties. Pinot Noir is especially soft and velvety, with superb bouquet. Gamay is often a little lighter in body and color.	**CLARET:** Dry, tart, zestful; usually light or medium-bodied, ruby red. Cabernet, Zinfandel and Grignolino are varietals, named for their grapes. Zinfandel is fresh and fruity; Grignolino often more like a Rosé. Cabernet differs from most Clarets in its fuller body, deeper, more sumptuous color and bouquet.	**ROSÉ:** Gay pink, fruity, light-bodied, dry or slightly sweet. **"VINO" TYPES** often have Italian names, are mellow, soft in flavor, slightly sweet, quite full. **CHIANTI:** Dry, slightly tart, full-bodied, "Italian" in flavor.	*Serve at cool room temperature, in 6 to 9-ounce glasses, with* **STEAKS, ROASTS, CHOPS, CHEESES OR SPAGHETTI** Also good as part of the liquid in stews, pot roasts; in marinating economy meats; and in making delicious wine jellies and punches. *(Exception is Rosé or pink: serve chilled, with all foods.)*
SAUTERNE: Golden-hued, full-bodied, fragrant, ranging from dry to sweet. Semillon (dry or sweet) and Sauvignon Blanc (usually dry) are varietal Sauternes, named for their grapes. Haut Sauterne is sweet, with delightfully rich aroma. This type is also popular as a dessert wine.	**RHINE WINE:** Thoroughly dry, tart, with flowery bouquet, light body; pale or green-gold in color. Rieslings are Rhine-type varietals, delicate in flavor, usually named for their grapes, such as Johannisberg (White) Riesling or Grey Riesling. (Sylvaner is a Franken Riesling.) Traminer is another varietal, spicy, fresh.	**CHABLIS:** Soft, dry, less tart and fuller-bodied than Rhine Wines. The delicately flavored and smoothly aristocratic Pinots are the best-known varietals, named for the grape varieties from which they are made.	*Serve well chilled, in 6 to 9-ounce glasses, with* **SEAFOODS, CHICKEN, OMELETS OR OTHER LIGHT DISHES** Also used in cooking fish, white meats; and in making punches.
PORT: All Ports are rich, sweet, fruity, fairly full-bodied. They may be deep red, white (pale gold) or tawny (autumn-leaf color). The red is usually heavier-bodied.	**MUSCATEL:** Sweet, fruity, full-bodied, with the pronounced flavor and aroma of Muscat grapes. Color may range from golden and dark amber to red.	**TOKAY:** Pinkish amber, with slightly "nutty" or Sherry-like flavor. Less sweet than Port. **ANGELICA:** Straw or amber-colored. Very sweet, resembling White Port.	*Serve chilled or at cool room temperature, in 2½ to 4-ounce servings, with* **FRUITS, COOKIES, NUTS OR CHEESES** Also used in cooking, like basting ham or making wine jellies; or poured over fruit desserts.
CHAMPAGNE: Gay, festive, naturally effervescent. Ranges from very dry ("brut") to semi-dry ("sec") to sweet ("doux"). The pink is sometimes called Sparkling Rosé.	**SPARKLING BURGUNDY:** Ruby-red, sweet or semi-sweet, fruity, gay and bubbling, from the same type of natural secondary fermentation that produces Champagne.		*Serve well chilled, in 5 to 9-ounce glasses. Good with all foods:* **APPETIZERS, MAIN COURSE OR DESSERTS** And especially fine for festive "special occasion" punches.

Most people prefer the combinations shown in the right-hand column. But the "correct" wine is the one YOU like best.

When you want to try California wine in your own recipes, this quick-reference chart will serve as a "safe" general guide to the wine type and amount to be added. However, there are no hard-and-fast rules. Don't be afraid to experiment. It's easy, rewarding and fun — and can make you famous with your friends!

WINE COOKERY CHART

	FOODS	AMOUNT	WINES
SAUCES	Cream Sauce	1 T. per cup	Sherry or Sauterne
	Brown Sauce	1 T. per cup	Sherry or Burgundy
	Tomato Sauce	1 T. per cup	Sherry or Burgundy
	Cheese Sauce	1 T. per cup	Sherry or Sauterne
	Dessert Sauce	1 T. per cup	Port or Muscatel
MEATS	Pot Roast	¼ cup per lb.	Burgundy
	Gravy for Roasts	2 T. per cup	Burgundy, Sauterne or Sherry
	Stew — Beef	¼ cup per lb.	Burgundy
	Stew — Lamb or Veal	¼ cup per lb.	Sauterne
	Ham, Baked	2 cups (for basting)	Port or Muscatel
	Liver, Braised	¼ cup per lb.	Burgundy or Sauterne
	Tongue, Boiled	½ cup per lb.	Burgundy
FISH	Broiled, Baked or Poached	½ cup per lb.	Sauterne
POULTRY AND GAME	Chicken	¼ cup per lb.	Sauterne or Burgundy
	Gravy for Roast or Fried Chicken, Turkey	2 T. per cup	Sauterne, Burgundy or Sherry
	Duck, Roasted	¼ cup per lb.	Burgundy
	Venison	¼ cup per lb.	Burgundy
	Pheasant	¼ cup per lb.	Sauterne, Burgundy or Sherry
FRUIT Fresh, Canned or Frozen	In syrup or juice (Fruit cups, compotes, etc.)	2 T. per cup *over fruit or in syrup or juice*	Port, Muscatel, Sherry, Rosé, Sauterne or Burgundy
	(or) Drained	*At the table, pour over fruits without dilution*	Champagne or other Sparkling Wines

NOTE: Where Sauterne is suggested above, any California white dinner wine, such as Rhine or Chablis, may be substituted. Where Burgundy is suggested, any red dinner wine may be used instead, such as California Claret or Zinfandel.

(T = TABLESPOON)

HORS D'OEUVRES

At cocktail time, wine itself, alone, can serve as appetizer. The nutlike tang of a chilled California Sherry, or the piquancy of a Vermouth or flavored wine on-the-rocks, can make the dinner to follow even more enjoyable. But a few nibbles or snacks are also often desirable. These appetizers can be the simplest. Even cheese spread out of a jar has a festive flavor when it has been mixed with wine in the kitchen — and served with wine in the living room. Wine-flavored cheese spreads are also delightful as a dessert or any-hour refreshment, served with fruit and California Port (or with other dessert wines).

CARAWAY CHEESE LOG

(1-lb. log; about 20 servings)

C. E. Gibson, Weibel Champagne Vineyards, Mission San Jose

- 1 (8-oz.) pkg. cream cheese
- ⅓ cup California Sauterne, Rhine or other white dinner wine
- ½ lb. Jack or Swiss cheese, grated
- 1 tablespoon caraway seed
- 1 (2½-oz.) jar shredded Parmesan cheese

Beat cream cheese until soft; blend in wine. Add Jack cheese and caraway seed. Sprinkle layer of Parmesan cheese in an unfolded 1-lb. butter carton; spoon the caraway-cheese mixture over Parmesan cheese to form brick. Pat top and sides of brick with remaining Parmesan cheese. Close butter carton; chill until firm enough to slice (about 1 hour). Garnish with chopped parsley, if desired. Serve with crackers.

NOTE: *This is a soft, creamy cheese mixture, and may be packed into any suitable container, or rolled up in foil, to chill. Served with California Champagne, it would be a delightful hors d'oeuvre for a festive dinner.*

STUFFED CELERY is better than ever when the cheese stuffing is blended from a jar cheese spread and California wine. Try White Port, Port or Sherry with Cheddar or American; Claret or Burgundy with blue cheese; and Chablis or Sauterne with pimiento. Usual proportion: 2 tablespoons wine to each 5-oz. jar. Thinned down still more with wine, these cheeses also provide enjoyable dips for potato chips or crackers. It's fun to provide an assortment of several flavors.

GOLD COAST NUGGETS

(About 36 cubes)

Mrs. Stanley Strud, California Wine Association, Lodi

- 2 (5-oz.) jars Cheddar cheese spread
- ¼ cup California Sherry
- 2 tablespoons mayonnaise
- ½ teaspoon Worcestershire sauce
  Salt
  Dash of cayenne pepper
- 36 (1-inch) bread cubes (approximately) (see below)
  Paprika

Place cheese spread in mixing bowl; gradually blend in Sherry. Add mayonnaise, Worcestershire sauce, salt and cayenne; mix well. With a fork, dip each cube into cheese mixture, coating all but one side. Place cubes, uncoated side down, on greased baking sheet. Sprinkle with paprika. Broil until delicately browned. Serve hot.

TO MAKE BREAD CUBES: remove crusts from unsliced loaf of sandwich bread. Cut bread in 1-inch slices; cut each slice into 1-inch squares.

NOTE: *A refreshing change at hors d'oeuvre time, and ideally teamed with chilled California Sherry.*

3-CHEESE RING WITH FRUIT

(1 quart mold)

Philo P. Biane, Assumption Abbey Winery, Guasti

> 1 lb. Cheddar cheese, grated
> ½ lb. Jack cheese, grated
> 4 oz. blue cheese
> ½ cup mayonnaise
> ¼ cup California Sherry
> ¼ teaspoon curry powder
> ½ teaspoon grated lemon rind
> Melon balls (cantaloupe, Persian, honeydew) or other bite-size pieces of fruit

Combine grated Cheddar and Jack cheeses with crumbled blue cheese and mayonnaise; beat until blended thoroughly. Beat in Sherry, curry and lemon rind. Pack into buttered 1-quart tube mold. Chill, covered, in refrigerator several hours or overnight, so that mold becomes firm and flavors blended. Turn out onto serving dish. Fill center of mold with melon balls or other fruit. Serve with crackers, for a dessert or evening refreshment.

My choice of wine to accompany this dish:
CALIFORNIA PORT OR OTHER DESSERT WINE

HERBED CHEESE SPREAD CHABLIS

(3 cups)

Keith V. Nylander, Di Giorgio Wine Company, Di Giorgio

> ½ lb. Port d' Salut or Jack cheese
> 2 (8-oz.) pkgs. cream cheese
> 1 (2½-oz.) jar shredded Parmesan cheese
> ½ teaspoon crumbled dry marjoram
> ½ teaspoon dried dill
> ½ teaspoon hickory smoke salt or seasoned salt
> 3 tablespoons soft butter
> ½ cup California Chablis or other white dinner wine
> Crisp crackers and fresh grapes

Grate very finely the Port d' Salut or Jack cheese; soften cream cheese. Combine all cheese with herbs, salt and soft butter. Beat until well blended. Beat in wine until mixture is quite smooth. Pack into lightly oiled 3-cup mold. Cover and chill in refrigerator several hours or overnight, until mold firms and flavors mellow. Turn out on serving platter; surround with crisp crackers and tiny bunches of fresh grapes. Serve as a refreshment anytime or dessert.

My choice of wine to accompany this dish:
A MELLOW CALIFORNIA PORT

LODI BLUE CHEESE DIP

(About 1 cup)

Mrs. Alvin Ehrhardt, United Vintners, Inc., Lodi

> 2 oz. blue cheese
> 2 (3-oz.) pkgs. cream cheese
> California Dry Sherry

Combine cheeses in bowl; soften with Sherry; mix thoroughly. Let stand several hours before serving.

NOTE: A perfect example of the great ease of blending cheeses with wine for a more tantalizing flavor. Another good blend is used by Mrs. Reginald Gianelli of East-Side Winery, Lodi, who mixes Sherry with a sharp Cheddar cheese spread (from a jar) until dipping consistency is reached, for either crackers or potato chips. Any appetizer wine would be good with these dips—chilled California Sherry or Vermouth, or a flavored wine on-the-rocks.

MODESTO CHEESE MASTERPIECE

(About 2 cups)

Mrs. Charles M. Crawford, E. & J. Gallo Winery, Modesto

This makes a good cheese spread for a snack anytime, or before dinner.

> 1 lb. ripe Camembert cheese
> ½ cup California Dry Sherry
> 1 lb. unsalted butter
> 3 tablespoons dry bread crumbs

Remove rind from cheese, press into bowl and cover with Sherry; let stand in cool place overnight. Cream unsalted butter in a warm bowl. Drain Sherry from cheese and reserve. Mash the cheese with fork, add butter and blend thoroughly. Blend in Sherry; place bowl in refrigerator about an hour, or until cheese sets. Immerse bowl to rim in warm water to unmold neatly onto serving plate. Garnish with dry bread crumbs, and serve with melba toast or crackers.

My choice of wine to accompany this dish:
CALIFORNIA PALE DRY COCKTAIL SHERRY

NOTE: Chopped toasted almonds would also be an interesting garnish for this sophisticated mixture.

CHRISTMAS CHEESE BALL

(1 ball, about 3" diameter)

Mrs. Pete Peters, Fresno

This may be made up several days ahead and refrigerated, with the rolling in chipped beef (if desired) done just before serving. It's good anytime guests serve themselves: as a prelude to dinner, or on a buffet. I usually double the recipe, for a larger-size cheese ball.

    ½ lb. Cheddar cheese, grated
    1 (3-oz.) package cream cheese
    ¼ cup California Sherry
    ¼ cup coarsely chopped pitted black olives
    ½ teaspoon Worcestershire sauce
       Dash each: Onion, garlic and celery salts
    ½ cup coarsely snipped dried beef (optional)

Have cheeses at room temperature. In large bowl, combine cheeses, Sherry, olives, Worcestershire sauce and salts; mix with electric beater at medium speed. Shape mixture into a ball; wrap in foil; refrigerate until needed. Before serving, remove foil and roll ball in dried beef.

NOTE: The dried beef would be an attractive finishing touch for a Christmas cocktail party. The recipe would be perfect any time of year, however; the cheese ball could also be rolled in finely chopped parsley, sesame seeds or caraway seeds. Chilled California Sherry would be an appetizing accompaniment.

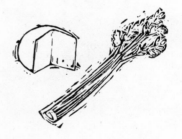

ANCHOVY WINE CHEESE SPREAD

(About 1½ cups)

Peter Scagliotti, Live Oaks Winery, Gilroy

    1 (2-oz.) can anchovies, drained
    2 (8-oz.) pkgs. cream cheese
    ¼ cup California Sherry
    2 tablespoons finely chopped
       stuffed green olives

Mash drained anchovies. Soften cheese and blend into fish. Beat in Sherry until mixture is smooth. Add olives. Cover and chill several hours to blend flavors. When ready to serve, pile into bowl and place bowl in cracked ice, if desired. Garnish spread with strips of anchovy and pimiento and top with a stuffed green olive. (Or, sprinkle with finely chopped green onion or chopped hard-cooked egg.) Serve as an appetizer with buffet rye bread or crackers.

My choice of wine to accompany this dish:
CHILLED CALIFORNIA SHERRY OR DRY VERMOUTH
ON-THE-ROCKS, OR CHAMPAGNE

SHERRIED CLAM-CHEESE DIP

(About 2 cups)

Mrs. Julius Jacobs, Wine Institute, San Francisco

    1 (8-oz.) can minced clams, undrained
    1 (8-oz.) pkg. cream cheese
    ¼ cup California Dry Sherry
       Worcestershire sauce
       Paprika

Drain clams, reserving liquid; chop clams very fine. Soften cheese; thin with clam juice and Sherry. Add clams, Worcestershire sauce and paprika. Mix well; chill.

My choice of wine to accompany this dish:
CHILLED CALIFORNIA CHABLIS, ROSÉ OR SHERRY

TUNA RAREBIT DIP

(About 3½ cups)

Mrs. Peter Mirassou, Mirassou Vineyards, San Jose

    1 (8-oz.) package process Cheddar cheese
    ⅓ cup California Sherry
    ⅓ cup evaporated milk
    1 (10½-oz.) can condensed tomato soup
    3 strips bacon, crisp cooked
    2 (7-oz.) cans tuna, drained and flaked

Slice cheese into top of double boiler; melt cheese over boiling water. Blend in Sherry, milk and soup. Crumble crisp bacon; add with tuna to cheese mixture. Serve hot in chafing or warming dish with cubes of French bread for dipping. Or, fill bite-size cream puffs or pastry shells with the mixture; heat through in moderate oven (350°).

NOTE: Would be appetizing with a chilled California Sherry or Vermouth on-the-rocks.

THE TUNA-SHERRY CAPER

(About 3 cups)

Jessica McLachlin Greengard, Public Relations, Wines & Food

Serve this as a dip with chips, melba toast, crisp crackers or raw vegetables.

1 (8-oz.) package cream cheese
3 tablespoons mayonnaise
5 tablespoons California Sherry
2 (6 or 7-oz.) cans chunk-style tuna
3 tablespoons capers
3 tablespoons chopped parsley
1 teaspoon Worcestershire sauce
½ teaspoon *each:* garlic salt
and onion salt
Dash Tabasco sauce
Paprika

Mash cheese with fork; blend in mayonnaise. Gradually blend in Sherry, beating until smooth. Add the remaining ingredients; mix well. Heap in bowl; chill several hours. Dust with paprika.

My choice of wine to accompany this dish:
CALIFORNIA SHERRY

HOT CRAB HORS D'OEUVRE

(16 servings)

Tony Kahmann, Wine Public Relations Consultant

½ cup butter
4 small onions, minced
1 lb. sharp Cheddar processed
cheese, cubed
¾ cup catsup
¼ cup Worcestershire sauce
Cayenne pepper
4 (7-oz.) cans crabmeat, drained
¼ cup California Sherry
Crackers or melba toast

In blazer or top pan of chafing dish, over direct heat, melt butter and sauté onions slightly. Add cheese; stir until melted. Blend in catsup, Worcestershire sauce, cayenne and drained crabmeat. When hot, add Sherry. Set blazer over hot water to keep warm. On individual serving plates, put crackers or melba toast. Spoon hot crab mixture over and serve with a fork. Thin mixture with additional Sherry if it becomes too thick. Makes about 5 cups.

NOTE: *Your favorite California appetizer wine could be served with this. A Dry Vermouth on-the-rocks would be particularly good with it. Tony says the recipe is extremely simple to make and serve; guests always enjoy it.*

MOLDED CRAB CANAPÉS are an easy do-ahead party pleaser. To make 36 to 40: Soften 2 envelopes unflavored gelatin in ⅓ cup California Sherry 5 minutes; then dissolve in top of double boiler, over hot water. Cool. Blend 1 cup mayonnaise, 2 tablespoons chili sauce, 1 teaspoon lemon juice and 2 tablespoons chopped parsley. Stir in cooled gelatin mixture. Fold in ½ cup heavy cream, whipped; add salt and pepper to taste. Chill until mixture begins to thicken, then fold in 1 (6½-oz.) can crabmeat, flaked, **or** 1 cup fresh crabmeat. Spoon mixture into 4 (5-oz.) cheese glasses, lightly oiled. Chill several hours or overnight. Just before serving, unmold and slice in thin slices, to top toast rounds or crackers.

SONOMA SHRIMP-CRAB DIP

(About 2½ cups)

Rod Strong, Windsor Winery, Windsor

1 cup mayonnaise
1 teaspoon instant minced onion
¼ teaspoon Worcestershire sauce
2 tablespoons finely chopped green pepper
¼ cup California Sherry
1 (6½-oz.) can crabmeat
1 (4½-oz.) can shrimp

Combine all ingredients, stirring lightly. Serve chilled with crisp crackers.

My choice of wine to accompany this dish:
CALIFORNIA JOHANNISBERG RIESLING

SHRIMP COCKTAIL SAUCE or dip (great also for crabmeat or lobster) blends 1 cup bottled cocktail sauce with ⅓ cup California Claret or other red dinner wine, ¼ cup cream, 1 teaspoon lemon juice and salt to taste. This makes about 1⅔ cups for zestful dipping.

HOT SHRIMP APPETIZER

(6 to 8 servings)

Esther Gowans, Glen Ellen Winery & Distillery, Glen Ellen

1½ lbs. raw shrimp or prawns
¼ cup California Dry Sherry
¼ cup butter or margarine
½ teaspoon garlic salt
¼ cup grated Parmesan cheese

Peel and devein shrimp; place in bowl. Pour over Sherry; marinate several hours. Melt butter in heavy skillet over low heat; add shrimp and Sherry. Sprinkle with garlic salt; simmer 10 to 15 minutes. Just before serving, sprinkle cheese over shrimp; place under broiler for 2 or 3 minutes or until cheese is lightly browned. Serve hot, with cocktail pick in each, and cold Shrimp Sauce on side.

SHRIMP SAUCE: Combine ½ cup mayonnaise, 1 tablespoon tomato paste, 1 teaspoon Worcestershire sauce and 1 teaspoon prepared mustard. Refrigerate until ready to serve.

NOTE: *Different and good. Delectable with any favorite California appetizer wine or Champagne.*

SHRIMP MOUSSE

(6 servings)

Mrs. August Sebastiani, Samuele Sebastiani, Sonoma

This is an excellent hors d'oeuvre to serve before any type of meal, as a cracker spread. It may also be used as a salad.

1½ teaspoons plain gelatin
½ cup cold water
¾ cup California Chablis or other white dinner wine
1 (7-oz.) can shrimp
1 tablespoon chopped onion
1 teaspoon lemon juice
½ teaspoon dry mustard
1 cup mayonnaise
Salt and pepper
Dash cayenne pepper

Soften gelatin in water. Heat wine; stir in gelatin until dissolved. Put remaining ingredients in blender; mix until smooth. Stir in wine mixture; pour into mold. Chill until firm. Unmold on cold platter garnished with lettuce. Decorate with capers and lemon peel, if desired.

NOTE: *A very pleasing flavor. Would be enjoyable with Sherry, Vermouth-on-the-rocks or Champagne.*

EASY LOBSTER CANAPÉS

(About 1½ cups of spread)

Robert S. McKnight, Di Giorgio Wine Company, Di Giorgio

This recipe is a bachelor's delight. You can make it in five minutes and it's wonderful!

⅓ cup mayonnaise
3 or 4 tablespoons California Dry Sherry
Salt and paprika
1 cup canned or fresh cooked lobster meat

Combine all ingredients in mixer or blender; mix well. Chill; serve as a spread, on crackers or toast rounds.

My choice of wine to accompany this dish:
CALIFORNIA CHAMPAGNE COCKTAIL, DRY SHERRY OR VERMOUTH COCKTAIL (DRY OR MIXED WITH SWEET)

CALIFORNIA BOUNTY BOWL combines chilled crab legs, lobster cubes, cooked prawns or shrimp, avocado balls, raw cauliflowerets, green and red pepper strips, and / or tiny red or yellow tomatoes, arranged on serving platter. (Insert wooden cocktail picks as needed.) In center of platter, place bowl of dipping mixture, made as follows: Mix 1 cup mayonnaise wtih ⅓ cup chili sauce and ¼ cup California Sherry. Add 2 tablespoons chopped parsley, 1 teaspoon grated onion, ½ teaspoon Worcestershire sauce and salt to taste. Blend mixture well and chill until serving time.

WINEMAKER COCKTAIL 'BURGERS

(About 4½ dozen)

Richard Norton, Fresno State College Dept. Vitic. & Enology

1 lb. ground beef chuck or round steak
½ cup fine dry bread crumbs
¼ cup California Sherry
¼ cup milk
1 tablespoon instant minced onion or 3 tablespoons finely chopped green or mild onion
1 teaspoon seasoned salt
1 teaspoon seasoned pepper
Heated shortening or oil
4½ dozen tiny biscuits (see below)
Dipping Sauce (see below)

Combine meat with bread crumbs, Sherry, milk, onion, salt and pepper. Mix until well blended. Shape into bite-size meat balls. Cover and refrigerate until ready to use. Sauté meat balls in a little heated shortening or oil, until cooked and nicely browned. Drain on paper towels and keep hot until ready to serve. Serve each meat ball on a tiny biscuit, secured by a toothpick, with Dipping Sauce on the side.

COCKTAIL BISCUITS: Separate biscuits from 8-oz. pkg. refrigerated biscuits. Flatten to about ¼" and cut into tiny biscuits with 1" cutter (or, divide each biscuit into quarters and round up into small balls). Bake in a hot oven (450°) until crisp and nicely browned, about 5 minutes. Makes about 4½ dozen.

DIPPING SAUCE: Blend 1 cup chili sauce or catsup with 2 tablespoons prepared mustard. If thinner sauce is desired, add a little California Sherry. Makes about 1¼ cups sauce.

My choice of wine to accompany this dish:
CALIFORNIA SHERRY OR VERMOUTH

RIPE OLIVES, drained and marinated in California Sherry mixed with a little salad oil, are extra good for before-dinner nibbling. Add a clove of garlic to the marinade, and marinate overnight in the refrigerator. Discard garlic just before serving, and drain off marinade.

NO-FUSS COCKTAIL SPREAD combines deviled ham with California Sherry, blended in seconds. Or, mix deviled ham with cream cheese and moisten with Sauterne.

SONOMA STEAK POT

(8 to 10 servings)

John Pedroncelli, John Pedroncelli Winery, Geyserville

2 lbs. tender beef steak
(cut about 1" thick)
¼ cup butter
1½ teaspoons plain or seasoned salt
⅔ cup California Sauterne or other
white dinner wine, or Rosé
¼ cup catsup
2 teaspoons cornstarch
¼ teaspoon dried dill
Freshly ground black pepper
Assorted Go-Alongs (see below)

Trim all excess fat from meat. Cut steak into bite-size cubes, about ½" thick (should be about 48 cubes). Brown steak quickly in heated butter, turning and sprinkling meat with salt during browning. Do not crowd skillet; meat should brown nicely, just to rare or medium-rare stage. Remove steak cubes to heated chafing dish or other serving dish over a candle-warmer. Blend wine, catsup, cornstarch, dill and pepper to taste; stir into rich pan drippings. Cook and stir until mixture boils and thickens. Pour over steak cubes, stirring to combine meat and sauce. Serve with fondue forks or bamboo picks or other cocktail picks for spearing meat. Each guest spears a piece of meat and dips it into desired Go-Along.

GO-ALONGS: Finely chopped green onion or parsley; toasted sesame seeds; half-and-half mixture of prepared mustard and catsup or chili sauce; sour cream mixed with chopped chutney or canned green chile.

NOTE: *This is a great conversation dish, and one that men particularly like. Good with any appetizer wine: California Sherry, Vermouth or flavored wine over ice.*

PARTY PATÉ

(1 large loaf pan)

Mrs. Jack F. M. Taylor, Mayacamas Vineyards, Napa

1½ lbs. liver (see Note below)
½ cup California Sweet Vermouth
½ cup water
1 (5-oz.) jar sweet pickled onions
¼ lb. boiled ham
1½ cups bacon fat or margarine
2 tablespoons mixed herbs, such as
rosemary, marjoram and basil
4 teaspoons savory salt
¼ cup California brandy
1 small can chopped ripe olives

Slice liver; simmer very gently 15 minutes in Vermouth and water. Meanwhile chop onions and ham very fine. When liver is done, place in blender, adding a little of the cooking liquid as needed for easy blending. (If any liquid is left, save for soup.) Melt fat; combine with liver and all other ingredients; mix well. Press firmly into a large loaf pan lined with waxed paper or saran. Chill until firm. Remove from pan; cut into 4 or 5 small cakes. Wrap each cake and freeze, to be used as needed as a very special hors d'oeuvre. To serve, slice very thin and serve on melba toast or crackers.

NOTE: *Or let guests spread their own; it spreads easily. Wonderful with a dry California Sherry, Vermouth-on-the-rocks or, of course, Champagne. (Mrs. Taylor says that she has made this recipe with many kinds of liver. She prefers venison liver, if available; or, next best, chicken livers. Baby beef, calves or pork liver may also be used.)*

HOT SHERRIED CHICKEN LIVERS

(About 16 livers, for 4 to 8 persons)

J. B. Cella, II, Cella Wineries, Fresno

We enjoy these as hors d'oeuvre at our home during "Champagne Hour" before dinner.

1 pound chicken livers
4 tablespoons butter
½ cup California Dry Sherry or brandy
2 teaspoons chopped parsley
½ teaspoon salt
Few grains pepper

Sauté livers in butter over low heat until brown. Add other ingredients; simmer for 10 minutes. Serve hot with cocktail pick in each piece.

NIPPY WINE-CHEESE SAUCE also provides a good dip for little hot cocktail sausages, or chunks of hot frankfurters. Start with your favorite "store-bought" cheese sauce, and blend in California Sherry to taste, or Claret or Burgundy. Keep sauce hot over a candle-warmer or in chafing dish.

MINIATURE TURKEY TURNOVERS

(48 turnovers)

W. E. Kite, Alta Vineyards Company, Fresno

Prepare pastry crust, using 2 (9-oz.) pkgs. pie crust mix; follow directions on carton. Roll out thin and cut in 3" rounds. Place some Turkey Filling (see below) in center of each round. Moisten edges with water; fold pastry over to form a semi-circle; press edges together and prick tops with fork. Brush tops with milk, for glaze. Bake in hot oven (450°) 15 to 20 minutes. Serve hot.

TURKEY FILLING: Melt 3 tablespoons butter, stir in same amount flour. Add ⅓ cup **each** chicken stock and California Sauterne, or other white dinner wine. Cook, stirring constantly, until mixture boils and thickens. Stir in 1 cup finely chopped cooked or canned turkey (or chicken); ½ cup finely chopped canned or sautéed fresh mushrooms; ¼ cup grated Parmesan cheese; 2 tablespoons chopped parsley; ½ teaspoon **each** lemon juice and Worcestershire sauce; dash of mace; and salt and pepper to taste. Refrigerate until ready to make turnovers.

NOTE: Hot hors d'oeuvre such as these are always favorites. Keep them hot, or bake only half a batch at the start of your party, and the other half later on for a second serving. Wonderful with chilled California Sherry or other appetizer wine.

HOT MINIATURE TURNOVERS such as the above are an international favorite for the Sherry hour. Other fillings, popular in the Latin American version (empanadas), include ground beef moistened with Burgundy; or grated Cheddar cheese moistened with Sherry or Sauterne. Follow same procedure above, and serve very hot, with any chilled California appetizer wine or Champagne.

HOT SEAFOOD TARTLETS (36 total) are also made from a 9-oz. pkg. pie crust mix. Cut unbaked crust in 2½" rounds; fit over **backs** of tins for tiny 2" muffins. Prick pastry and bake in hot oven (450°) 10 to 12 minutes or until lightly brown. Cool and fill with seafood filling, made as follows: Melt 4 tablespoons butter, stir in same amount flour, add ½ cup **each** cream and chicken stock. Stir constantly until mixture boils and thickens, then stir in ½ cup California Sauterne or other white dinner wine. Add ½ cup finely diced celery, 2 tablespoons chopped parsley, ¼ teaspoon grated lemon rind, salt, pepper and paprika to taste. Add 1 cup flaked crabmeat (6½-oz. can) and 1 cup shrimp (5-oz. can). (Cut up shrimp if large.) Fill tartlet shells; bake 10 to 15 minutes at 350° or until hot.

MUSHROOMS MAGNIFIQUE

(About 30 mushrooms)

Marvin B. Jones, Gibson Wine Company, Elk Grove

These are especially nice served in a chafing dish, and the recipe is easy to enlarge in any amount.

    1 (4-oz.) can button mushrooms, **or**
      30 fresh cooked button mushrooms
  ¼ cup butter or margarine
  ⅓ cup California Sherry
    Finely chopped fresh parsley or chives

Drain mushrooms; heat in butter in shallow pan. Add Sherry; simmer gently until liquid is almost completely evaporated. Sprinkle with chopped parsley or chives. Serve hot with cocktail picks.

NOTE: Always a winner at any cocktail-hour gathering. Serve with Vermouth or Sherry on-the-rocks, or California Champagne.

TOASTED MUSHROOM ROLLS are different and delicious. (Make in advance and toast just before serving.) To make filling: Sauté sliced fresh mushrooms in butter, with chopped shallots or finely minced green onion. Add flour to thicken, then equal parts of chicken broth and cream. Cook, stirring constantly, until reduced and thickened, and finally add a few tablespoons California Marsala or Sherry. Mixture should be like a thin paste in consistency. Spread on thin slices of white bread with crusts removed. Roll up, fasten with cocktail picks, and place on buttered cookie sheet. Bake in moderately hot oven (375°) until bread is toasted. Serve hot with glasses of chilled Sherry.

MEATS

Beef, Veal, Pork, Lamb, Variety Meats

Here is probably the most important of wine's many functions in the kitchen: to enrich the flavor of meats, adding subtle new aromas and a succulent tenderness. There's no meat known that cannot easily be improved in some way by a little wine, whether directly applied during cooking, or stirred into the pan drippings to make a wonderful sauce or gravy. And, of course, served **with** a wonderful California wine at the table. (For favored sauce recipes, see the section starting on Page 57. Helpful marinating tips are on Page 90, and a quick-reference cooking chart appears on Page 8.)

BEEF WITH HORSERADISH SAUCE

(8 to 10 servings)

Dr. Emil M. Mrak, University of California, Davis

    4 lbs. top round steak, cut in 1½" cubes
    6 tablespoons butter or margarine
    2 large onions, thinly sliced
    2 teaspoons curry powder
      1-inch square fresh ginger root, pressed,
      or 1 teaspoon ground ginger
    2 tablespoons Worcestershire sauce
    1 teaspoon salt
    ½ teaspoon freshly-ground pepper
    ½ to 1 cup California Sauterne or
      other white dinner wine
    1 cup sour cream
    2 tablespoons prepared horseradish
    2 tablespoons freshly-chopped parsley

Brown meat in 4 tablespoons butter; remove to casserole. Brown onions in remaining 2 tablespoons butter. Add to casserole along with curry powder, ginger, Worcestershire sauce, salt, pepper and wine. Bake, covered, in slow oven (300°) about 3 hours, or until meat is tender. Just before serving, combine sour cream and horseradish; stir into meat along with parsley. Serve on rice.

NOTE: *Mrs. Mrak says her husband always uses fresh ginger, put through a garlic press, for this dish. (Fresh ginger root can be sliced and frozen for use later, a slice at a time.) For an accompanying wine, California Burgundy would be perfect.*

A PRESSURE COOKER works quick magic on stews, for those who are short on cooking time. Cuts out hours. Even faster: canned or frozen stew, heated in oven, and sparked with California red dinner wine for flavor and that personal touch.

BEEF STEW BURGUNDY

(6 servings)

Mrs. Ronald G. Hanson, Di Giorgio Wine Co., Di Giorgio

    5 medium-size onions, peeled and sliced
    2 tablespoons bacon drippings
    3 lbs. lean beef stew meat, cut in 1" cubes
    1½ tablespoons flour
      Salt and pepper
      Pinch each of marjoram and thyme
    ½ cup beef bouillon (canned or
      bouillon-cube broth may be used)
    1 cup California Burgundy, Claret
      or other red dinner wine
    ½ lb. fresh mushrooms, sliced

In a large heavy skillet, sauté onions in bacon drippings until brown. Remove onions. Brown meat on all sides in same drippings, adding a little more fat if necessary. When browned, sprinkle with flour and seasonings. Add bouillon and wine; mix well. Simmer very slowly 3¼ hours. (Add more bouillon or wine as necessary to keep meat barely covered.) Return onions to skillet along with mushrooms; stir well. Simmer 1 hour longer, or just until meat is tender.

NOTE: *Robust rich flavor. To bring out more wine taste, about ¼ cup of wine may be saved out and stirred in just before serving, if desired. Would be marvelous with rice or noodles and any of California's many good red dinner wines accompanying. Beef stew is one of the most popular dishes cooked with red wine. It's a favorite also with Mrs. E. F. Handel of East-Side Winery, Lodi; Mrs. Joseph Roullard of Petri Wineries, Escalon; and W. W. Owen of California Grape Products Corp., Delano.*

BOEUF MIRONTON

(8 servings)

Mrs. Walter H. Sullivan, Jr., Beaulieu Vineyard, Rutherford

This casserole of beef a la Mironton is an old Gascon recipe.

- 1 (4-lb.) piece rump or cross rib of beef
- 3 or 4 carrots
- 7 to 9 medium-size onions
- 1 bay leaf
- 8 to 10 peppercorns
  Butter or margarine
  Salt and pepper
  California Chablis, Sauterne or other
  white dinner wine
  Bread crumbs

Place meat in large container; add carrots, 2 onions, bay leaf and peppercorns. Cover with water; simmer 3 to 4 hours. Skim off foam from time to time. Cool meat in cooking liquid. Remove meat, reserving broth; pick meat to pieces with two forks. (DO NOT CUT!) Thinly slice remaining onions; sauté in butter until golden brown. Mix well with shredded beef; season with salt and pepper. Place in 2 to 3-inch deep baking dish. Measure cooking broth; add an equal amount of wine. Pour into pan in which onions were sautéed. Bring to boiling twice; cook until liquid will cover ¾ of meat and onion mixture (about 5 minutes). Pour liquid over meat; sprinkle generously with bread crumbs; dot with butter. Bake in moderate oven (350°) about 45 minutes. Serve piping hot. Menu might include a jellied consommé with sour cream and caviar; mashed potatoes with the beef casserole; mixed green salad; sliced strawberries and toasted pound cake.

My choice of wine to accompany this dish:
CALIFORNIA BURGUNDY OR ROSÉ

EASY BAKED STEW

(6 to 8 servings)

Diana Herrin, California Growers Wineries, Cutler

- 2 lbs. lean beef stew meat
  Salt, pepper and paprika
- 2 tablespoons dry onion soup mix
- 6 medium-size potatoes
- 8 white boiling onions
- 3 carrots, quartered
- 1 (10½-oz.) can cream of celery soup
- ½ cup water
- ½ cup California Sherry

Season meat with salt, pepper, paprika and onion soup mix. Place meat in Dutch oven; add whole potatoes and onions and quartered carrots. Blend celery soup with water and wine; pour over meat. Cover; bake in slow oven (250 to 300°) for 5 hours.

NOTE: *This is an exceptionally easy recipe, with no browning of meat or watching necessary. For those who like increased wine flavor, a little extra wine could be poured over at the last minute. Would be tops with a hearty California red dinner wine such as Zinfandel, Claret, Burgundy, or a "vino" type, served with the meal.*

VINTNER'S STEW

(6 servings)

Paul Huber, E. & J. Gallo Winery, Fresno

This is one of the easiest of all beef stews. The meat needs no browning before it is baked.

- 2 lbs. stewing beef, cut in 1½" chunks
- 1¼ cups California Burgundy, Claret
  or other red dinner wine
- 2 (10½-oz.) cans condensed consommé,
  undiluted
- 1 teaspoon salt
- ½ teaspoon garlic salt
- ¼ teaspoon pepper
- 1 large onion, sliced
- ½ cup fine dry bread crumbs
- ½ cup sifted all-purpose flour

Combine beef, 1 cup of wine, consomme, salts, pepper and onion in a heavy casserole. Mix flour with crumbs; stir into casserole mixture. Cover; bake in slow oven (300°) for 3 hours, or until meat is tender. Just before serving, stir in remaining ¼ cup wine for additional wine flavor.

My choice of wine to accompany this dish:
CALIFORNIA BURGUNDY OR VIN ROSÉ

ANOTHER TRICK that adds subtle flavor to beef stew is to flame the meat with a little California brandy, just after browning it, before long cooking. Barely warm brandy first, carefully, in double boiler. Ignite and pour over meat. Spoon flaming brandy over meat until flames die out, then proceed with cooking. Two Wine Land cooks favoring this method are Mrs. Harold Berg, U. C. Dept. of Viticulture & Enology, Davis, and Mrs. Joseph Heitz, Heitz Wine Cellar, St. Helena.

STEW WITH POLENTA

(7 servings)

Peter Scagliotti, Live Oaks Winery, Gilroy

For a cold-weather menu, Northern Italy style, this combination is wonderful. First make your favorite wild game stew, or one made of beef or veal. Use at least ¼ cup of California red dinner wine for each pound of meat, and not too many vegetables. Serve stew on top of thick slices of polenta, which is easy to make, as follows:

- 3 quarts cold water
- 4 cups yellow corn meal
- ½ cup butter or margarine
  Olive oil

Bring water to rolling boil in heavy kettle. (Copper kettle is traditional.) Stir corn meal in gradually. Cook over medium heat 1 hour, stirring often to prevent burning. Slice in butter, stirring until absorbed. Reduce heat; cook until very thick. Remove from heat and brush edges of polenta with a little olive oil, by pushing a spatula against side of pot and following with oil. Polenta will then drop out of pan in nice round firm mold. Slice at least 1" thick in 3" squares, to serve under stew. A romaine or endive salad made with good wine vinegar and a half-clove of garlic adds to the delicacy of this meal.

My choice of wine to accompany this dish:
CHILLED CALIFORNIA ROSÉ OR BURGUNDY

BEEF POT PIE

(6 servings)

Mrs. Robert Weaver, U. of Calif. Dept. Viticulture & Enology

2 lbs. round steak, cut in 1-inch cubes
1 teaspoon salt
¼ teaspoon pepper
3 level tablespoons flour
¼ cup olive oil
2 tablespoons butter or margarine
4 cloves unpeeled garlic
1 lb. fresh mushrooms, cut in halves
1 (4-oz.) can green chiles, minced
¼ teaspoon marjoram
½ teaspoon dried dill weed
1 cup California Burgundy or other
   red dinner wine
1 (10½-oz.) can consommé
1 tablespoon California wine vinegar
2 (10-oz.) pkgs. frozen artichoke bottoms or
   hearts, cooked as directed on pkg.
   Parmesan Biscuit Crust (see below)

Sprinkle meat with salt and pepper; roll in flour. In large heavy skillet, heat oil and butter with garlic; brown meat. Remove meat to warm platter; discard garlic. In same skillet, add mushrooms; cover and simmer 7 minutes. Add chiles; return meat to pan. Add marjoram, dill weed, wine, consommé and vinegar; simmer, covered, very slowly for 1½ hours, stirring occasionally. Add cooked artichokes. Pour mixture into a 2 to 2½-qt. baking dish. Top with Parmesan biscuits around outer edge of casserole. Bake in moderately hot oven (400°) 10 to 15 minutes, or until biscuits are well browned. As the vegetables, meat and starch are already in the Pot Pie, I make a tangy tomato aspic with chopped celery, green pepper and chopped hard-cooked eggs in it, to add color served alongside; and plenty of Parmesan biscuits for the gravy.

PARMESAN BISCUIT CRUST: Separate 1 (8-oz.) pkg. refrigerator biscuits. Dip each biscuit in melted butter; roll in shredded Parmesan cheese; sprinkle lightly with dill weed. I make extra biscuits for bread and bake them on a cookie sheet, along with those on top of the Pot Pie.

My choice of wine to accompany this dish:
CALIFORNIA CABERNET SAUVIGNON OR BURGUNDY

MANY LIKE a pronounced wine flavor which can be added without fuss, at the very last minute, to any stew or meat dish where liquid or gravy is a basic element. Simply pour a little EXTRA wine into the dish, and serve promptly. Since this final wine is not cooked, the alcohol does not volatilize, hence flavor remains more intense. (Usually in cooking, the wine flavor does not dominate, but "marries" or blends with the other food flavors, bringing out their natural best, delicately enriched.)

BEEF MAGNIFIQUE

(8 servings)

Mrs. Frank H. Bartholomew, Buena Vista Vineyards, Sonoma

This Burgundian dish was served to us in the heart of the Cote d'Or vineyard district, when we were guests at Chateau Grivelet in Chambolle-Musigny.

½ lb. salt pork, thinly sliced
   and cut in 1" squares
2 dozen small white onions
4 lbs. lean beef, cut in 2" cubes
1 teaspoon flour
½ teaspoon salt
¼ teaspoon freshly-ground pepper
1 clove garlic, pressed
1 slice orange peel
1 bouquet garni (see below)
2 cups California Pinot Noir,
   Burgundy or other red dinner wine
1 cup fresh small button mushrooms, or
   1 (4-oz.) can button mushrooms, drained
   Fresh parsley, finely chopped

Brown salt pork in Dutch oven until crisp. Remove pork; brown onions in remaining fat. Remove onions. Brown meat on all sides in same fat. Sprinkle salt pork with flour; return to Dutch oven. Season with salt and pepper. Add garlic, orange peel and bouquet garni. Heat wine; pour over meat. Cover and place in slow oven (250 to 300°) about 3 hours. Add more wine as necessary. Meanwhile, sauté fresh mushrooms in a little butter, until soft. Add mushrooms and onions 15 minutes before beef is done. Before serving, remove herb bouquet and orange peel; sprinkle lavishly with parsley. Serve with hot, buttered, crusty, sour dough French bread.

TO MAKE BOUQUET GARNI, tie 2 small bay leaves, 1 sprig thyme, ½ teapoon freshly-ground nutmeg, ½ teaspoon marjoram and small bunch parsley in piece of cheesecloth.

My choice of wine to accompany this dish:
CALIFORNIA PINOT NOIR

EASY OVEN POT ROAST

(4 servings)

Mrs. Vincent Indelicato, Sam-Jasper Winery, Manteca

3 lbs. chuck or pot roast
1 (10½-oz.) can cream of mushroom soup
1 cup California Burgundy or
   other red dinner wine
1 large onion, finely chopped
1 small clove garlic, crushed
2 tablespoons finely-chopped parsley
   Salt and pepper
4 medium-size potatoes
4 medium-size carrots

Place meat in Dutch oven or small roaster. Blend soup and wine; pour over meat. Add onion, garlic, parsley, salt and pepper. Cover and bake in moderately slow oven (325°) 5 hours. During last hour, add potatoes and carrots. Serve with garlic bread, tossed green salad and gelatin dessert with fruit.

My choice of wine to accompany this dish:
CALIFORNIA BURGUNDY OR VIN ROSÉ

SWISS STEAK SUPREME

(6 servings)

Mrs. Allen Pool, Bear Creek Vineyard Association, Lodi

This is not an original recipe, but I have made it for years. When I became interested in wine cookery, I simply added wine to the recipe, and found that I liked it much better.

    ¼ cup flour
    1 teaspoon salt
    ¼ teaspoon pepper
    2 lbs. round steak, ¾ to 1" thick,
        cut in 6 serving-size pieces
    ¼ cup oil
    1 onion, sliced
    1 tomato, sliced (or 1 tablespoon
        tomato paste)
    1 cup California Burgundy, Claret
        or other red dinner wine
        Pinch *each*: powdered bay leaf,
            oregano, rosemary
    6 small potatoes, peeled
    12 small carrots, peeled
    12 small white onions, peeled
    1 (10½-oz.) can cream of mushroom soup,
        or 1 (6-oz.) can whole mushrooms

Mix flour, salt and pepper; coat meat well, pounding in as much flour as possible. In a large heavy skillet, brown meat well in oil over high heat. Reduce heat. Top each piece of meat with a slice of onion and tomato; add wine and enough water to almost cover meat (or, if desired, use all wine). Add herbs. Simmer, covered, 2 hours. Place vegetables around meat; add mushroom soup or mushrooms. Simmer again until vegetables are tender (about 45 minutes). Since this is a whole meal in a skillet, menu might simply include a tossed green salad with wine vinegar and oil dressing and apple pie.

My choice of wine to accompany this dish:
CALIFORNIA BURGUNDY OR
ONE OF THE RED "VINO" TYPES

SWISS STEAK SAUTERNE

(6 servings)

Mrs. Louis W. Pellegrini, Sr., Italian Swiss Colony, Asti

    2 lbs. round steak, cut ½" thick
    1 teaspoon salt
    ⅛ teaspoon pepper
        Flour
        Oil
    ½ medium-size onion, chopped
    1 cup California Sauterne or
        other white dinner wine
    1 (6-oz.) can sliced mushrooms, undrained

Pound steak; cut in 6 serving-size pieces. Sprinkle with salt and pepper; dip in flour. In heavy skillet, brown meat in heated oil along with onions. When well browned, add wine and mushrooms. Cover; cook over low heat 1 to 1½ hours or until meat is tender.

My choice of wine to accompany this dish:
CALIFORNIA ROSÉ, BURGUNDY OR
SPARKLING BURGUNDY

BAKED SHORT RIBS

(4 servings)

Mrs. Joseph Stillman, Paul Masson Vineyards, Saratoga

This was my own experiment, and proved to be a favorite dish with my family.

    2 pounds English-cut short ribs
    2 tablespoons flour
    ½ teaspoon paprika
    1 teaspoon salt
    ¼ teaspoon pepper
    2 cups California Burgundy or
        other red dinner wine
    1 clove garlic, diced

Roll ribs in flour seasoned with paprika, salt and pepper. Brown in hot fat. Place ribs in casserole; add wine and garlic. Cover and bake in slow oven (300°) 2½ hours, or until tender. Serve with baked potatoes, green beans, tossed green salad, French rolls, dessert.

My choice of wine to accompany this dish:
ANY CALIFORNIA RED DINNER WINE

ROUND OF BEEF WITH SHERRY

(6 servings)

Mrs. Alvin Ehrhardt, United Vintners, Inc., Lodi

    4 lbs. bottom round steak
    2 medium-size onions, sliced
    1 clove garlic, chopped
    1 bay leaf
    ¼ teaspoon thyme
    1 teaspoon salt
        Dash Tabasco sauce
    ¾ cup California wine vinegar
    ¾ cup water
    3 tablespoons fat from meat or shortening
    8 small white onions
    2 tablespoons flour
    ½ cup meat stock (may be made with
        1 teaspoon meat-extract paste
        and ½ cup water)
    ¼ cup California Sherry

Trim fat from meat; wipe meat with damp cloth; place in small crock or covered dish. Combine onions, garlic, bay leaf, thyme, salt, Tabasco sauce, vinegar and water; pour over meat. Cover; refrigerate 2 days, turning several times each day. Remove meat, reserving marinade; drain. Brown well in heated fat in a heavy soup pot or Dutch oven. Add small onions; cover and cook over very low heat for 30 minutes, turning once. Remove meat. Add flour to fat in pan; cook, stirring constantly, 3 minutes. Strain marinade; stir into flour mixture along with stock. Simmer meat in thickened gravy, covered, 1½ hours. Add Sherry; simmer 1 hour more, or until meat is tender.

My choice of wine to accompany this dish:
CALIFORNIA BURGUNDY

SAUERBRATEN

(6 to 8 servings)

Mrs. Lewis A. Stern, E. & J. Gallo Winery, Modesto

Our friends usually look forward to some good old German cookery when they come to our house. This is Lew's favorite meal—the way "mother used to make it."

        4 to 6 lbs. top round steak
        4 slices bacon
        1½ cups California wine vinegar
        2 teaspoons salt
        10 whole peppercorns
        3 cloves
        2 bay leaves
        2 onions, chopped
        2 carrots, sliced
        3 tablespoons butter or margarine
        ½ cup boiling water
        1 cup California Burgundy or
            other red dinner wine
        1 cup sour cream

Lard meat by cutting a gash through the meat in about 6 places; insert a piece of bacon in each gash. In a saucepan, combine vinegar, salt, peppercorns, bay leaves, onions and carrots; bring to boiling. Remove from heat; cool about ½ hour. Place meat in glass or porcelain bowl; pour over vinegar mixture. Marinate 3 to 5 days in refrigerator, turning meat several times. Baste occasionally. Drain meat, saving marinade; blot dry with paper towels. Melt butter in Dutch oven. Brown meat all over. Add marinade and boiling water; simmer 2½ hours. Add wine; simmer 30 minutes longer, or until meat is tender. Add sour cream, stirring constantly; simmer 15 minutes longer. Slice and serve with the gravy and Potato Pancakes (Kartoffelpuffer—see below); also sweet-and-sour red cabbage, tossed green salad, French bread and apple pie with cheese.

POTATO PANCAKES (KARTOFFELPUFFER): Peel and grate 6 medium-size potatoes and ½ onion. Drain off liquid; combine potato-onion mixture with 2 tablespoons flour, 2 beaten eggs, 1½ teaspoons salt, ¼ teaspoon white pepper, ¼ teaspoon nutmeg and 2 tablespoons minced parsley. Beat well. Drop mixture by spoonfuls on hot, lightly buttered griddle; fry until brown and crisp on both sides, turning only once. Serve hot.

Our choice of wine to accompany this meal:
CALIFORNIA BURGUNDY OR CLARET

LOW BUDGET T-BONE STEAK

(2 or 3 servings)

Walter S. Richert, Richert & Sons, Morgan Hill

Buy tough chuck roast and serve meat as tender as T-bone. This method also works beautifully with any wild game: deer, rabbit, squirrel, duck, etc.

        Chuck or pot roast, cut ¾" thick
        1¾ cups California Burgundy, Claret
            or other red dinner wine
        ½ teaspoon salt
        ½ teaspoon seasoned salt
        ¼ teaspoon freshly-ground pepper

Cover meat with wine in glass or porcelain dish; marinate from 12 hours to 3 days, turning occasionally. (Marinate at room temperature for short period of time, or in refrigerator for longer period.) Remove meat from marinade, season and broil. Serve with tomato and onion salad marinated in wine vinegar; mayonnaise optional.

My choice of wine to accompany this dish:
ANY FULL-BODIED CALIFORNIA RED DINNER WINE

WINEBRATEN

(4 servings)

Mrs. Don Bonhaus, Wine Advisory Board, Detroit

This started in my mother's kitchen, as a substitute for Hasenpfeffer. By mixing recipes for Sauerbraten and Hasenpfeffer, and adding the most necessary "secret touch" of California Port, we have what I now call Winebraten.

        2 cups "carelessly cut cubes" of
            leftover pork or beef roast
        ¼ cup California wine vinegar
        2 tablespoons mixed pickling spices,
            tied in small piece cheesecloth
        ¼ teaspoon meat sauce
        ½ teaspoon salt
        ⅛ teaspoon pepper
        ¼ teaspoon monosodium glutamate
        1 cup leftover roast gravy or canned gravy
        1 medium onion, chopped
        ½ cup California Port
        1 tablespoon cornstarch

Combine all in a saucepan. Simmer, covered, 1 hour or longer, stirring occasionally. If more thickening is desired, add a little more cornstarch blended with water; cook, stirring, until thickened. Serve over boiled noodles, with potato pancakes, small peas, lots of crisp celery, and fruit for dessert. Although this complete menu is not a balanced meal, it is a family tradition, and when it is served everyone forgets "the rules" and just enjoys it.

My choice of wine to accompany this dish:
CALIFORNIA CLARET, ZINFANDEL OR BURGUNDY

EASY CABERNET POT ROAST

(4 to 6 servings)

Mrs. Guy Baldwin, Jr., Mont La Salle Vineyards, Napa

        4-lb. chuck or pot roast
        2 tablespoons flour
        2 teaspoons salt
        3 tablespoons oil
        1 (8-oz.) can tomato sauce
    1½ cups water
        1 cup California Cabernet Sauvignon,
            Claret or other red dinner wine
        ½ teaspoon dried oregano
        ½ teaspoon dried rosemary

Dredge meat with flour and salt. Brown on all sides in heated oil. Pour in tomato sauce, water and wine; add herbs. Cover and simmer gently 3 hours, or until meat is tender. Thicken gravy, if desired; add salt to taste; serve with meat. Menu could include noodles or rice; parsley-sprinkled carrots; tossed green salad; radishes, celery sticks and olives; buttered biscuits and strawberry preserves; and angel food cake.

My choice of wine to accompany this dish:
CALIFORNIA PINOT NOIR OR CABERNET SAUVIGNON

ROAST BEEF MAÑANA

(4 servings)

Mrs. Dale R. Anderson, Di Giorgio Wine Co., Di Giorgio

Mrs. Chet Steinhauer gave us this recipe several years ago when we lived in Delano, and it is our favorite way of using leftover roast beef—juicy and flavorful.

        1 tablespoon butter or margarine
        1 medium-size onion, chopped
        1 level tablespoon flour
        1 cup bouillon (canned or
            bouillon-cube broth may be used)
            Salt and pepper
            Worcestershire sauce
        ½ cup California Claret, Burgundy
            or other red dinner wine
            Thick slices cold cooked roast beef

Melt butter in saucepan; sauté onion until golden brown. Blend in flour. Slowly stir in bouillon; cook, stirring constantly, until well blended. Season with salt, pepper and Worcestershire sauce. Stir in wine. Add slices of cooked beef; heat thoroughly over low heat. Good with mashed potatoes, vegetable, tossed green salad and fruit for dessert.

My choice of wine to accompany this dish:
ANY CALIFORNIA DRY RED DINNER WINE

SAVORY ROAST OF BEEF

(16 servings)

Richard O'Hagan, Charles Krug Winery, St. Helena

        9-lb. standing 3-rib roast of beef,
            with bones in
        ¼ teaspoon dried marjoram
        ¼ teaspoon dried thyme leaves
        ¼ teaspoon rubbed savory
        ¼ teaspoon dried basil leaves
        ½ teaspoon salt
        ⅛ teaspoon pepper
        1 teaspoon meat extract paste dissolved
            in ½ cup hot water
    1½ cups California Burgundy or other
            red dinner wine
        6 tablespoons all-purpose flour
    1¼ cups water

Preheat oven to 325°. Place beef, fat side up, in shallow roasting pan. Do not use rack; let beef rest on bones. Combine herbs, salt and pepper; mix well. Rub into surface of beef on all sides. Insert meat thermometer through outside fat into thickest part of muscle; point should not rest on fat or bone. Combine meat broth with ½ cup of wine; use a little to baste beef. Roast meat, uncovered, basting several times with remaining wine mixture. Roast until thermometer reads 140° for rare, 3¼ to 3¾ hours; 160° for medium, 3¾ to 4¼ hours; 170° for well done, 4½ to 4¾ hours. Remove meat to heated platter; let stand 20 minutes before carving. Meanwhile, make gravy. Pour off drippings from roasting pan into measuring cup. Return 6 tablespoons to pan; stir in flour until smooth. Gradually add water and remaining 1 cup wine, stirring until smooth and scraping up browned bits. Bring to boiling, stirring constantly, for 5 minutes. Taste; add more salt and pepper, if needed. Serve gravy along with beef. Preferred menu with this would include oven-browned potatoes, fresh steamed buttered carrots, combination vegetable salad, soft French rolls, and raspberry Bavarian cream for dessert.

My choice of wine to accompany this dish:
CALIFORNIA ROSÉ OR CABERNET SAUVIGNON

POT ROAST PIEMONTESE

(6 to 8 servings)

Ferrer and Mildred Filipello, Calif. Wine Association, Lodi

> 4 to 5-lb. beef rump roast
> ¼ lb. precooked ham, sliced
>   into thin strips
> 4 strips bacon
> 2 cloves garlic, minced
> 2 medium onions, minced
> 2 stalks celery, minced
> 2 medium carrots, thinly sliced
> 1 cup California Chablis, Rhine
>   or other white dinner wine
> 1 cup California Burgundy, Claret
>   or other red dinner wine
> 1 teaspoon salt
> ¼ teaspoon pepper
> 1 sprig fresh rosemary

Lard roast with ham strips. Line casserole or Dutch oven with bacon strips. Add meat; brown on all sides over high heat (about 10 minutes). Add remaining ingredients. Cover and simmer, turning meat occasionally, about 3 hours or until tender. This is best served with gnocchi on the side, covered with the meat sauce, or buttered tagliarini. A tossed green salad is always appropriate.

Our choice of wine to accompany this dish:
CALIFORNIA CLARET OR ZINFANDEL

BARBECUED POT ROAST

(4 to 6 servings)

Phil Hiaring, Wine Institute, San Francisco

> 1 (4 to 5-lb.) chuck or pot roast
>   California Burgundy or other red
>   dinner wine
> 5 cloves garlic, chopped
>   Juice of 3 large lemons
> 4 tablespoons oregano
> ¾ cup olive oil
> ¼ cup chopped parsley
>   Pinch of rosemary
>   Salt and pepper

Cover meat with wine; marinate several hours or overnight, turning occasionally. Combine remaining ingredients; use to baste meat while barbecuing over hot coals. (Or, combine wine with other ingredients and use as both marinade and baste.)

My choice of wine to accompany this dish:
THE SAME CALIFORNIA RED DINNER WINE

NOTE: *This is a man's dish, robust and aromatic from the garlic and oregano. Those who prefer milder seasoning might want to cut down a little on these two ingredients in the initial marinating. More can be added later to the baste, if you're brave.*

LAZY SUNDAY OVEN DINNER

(4 to 6 servings)

Mrs. Richard Dettman, Mont La Salle Vineyards, Napa

This is a dinner which almost prepares itself — once it's in the oven, you can almost forget it.

> 4-lb. chuck roast
> 4 stalks celery, finely chopped
> 6 carrots, finely chopped
> 2 cloves garlic, finely chopped
>   Salt and pepper
> 1½ cups California Burgundy or other
>   red dinner wine

Place roast on large piece foil in shallow baking pan. Brown meat well on both sides under broiler. Remove from oven; top meat with chopped vegetables and season with salt and pepper. Add 1 cup wine; fold foil tightly around meat. Bake in moderately slow oven (325°) for 2 hours. Half an hour before done, partially unwrap foil and add remaining ½ cup wine; rewrap. This is not absolutely necessary, but a certain amount of evaporation sometimes occurs and this eliminates any chance of dryness. Also, the added wine provides an excellent gravy when slightly thickened with flour. Good with corn soufflé, green salad, and ice cream or sherbet for dessert.

My choice of wine to accompany this dish:
CALIFORNIA BURGUNDY, PINOT NOIR OR
CABERNET SAUVIGNON

SPICY POT ROAST OF VEAL

(4 servings)

Mrs. Sydney Whiteside, Del Rio Winery, Lodi

> 5-lb. veal rump roast with bone
> 1 tablespoon dry mustard
> 1 teaspoon poultry seasoning
> 2 tablespoons flour
> 1 tablespoon brown sugar
> 1 tablespoon salt
>   Pepper
> 3 tablespoons shortening or other fat
> ½ cup California Burgundy or other
>   red dinner wine
> 1 onion, sliced
>   Garlic (optional)

Dredge meat with mixture of mustard, poultry seasoning, flour, brown sugar, salt and pepper. Brown well on all sides in heated shortening. Add wine, onion and garlic, if desired. Cover tightly; simmer about 2½ hours, or until meat is tender. Good with a corn casserole, any vegetable in season, green salad with your favorite dressing, hot biscuits and relishes, and warm apple pie.

My choice of wine to accompany this dish:
CALIFORNIA CLARET OR A ROSÉ

GROUND BEEF WITH GLAMOUR

(4 to 6 servings)

Mrs. Wm. V. Cruess, U. of Calif. Dept. of Food Technology

Lean ground beef or hamburger is not very glamorous or attractive in flavor. Wine adds "the touch," and greatly improves it.

- 1 lb. ground lean beef
- 1 egg, beaten
- 1 cup cooked rice
- ½ onion, chopped
- 1 small clove garlic, chopped
- ½ teaspoon salt
- ⅛ teaspoon pepper
- 1 tablespoon oil
- ½ cup California Burgundy, Claret or other red dinner wine
- 1 (10¾-oz.) can prepared gravy

Combine beef, beaten egg, rice, onion, garlic, salt and pepper; mix just enough to blend. Shape into thick patties and brown lightly in heated oil. Pour off excess fat; add wine and gravy. Simmer about ½ hour, basting often. Thicken gravy with a little cornstarch mixed with cold water before serving, if desired.

My choice of wine to accompany this dish:
ANY DRY CALIFORNIA RED OR WHITE, OR DRY SHERRY

WINEDERFUL MEAT LOAF

(6 to 8 servings)

Larry Cahn, Wine Institute, San Francisco

Our meat loaves had lacked a distinctive flavor, so one night I suggested we use wine rather than water in them. My wife hinted that as long as I didn't like the way she did it, why didn't I try it myself. No sooner said than done. The wine made all the difference, and if a testimonial is needed, my wife will happily supply same.

- 2 lbs. ground beef
- 1 (1⅜-oz.) pkg. onion soup mix
- 1 cup California Burgundy, Claret or other red dinner wine
- 1 cup tomato juice
  Bacon slices

Mix meat, soup mix, ½ cup wine and ½ cup tomato juice. Shape into loaf. Place in baking pan; top with bacon slices. Bake in moderate oven (350°) for 45 minutes. Drain off fat; add remaining wine and tomato juice. Bake and baste 15 minutes longer. If desired, thicken pan juices slightly with a little cornstarch mixed with cold water or additional wine. Serve with baked potatoes, buttered fresh peas, and hearts of lettuce with blue cheese dressing.

My choice of wine to accompany this dish:
THE SAME CALIFORNIA BURGUNDY

NOTE: This easy-to-make meat loaf has unusual flavor, and is very moist, with lots of pan juices to make a luscious wine gravy. Another good red wine-flavored meat loaf is made by Mrs. Pete Peters, Fresno, who uses horseradish and chopped green pepper in hers.

BEEF STROGANOFF

(6 to 8 servings)

Richard O'Hagan, Charles Krug Winery, St. Helena

- 2 lbs. fillet of beef
- 4 tablespoons butter or margarine
- 1 cup chopped onion
- 1 clove garlic, finely chopped
- ½ lb. fresh mushrooms, sliced ¼" thick
- 3 tablespoons flour
- 2 teaspoons meat-extract paste
- 1 tablespoon catsup
- ½ teaspoon salt
- ⅛ teaspoon pepper
- 1 (10½-oz.) can beef bouillon, undiluted
- ½ cup California Sauterne, Chablis or other white dinner wine
- 1 tablespoon snipped fresh dill, or ¼ teaspoon dried dill
- 1½ cups sour cream
  Wild & White Herb Rice (see below)

Trim fat from beef; cut fillet crosswise into ½" thick slices. Cut each slice, across grain, into ½" wide strips. Heat a large, heavy skillet; melt 1 tablespoon of the butter. Add beef strips a few at a time; brown quickly on all sides over high heat. Remove beef as it browns—should be browned outside and rare inside. Brown rest of meat; set aside. In same skillet, melt remaining 3 tablespoons butter; sauté onion, garlic and mushrooms until onion is clear—3 to 5 minutes. Remove from heat and add flour, meat-extract paste, catsup, salt and pepper. Stir until smooth. Gradually add bouillon; bring to boiling point, stirring constantly. Reduce heat; simmer 5 minutes. Stir in wine, dill and sour cream. Add beef strips; heat thoroughly. Serve with Wild & White Herb Rice (or fresh tagliarini, for a change). Menu might also include beef consommé with croutons, avocado and grapefruit wedges with French dressing, green beans with little white onions, hard French rolls and Grecian pears.

WILD & WHITE HERB RICE: Lightly toss 1½ cups cooked wild rice and 4 cups cooked white rice. Surround Beef Stroganoff with rice. Snip 2 tablespoons fresh dill or 3 tablespoons parsley over the top for garnish.

My choice of wine to accompany this dish:
CALIFORNIA JOHANNISBERG RIESLING,
ROSÉ OR CABERNET SAUVIGNON

NOTE: This is an outstanding dish, well worth the price of the beef fillet indicated. However, for a lower cost Stroganoff, top sirloin may be used instead. Sherry may also be substituted for the white wine in the recipe, for a pleasant flavor variation. And an interesting Stroganoff is made with Burgundy by Mrs. L. J. Berg of Mont La Salle Vineyards, Napa.

PAPER-THIN STEAKS POIVRADE

(4 servings)

Louis A. Benoist, Almaden Vineyards, Los Gatos

2 lbs. boneless beef steak, cut ¼" thick
1 teaspoon cracked black pepper
½ teaspoon soft butter or margarine
   for each side of each steak
⅛ teaspoon salt for each side
⅛ teaspoon ground pepper for each side
   Butter and oil (half and half)
3 tablespoons butter or margarine
1 teaspoon chopped green onions
½ cup California Burgundy, Claret
   or other red dinner wine
   Finely-chopped parsley

Sprinkle both sides of steaks with cracked pepper; press into meat. Cover each side of steaks with ½ teaspoon butter; sprinkle each side with salt and ground pepper. Heat butter and oil in large heavy skillet; brown steaks quickly over high heat. Place steaks on a hot platter. Discard cooking oil. In same skillet, blend 2 tablespoons butter with green onions, salt to taste and wine. Bring to boiling. Dip each steak into liquid for ½ minute. Boil liquid until almost all evaporated. Remove pan from heat; stir in remaining tablespoon butter a little at a time. Taste; correct seasoning. Pour sauce over steaks; sprinkle with parsley.

My choice of wine to accompany this dish:
CALIFORNIA CABERNET SAUVIGNON

NOTE: These thin, well-seasoned steaks are really delicious. The sauce is a simplified version of the famous Marchand de Vin or Wine Merchant Sauce, traditional for many dishes.

BOEUF SALMI

(4 to 6 servings)

Mrs. William Bonetti, Charles Krug Winery, St. Helena

This is an original recipe, and a very easy meat treatment.

3-lb. chuck roast
   Salt
1 carrot, diced
1 small onion, chopped
2 stalks celery, diced
   Sprig parsley
¼ teaspoon coarse black pepper
3 cloves
   Pinch *each:* sage, rosemary, marjoram,
   sweet basil and bay leaf
3 cups California Burgundy or other
   red dinner wine
3 tablespoons butter or margarine

Season roast on both sides with salt. Place meat in a glass or porcelain dish. Add all other ingredients except butter (meat should be covered by wine). Cover dish; refrigerate 2 days, turning once a day. Drain meat, reserving marinade. Brown meat on both sides in melted butter; add wine marinade; simmer 2 to 2½ hours or until meat is tender. Serve with spaghetti, rice, mashed potatoes or polenta.

My choice of wine to accompany this dish:
CALIFORNIA CABERNET SAUVIGNON OR PINOT NOIR

NOTE: For a good polenta recipe to go with the beef, see Page 34.

PEPPER STEAK BARBECUED

(6 servings)

Mrs. John Paul, California Products Co., Fresno

3 lbs. chuck or pot roast, 2" thick
2 teaspoons unseasoned meat tenderizer
2 tablespoons instant minced onion
   (or ½ cup finely-chopped onion)
2 teaspoons thyme
1 teaspoon marjoram
1 bay leaf, crushed
½ cup California wine vinegar
½ cup California Burgundy or
   other red dinner wine
½ cup oil
3 tablespoons lemon juice
2 tablespoons coarse ground pepper

Sprinkle tenderizer on both sides of meat; pierce deeply with fork. Combine remaining ingredients; pour over meat in a glass or porcelain dish. Marinate the meat 1 to 2 hours, turning occasionally. Grill on rack about 6 inches above coals, 15 to 20 minutes per side. Baste with remaining marinade while cooking. Slice diagonally ½ inch thick to serve. Serve with rice baked in consommé, creamed spinach, tossed salad with tomatoes and apple pie.

My choice of wine to accompany this dish:
CALIFORNIA CABERNET SAUVIGNON

BEEF-RICE CASSEROLE

(6 to 8 servings)

Mrs. J. W. Fleming, Lockeford Winery, Lodi

2 large onions, sliced
1 green pepper, finely chopped
3 tablespoons shortening
¾ pound ground beef
1 cup raw rice
½ teaspoon chili powder
2 teaspoons salt
1½ cups tomato juice
¾ cup California Sauterne, Chablis
   or other white dinner wine

Sauté onions and green pepper in shortening until onions are clear. Add meat; cook until brown and crumbly. Add rice, chili powder, salt, tomato juice and ½ cup of wine. Turn into casserole, cover and bake in a moderate oven (350°) for 45 minutes. Remove cover, stir in remaining ¼ cup wine; cook, uncovered, 15 minutes more to brown.

NOTE: A sprightly California Claret or Rosé served alongside would be the ultimate in appetite-appeal.

BEEF ROLL-UPS, MILANESE

(6 to 8 servings)

Ferrer and Mildred Filipello, Calif. Wine Association, Lodi

- 3 lbs. round steak, cut in ¼-inch slices
- 2 tablespoons soy sauce
- 1 clove garlic, peeled
- 2 (12-oz.) pkgs. frozen chopped spinach, thawed
- 2 cups bread crumbs
- ½ cup chopped Italian salami
- 1 cup grated Parmesan or other dry cheese
- 1 teaspoon salt
- 1 teaspoon thyme
- ½ teaspoon pepper
- 1 teaspoon paprika
- 1 teaspoon monosodium glutamate
- 2 tablespoons oil
- 1 cup California Sherry
- 1 to 4 large sprigs fresh rosemary, or
- ½ to 1 teaspoon dried rosemary

Pound meat until quite thin; cut in 3-inch squares. Moisten each piece with a little soy sauce; rub with garlic. Set aside. Press out and discard excess liquid from thawed spinach. In a mixing bowl, combine bread crumbs, salami, cheese, salt, thyme, pepper, paprika and monosodium glutamate. Mix thoroughly with hands. Mix in spinach. Add a little Sherry while mixing to hold dressing together. Spread thin layer of dressing on each piece of meat. Roll up meat; tie both ends with string. Heat oil in large heavy skillet; add roll-ups; salt lightly. Brown meat on all sides over medium heat. Reduce heat to very low; add Sherry and rosemary. Cover; cook over low heat 30 minutes or until tender, turning occasionally. Add a little more Sherry if necessary. Remove strings, if desired, before serving. Serve with cauliflower, mixed tossed green salad and garlic bread.

Our choice of wine to accompany this dish:
CALIFORNIA CABERNET, CLARET OR ZINFANDEL

BAKED CORNED BEEF

(10 to 12 servings)

Mrs. Hans Hyba, Paul Masson Vineyards, Saratoga

- 6 lbs. corned beef
- 10 whole cloves
- ½ cup brown sugar (packed)
- 1 cup California Cream Sherry

Wash corned beef under running water to remove brine. In large kettle, cover with cold water; bring to boiling. Drain; cover with fresh water. Bring to boiling; simmer slowly until tender (about 6 hours). Remove from kettle; place in baking dish. Insert cloves in meat; sprinkle with brown sugar; slowly pour Sherry over meat. Bake in moderate oven (350°) until brown. Baste occasionally with Sherry syrup in bottom of pan until thickly glazed. Serve hot or cold.

NOTE: *This is a simple yet flavorful glaze. Would be a luscious main course dish served with chilled California Rosé.*

BEEF ROULADES IN RED WINE

(6 servings)

Mrs. Joseph S. Vercelli, Italian Swiss Colony, Asti

- 1½ lbs. round steak, very thinly sliced and cut in 6 pieces
- 1 clove garlic, cut in half
- 1 teaspoon salt
- ⅛ teaspoon pepper
- ¾ lb. ground sausage
- 2 tablespoons finely-chopped parsley
- 2 tablespoons finely-chopped onion
- Flour
- 1½ cups California Burgundy, Claret or other red dinner wine
- 1½ tablespoons tomato paste
- ½ cup pitted olives

Rub each piece of meat with cut clove of garlic. Season with salt and pepper. Spread a thin layer of sausage over each piece of meat. Sprinkle with parsley and onion. Roll up each piece; tie securely at both ends. Dredge the rolls in flour; brown well in heavy skillet. Discard any fat left in pan. Add wine. Mix tomato paste with a little of the wine; stir into wine in pan. Cover; cook slowly for 1 hour, or until meat is tender. About 15 minutes before meat is done, add olives. Good with steamed rice, green beans sautéed with almonds and mixed tossed green salad.

My choice of wine to accompany this dish:
CALIFORNIA CHIANTI

NOTE: *Still another good rolled beef dish is made by Mrs. Dan C. Turrentine, Wine Advisory Board, San Francisco. She uses a packaged bread stuffing and canned gravy with Burgundy and sour cream added — an "easy do-ahead recipe that seems company-prone."*

BURGUNDY MEATBALLS

(6 servings)

Mrs. John Parducci, Parducci Wine Cellars, Inc., Ukiah

- 1 lb. ground beef
- ½ cup fine dry bread crumbs
- 1 small onion, minced
- ¾ teaspoon cornstarch
- Dash allspice
- 1 egg, beaten
- ¾ cup light cream
- ¾ teaspoon salt
- ¼ cup oil
- 3 tablespoons flour
- 2 cups water
- 1 cup California Burgundy or other red dinner wine
- 2 beef bouillon cubes
- ½ teaspoon salt (additional)
- ⅛ teaspoon pepper

Combine beef, crumbs, onion, cornstarch, allspice, beaten egg, cream and ¾ teaspoon salt. Shape into small balls about the size of a walnut. Brown well on all sides in heated oil; remove from pan. Blend remaining ingredients into oil remaining in pan. Cook, stirring constantly, until smooth. Add meatballs to sauce. Cover and simmer 30 minutes. Serve with mashed potatoes, rice or noodles.

NOTE: *Would be perfect with the same good red wine on the table.*

RULADINI

(4 servings)

Mrs. Frank J. Pilone, Cucamonga Vineyard Co., Cucamonga

- 2 to 2½ lbs. top sirloin, round or cube steak, cut in 12 pieces about 4" square and ¼" thick
- 1 teaspoon butter or margarine
- ¼ cup chopped parsley
- 1 clove garlic, minced
- 12 thin slices onion
- 12 thin slices carrot
- 12 thin slices celery
- 12 thin slices prosciutto or boiled ham
- Salt and pepper
- Flour
- Oil and butter
- ½ onion, chopped
- 2 tablespoons chopped parsley
- 1 (4-oz.) can sliced mushrooms, undrained
- ¼ cup California Sherry

Spread each piece of beef with butter, parsley and garlic, divided evenly. On each, place a slice of onion, carrot, celery and ham. Roll each slice; secure with a wooden pick or string. Roll in flour; brown in oil and butter. Remove rolls to baking dish. In same skillet, brown onion and parsley; sprinkle over meat. Add mushrooms and Sherry. Bake, covered, in moderate oven (350°) 1 hour, or until tender. Baste occasionally with Sherry. Preferred menu would include gnocchi, zucchini and green salad.

My choice of wine to accompany this dish:
CALIFORNIA BURGUNDY

VEAL SCALLOPINI MARSALA

(4 to 6 servings)

Mrs. Dorothy Winneberger, U. C. Dept. Viticulture & Enology

This Italian recipe is very simple to make, yet an exquisite main dish. Do actually squeeze the lemon wedges onto the meat; it adds a delightful touch of flavor.

- 2 lbs. veal top round steak, thinly sliced and cut in 2" strips
- Flour
- ½ cup butter or margarine (or half oil)
- 1 (4-oz.) can sliced mushrooms, drained
- California Marsala or Sherry
- Salt and pepper
- Lemon wedges

Pound veal strips with flour; brown meat quickly in heated butter. Cover with mushrooms; add wine to cover. Simmer, covered, 5 to 10 minutes or until tender. Season with salt and pepper; serve with lemon wedges. I usually also serve rice pilaf with it; very small frozen peas, buttered; a green salad; hot rolls; and an extravagant dessert, possibly angel food cake with chocolate whipped cream and slivered almonds.

My choice of wine to accompany this dish:
CALIFORNIA CABERNET SAUVIGNON OR PINOT NOIR

VEAL WITH ARTICHOKES

(6 servings)

Mrs. A. Jensen, Gemello Winery, Mountain View

This is a Gemello family recipe, which is a favorite of ours.

- 2 cloves garlic
- Oil (half olive oil, if preferred)
- 2 lbs. veal round (have butcher flatten to ¼")
- Flour seasoned with salt and pepper
- 1 (1-lb.) can solid-pack tomatoes
- ½ cup California Sherry or Sauterne
- ¼ teaspoon oregano
- 2 (10-oz.) pkgs. frozen artichoke hearts

In a heavy skillet, sauté garlic in oil. Dust veal with seasoned flour; brown in oil. Add tomatoes, wine and oregano; mix well. Add frozen artichoke hearts. Cover; simmer 45 minutes to 1 hour, or until meat is tender. Serve with steamed rice, tossed green salad, French bread and fresh fruit dessert.

My choice of wine to accompany this dish:
CHILLED CALIFORNIA VIN ROSÉ

NOTE: *Lots of eye-appeal as well as taste in this one.*

BAKED VEAL SCALLOPINI

(6 servings)

Mrs. Allen Pool, Bear Creek Vineyard Association, Lodi

I acquired this recipe at a wine tasting luncheon, and have used it often during the last few years.

- ¼ cup chopped onions
- ¼ cup oil
- 1½ lbs. boned veal steak, cut in serving-size pieces
- ¼ cup sifted flour
- ½ teaspoon salt
- ⅛ teaspoon pepper
- 1 (4-oz.) can button mushrooms, drained
- 1 cup tomato juice
- ½ teaspoon sugar
- 1 cup California Sauterne, Chablis or other white dinner wine

Sauté onions in heated oil; remove to casserole. Roll veal in flour seasoned with salt and pepper; brown in oil. Add mushrooms and brown slightly. Arrange veal and mushrooms over onions. Combine other ingredients; pour over meat. Cover; bake in moderate oven (350°) for 1¼ hours or until veal is tender. Remove cover last ½ hour. Serve with baked potatoes, green peas, Perfection Salad and spumoni.

My choice of wine to accompany this dish:
CALIFORNIA BURGUNDY OR SAUTERNE

JOE'S VEAL CROQUETTES AU VIN

(6 to 8 servings)

Mrs. Cesare Vai, Cucamonga Vineyard Co., Cucamonga

- ¼ cup butter or margarine
- 2 tablespoons flour
- 1 lb. lean ground pork
- 1 lb. lean ground veal
- 4 eggs
- 1 cup grated Parmesan cheese
- ½ cup finely-chopped parsley
- ¼ teaspoon nutmeg
- 3 tablespoons California brandy
- 12 slices Provolone cheese, cut 2 x 1 x ¼"
- 6 slices prosciutto, cut in half
- ½ cup flour
- ½ cup bread crumbs
- ½ cup California Sauterne or other white dinner wine
  Sautéed sliced fresh mushrooms

Melt butter and stir in 2 tablespoons flour; cool. Combine butter-flour mixture with pork, veal, 2 eggs (beaten), ½ cup grated Parmesan cheese, parsley, nutmeg and brandy. Form meat mixture into thin patties. Top a patty with a slice of Provolone cheese, a piece of prosciutto and a second patty; pinch edges of patties together to hold filling. Repeat with remaining patties. In 3 separate bowls, place ½ cup flour, 2 beaten eggs and a mixture of bread crumbs and remaining grated Parmesan cheese. Dip each patty in flour, then egg, then crumb-cheese mixture. Fry patties in butter or margarine. Remove patties to shallow baking dish; add wine. Bake in slow oven (300°) for 30 to 40 minutes. Garnish with sautéed mushrooms. Menu might include linguini with tomato sauce, buttered green vegetable, tossed green salad with Italian dressing, fresh strawberries or sherbet and cookies.

My choice of wine to accompany this dish:
CALIFORNIA BARBERA

VEAL CHOPS TARRAGON

(2 servings)

Mrs. Joseph J. Franzia, Franzia Brothers Winery, Ripon

- 2 veal chops
- ¼ cup bread crumbs
- 3 tablespoons butter or margarine
- 2 shallots or green onions, chopped
- 1 tablespoon chopped parsley
- 3 or 4 leaves fresh tarragon, chopped, *or* 1 teaspoon dried tarragon
- ¼ teaspoon salt
  Few grains freshly-ground pepper
- ½ cup California Sauterne, Chablis or other white dinner wine

Roll chops in bread crumbs; press in as many as will stick to the surface of chops. (Do not use egg or milk.) Brown chops in butter. Add shallots or green onions, parsley, tarragon, salt and pepper. Cook 5 minutes. Reduce heat; add ¼ cup of the wine. Cover; simmer 15 to 20 minutes. Add remaining ¼ cup wine; continue simmering 10 to 15 minutes longer.

My choice of wine to accompany this dish:
CHILLED CALIFORNIA CHABLIS OR SAUTERNE

GOURMET VEAL BIRDS

(3 to 4 servings)

Mrs. William Bonetti, Charles Krug Winery, St. Helena

This is an original recipe, also entitled UCCELLI SCAPPATI.

- 8 very, very thin slices veal, cut 2 x 4"
- 8 very thin slices prosciutto
- 8 (½") cubes veal or chicken liver
- 8 wooden toothpicks
- 8 (¼") cubes salt pork
- 8 fresh sage leaves
- 2 tablespoons butter
- ¼ cup California Dry Semillon, Sauterne or other white dinner wine

Top each slice of veal with slice of prosciutto and cube of liver; roll up and secure with toothpick. Place cube of salt pork on one end of pick, and sage leaf on other. Melt butter in heavy skillet. Add veal rolls; brown slowly. Add wine. Cook 5 minutes, then cover; simmer slowly for 20 minutes more, or until fork-tender. Serve with whipped mashed potatoes or small buttered lima beans.

My choice of wine to accompany this dish:
CALIFORNIA JOHANNISBERG RIESLING

SALTIMBOCCA

(1 serving)

Mrs. Frank H. Bartholomew, Buena Vista Vineyards, Sonoma

This is a favorite dish at world-famous Giannino's in Milano. The chef there would tell you "the better the wine, the better the dish." This can, of course, be multiplied to serve any number of persons.

- 2 thin veal cutlets
  Salt and pepper
  Powdered sage
- 1 thin slice cooked ham or prosciutto
- 1 thin slice Jack, Provolone or other mild cheese
  Oil (half butter, if desired)
- 2 or 3 fresh mushrooms, chopped
- 2 teaspoons finely-chopped parsley
  Dash garlic
- 1 cup California Green Hungarian, Rhine or other white dinner wine
- 1 tablespoon butter

Season 1 cutlet with salt, pepper and sage. On top of cutlet, layer ham, cheese and other cutlet. Press edges of veal together firmly to hold filling; secure with wooden picks. Brown both sides well in heated oil. Remove to warmed shallow pan, or chafing dish, if preferred. In small pan, sauté mushrooms and parsley in butter with slight squeezing from garlic press. To pan in which meat was browned, add wine; heat, scraping up remaining browned bits into wine. Add mushrooms and parsley. Pour wine sauce over meat. Add 1 tablespoon butter; cook slowly over low heat until tender. Decorate with truffles, if desired.

My choice of wine to accompany this dish:
CHILLED CALIFORNIA GREEN HUNGARIAN

VEAL PAPRIKA

(6 servings)

W. W. Owen, California Grape Products Corp., Delano

- 3 tablespoons oil
- 2 pounds cubed veal
- ¼ cup flour
- 1 cup hot water
- 1 cup California Sauterne or other white dinner wine
- 1 (4-oz.) can mushrooms, undrained
- 2 tablespoons chopped parsley
- 1 onion, thinly sliced
- 1 teaspoon paprika
  Salt and pepper
- 1 cup sour cream

Heat oil in heavy skillet. Add veal; brown slowly on all sides. Stir in flour, hot water and wine. Cook, stirring constantly, until mixture is thickened and smooth. Add mushrooms and liquid, parsley, sliced onion, paprika, salt and pepper. Simmer 1 hour, covered. Just before serving, pour in sour cream. Heat through.

NOTE: A chilled California Sauterne or Chablis would be an ideal wine-companion for this savory dish.

LUNCHEON CASSEROLE

(10 to 12 servings)

Mrs. Ernest A. Wente, Wente Bros., Livermore

- 3 lbs. boneless veal, or 2 (2-lb.) pheasants, or 1 (4 to 5-lb.) stewing hen
- 2 large onions
- 6 stalks celery
- 2 sprigs *each*: fresh rosemary and oregano, or 1 teaspoon dried rosemary and oregano
- 1 teaspoon salt
- ⅛ teaspoon pepper
- 2 cups California Sauterne or other white dinner wine
- ¼ cup oil
- ½ lb. fresh mushrooms, sliced
- 2 (10½-oz.) cans cream of mushroom soup
- 4 eggs, beaten
- 4 cups (½ lb.) soda crackers, coarsely crushed

Place veal or poultry in large kettle with 1 onion (sliced), 2 stalks celery with leaves, herbs, salt, pepper and 1 cup wine. Add enough hot water to barely cover. Simmer 1 to 1½ hours, or until meat is tender. Cool; cut meat in bite-size pieces. Strain broth; set aside. Mince remaining onion; sauté in 2 tablespoons oil until soft. Mince remaining celery; add to onion along with 1 cup of reserved broth; simmer until celery is tender. Sauté mushrooms in 2 remaining tablespoons oil. Combine meat, onion and celery broth, mushrooms, soup, remaining 1 cup wine, 1 additional cup broth, eggs, crackers, salt and pepper. Place in large casserole. Put casserole in a pan of hot water (or place pan of hot water on lower rack of oven); bake in moderate oven (350°) for 1 hour.

NOTE: Would be marvelous with any chilled California white dinner wine, such as Sauterne, Chablis or Rhine Wine.

VEAL SUPREME

(8 servings)

Mrs. John G. Laucci, Franzia Brothers Winery, Ripon

- 4 thin slices veal steak, cut in half
- ⅔ cup olive oil
- 1½ tablespoons wine vinegar
- ¼ teaspoon oregano
- ¼ teaspoon sweet basil
- 1 large onion
- 1 large carrot
- 1 small celery heart (or 3 stalks)
- 2 sprigs parsley
- ½ cup dry mushrooms
- 1 cup water
- 2 eggs, beaten
  Fine, dry bread crumbs
  Salt and pepper
- ½ cup California Dry Sherry
- 1 cup tomato juice
- 8 to 10 potatoes, quartered

One hour before cooking, marinate veal in 3 tablespoons olive oil, wine vinegar, oregano and sweet basil. Meanwhile, finely chop onion, carrot, celery and parsley. Soak mushrooms in water 15 to 20 minutes; drain. Dip veal in beaten eggs, then coat both sides with bread crumbs. Heat remaining oil in large heavy skillet; brown veal over medium heat until golden. Remove veal to warm platter. Add to skillet the onions, celery, carrots, parsley, drained mushrooms, salt and pepper. Sauté over low heat, stirring often. Add Sherry and tomato juice; cook about 5 minutes. Return veal to skillet; simmer about ½ hour or until tender. Meanwhile, deep-fat fry quartered potatoes; add to veal; cook 5 to 10 minutes longer. Place veal on large platter, arrange potatoes around it and pour sauce over all. Garnish platter with large black olives and sprigs of parsley if desired.

NOTE: Wine accompaniment might be a hearty red, such as California Burgundy, or a mellow red "vino" type; or a chilled Rosé or white.

BAKED HAM SLICE SAUTERNE

(4 servings)

Mrs. E. F. Handel, East-Side Winery, Lodi

- 1 (2-lb.) ham slice, cut 1½" thick
- ½ cup brown sugar, firmly packed
- 3 tablespoons cornstarch
- 1½ cups water
- 1 tablespoon butter or margarine
- ½ cup raisins
- ½ cup California Sauterne or other white dinner wine

Cover ham with cold water; bring to boiling. Remove ham to oiled baking dish. Mix sugar and cornstarch in saucepan. Mix in water and butter; cook, stirring constantly, 5 minutes. Remove from heat; stir in raisins and wine. Pour over ham; bake, uncovered, in moderate oven (350°) for 45 minutes or until tender.

NOTE: Different and delightful, especially with the same good wine accompanying — or perhaps a chilled pink California Rosé. A very similar treatment is recommended by Mrs. James Concannon, Concannon Vineyard, Livermore.

HAM WITH ORANGES

(3 to 5 servings)

Brother Gregory, Mont La Salle Vineyards, Napa

- 1 center slice of ham, ¾" thick
- 2 tablespoons butter
- 1 medium-size orange, peeled and sliced
- ½ cup California Light Muscat wine
  Salt, if desired

Trim any excess fat from ham. Brown ham in butter over moderately high heat. Add orange slices and cook about one minute (pushing ham to one side of pan). Add wine, lower heat and simmer 10 minutes. If wine cooks away, add just a little water, enough to capture essence in the pan. Remove ham; arrange on platter with orange slices. Scrape up gelatinous bits in pan; simmer until sauce is well blended (about 30 seconds). Ordinarily no salt is needed in sauce, but taste to make sure. Pour unthickened sauce over ham.

NOTE: *A California white dinner wine, served well chilled alongside, would be the final touch of perfection.*

BAKED HAM CHERRY-SHERRY

(8 to 10 servings)

Mrs. Otto E. Meyer, Paul Masson Vineyards, Saratoga

This recipe came from Finland. It is wonderful in cold weather.

- 1 (1-lb.) can pitted black cherries
- 2 oranges
- 1 lemon
- 1 teaspoon ginger
- 1 cup dark brown sugar (packed)
- 1 cup California Dry Sherry
- 1 canned ham (about 6-lb. size)
- ¼ cup California brandy

Drain juice from cherries into saucepan. Blend with pulp and juice of oranges and lemon, ginger, brown sugar and Sherry. Simmer until sugar dissolves. Place ham in baking pan; pour on warm sauce. Bake, uncovered, in slow oven (300°) 25 minutes per lb. Baste with sauce every 15 to 20 minutes. About 15 minutes before done, pour brandy over ham. At end of cooking period, pour pan juices into saucepan and bring to boiling. Add cherries; simmer 5 minutes. Slice ham and serve with sauce. For first course with this menu I prefer broiled grapefruit, dotted with butter and brown sugar; then the Ham with Cherry-Sherry Sauce, with shredded carrots baked in a ring with petite green peas in center, and popovers. For dessert, perhaps a fresh fruit cup.

My choice of wine to accompany this dish:
CHILLED CALIFORNIA RIESLING

NOTE: *An exceptionally fine ham treatment. If desired, sauce may be tihckened slightly with a little cornstarch mixed with cold water. For Mrs. Meyer's fruit cup idea, see Dessert section.*

BRAISED HAM FINANCIERE

(6 to 8 servings)

Rene Baillif, Buena Vista Vineyards, Sonoma

- 4 or 5 lbs. uncooked smoked boneless ham
- 1 medium-size onion
- 12 whole cloves
- 2 or 3 leeks
- 1 bouquet garni (tie together few sprigs parsley, bay leaf and sprig of thyme or little powdered thyme)
- 1 bottle California Sauterne, Chablis or other white dinner wine
- 10 to 12 whole peppercorns
- 2 cups California Sherry

Soak ham at least 24 hours, changing water several times. Place ham in large cooking utensil; cover with cold water; bring to boiling. Discard water; recover with fresh boiling water to which the onion (spiked with whole cloves), leeks and bouquet garni are added. Add white dinner wine; bring to boiling. Reduce heat; simmer 45 minutes to 1 hour. Add peppercorns last half hour of simmering. Remove ham to oven-proof dish or casserole; pour over Sherry. Bake covered in very slow oven (250°) 45 minutes to 1 hour longer, basting occasionally. Before serving, use remaining wine in pan as part of liquid to make a nice accompanying mushroom sauce, if desired. Should be served at a festive family dinner, with mashed potatoes, green beans and spinach.

My choice of wine to accompany this dish:
CALIFORNIA GREEN HUNGARIAN OR CABERNET ROSÉ

SHERRY-GLAZED HAM

(6 to 8 servings)

Mrs. Sydney Whiteside, Del Rio Winery, Lodi

- 1 (3 or 4-lb.) canned ham
- 1½ cups California Cream Sherry
- ½ cup apricot or peach jam
- ½ cup honey
  Dash nutmeg or cinnamon
- 1 tablespoon cornstarch

Place ham in shallow baking pan and pour over ½ cup of the Sherry. Bake 1 hour in moderately slow oven (325°). Meanwhile, combine jam with honey and generous dash of nutmeg or cinnamon, in saucepan. Stir in cornstarch and remaining cup of Sherry. Cook, stirring constantly, until thick. Spoon sauce over ham and bake about 20 minutes more or until ham is glazed, basting occasionally. Good with candied sweet potatoes; hot fresh asparagus (if in season) or any other green vegetable; cinnamon apple salad, or fruit salad; relishes; rolls and pineapple sherbet.

My choice of wine to accompany this dish:
CHILLED CALIFORNIA ROSÉ

NOTE: *Mrs. J. W. Fleming of Lockeford Winery, Lodi, recommends a very similar version of this taste-tempting sweet glaze. For a good sweet potato recipe for the menu, see Vegetable section.*

HAM PORTUGUESE STYLE

(4 servings)

J. H. "Mike" Elwood, Llords & Elwood Wine Cellars, Fremont

½ cup dark brown sugar (packed)
1 lb. thick ham slice
4 tablespoons prepared mustard
2 tablespoons butter or margarine
¼ cup California Port

Rub sugar into both sides of ham; coat both sides with mustard. Melt butter in a heavy skillet; fry quickly, turning several times. Reduce heat; cover; cook slowly until tender, turning once. Remove to hot platter. Skim off fat from pan juices; stir in Port; heat to boiling. Pour over ham.

NOTE: A cool California Rosé would be fine with this unusually good ham.

FRUIT-SHERRY PORK CHOPS

(6 servings)

Mrs. Richard D. Dettman, Mont La Salle Vineyards, Napa

6 loin or rib pork chops, cut ¾" thick
¼ cup sifted flour
1½ teaspoons salt
½ teaspoon pepper
1 large orange
¼ cup brown sugar (packed)
2 tablespoons concentrated orange juice, undiluted
2 teaspoons concentrated lemon juice, undiluted
¾ cup California Dry Sherry
6 rings canned pineapple
½ cup juice from canned pineapple

Trim all but thin layer of fat from chops. In large heavy skillet, render some of the trimmed fat to coat pan lightly; discard excess fat. Rub flour seasoned with salt and pepper into both sides of meat; brown on both sides over medium heat. Cut 3 (¼") slices from center of orange; cut each slice in half; top each chop with piece of orange. Sprinkle with brown sugar. Combine concentrated orange and lemon juice with Sherry; pour over and around chops. Cover pan tightly; bake in moderately slow oven (325°) for 1 to 1½ hours, or until meat is fork-tender. Add pineapple rings and juice last half hour of cooking. Remove chops and fruit; thicken pan juices slightly with a little cornstarch mixed with cold water, if desired. With this I like to serve baked potatoes and fresh or frozen French-cut green beans, with a salad of cottage cheese, lime gelatin and crushed pineapple. Salad can be made a day ahead.

NOTE: A chilled California Sauterne or Vin Rosé would make beautiful sipping with this.

ROAST PORK ROSEMARY

(6 to 8 servings)

Mrs. Domenic E. Viotti, Jr., Viotti Winery, San Gabriel

This is a family recipe, taught to me by my mother-in-law, Mrs. Virginia Viotti.

2 tablespoons oil
1 (5 or 6-lb.) pork shoulder or pork loin roast
2 cups California Sherry
2 cups water
2 to 4 tablespoons fresh rosemary, or 4 to 6 tablespoons dried rosemary
1 tablespoon garlic powder, or 3 or 4 cloves garlic, minced
1 teaspoon monosodium glutamate
1 teaspoon salt
¼ teaspoon black pepper
½ cup flour
¼ cup butter or margarine

Heat oil in roasting pan or large Dutch oven. Brown roast slightly on all sides. Add Sherry, water and seasonings. Ccok, covered, in slow oven (300°) for 4 to 5 hours (until very tender and meat pulls away from bone). Remove roast to platter. Skim off fat from pan juices; strain juices; set aside. Melt butter in saucepan. Blend in flour; mix well. Add juices slowly, stirring constantly. Cook over low heat until thickened. Thin to desired consistency with hot water or additional Sherry. Taste and correct seasoning, as desired. Slice onto serving platter, garnished with hot crab apples and parsley. Good with mashed potatoes, buttered green peas, mixed green salad and biscuits.

My choice of wine to accompany this dish:
CALIFORNIA CHAMPAGNE, SAUTERNE OR RHINE

EASY WINE PORK CHOPS

(6 to 8 servings)

Mrs. H. Peter Jurgens, Almaden Vineyards, Los Gatos

Trim excess fat from 6 to 8 thick loin pork chops; brown chops in heavy skillet. Season with salt and pepper. Add California Sauterne, Chablis or other white dinner wine to half-cover meat. Arrange quartered onions around chops. Bake in a moderate oven (350°) about 1 hour or until meat is fork-tender. Add more wine as needed.

NOTE: Sauterne is also used in PORK CHOPS ITALIANO, a recipe originated by Mrs. Domenic E. Viotti, Jr., of Viotti Winery, San Gabriel. Mrs. Viotti browns chops well, then transfers them to a casserole with a wine-tomato-garlic flavored sauce. She prefers either Rosé wine or Sauterne served alongside.

PORK TENDERLOIN IN WINE

(6 servings)

Mrs. Ronald G. Hanson, Di Giorgio Wine Co., Di Giorgio

6 serving-size pieces of
pork tenderloin
½ teaspoon salt
⅛ teaspoon pepper
2 cups California Sauterne or
other white dinner wine
½ bay leaf
1 onion with 2 cloves inserted
6 whole peppercorns
2 tablespoons butter or margarine

Lard pork; season with salt and pepper. Place in glass bowl; add wine, bay leaf, cloved onion, and peppercorns. Cover; marinate several hours. An hour before serving, remove meat, reserving marinade; drain and wipe dry. Heat butter in roasting pan; add meat. Roast in moderately hot oven (375°) until meat begins to brown, basting with pan drippings. Add 1 cup wine marinade, including spiced onion. Continue cooking until meat is tender and well done, basting frequently. Add more wine if necessary. Arrange on heated platter, garnished with border of cooked sauerkraut, plain boiled potatoes, and small glazed white onions.

NOTE: *And with a chilled bottle of California Sauterne or Rosé on the table, for maximum enjoyment. Pork chops may also be cooked this way.*

LODI JAMBALAYA

(4 to 6 servings)

Ferrer and Mildred Filipello, Calif. Wine Association, Lodi

This is a one-course meal.

1 lb. lean pork, cut in ¾" cubes
1 tablespoon olive oil
1 tablespoon butter or margarine
1 large onion, chopped
1 lb. ham, cut in ¾" cubes
4 cups water
½ cup California Sherry
1 teaspoon dry mustard
1 teaspoon celery salt
½ teaspoon savory
½ teaspoon thyme
¼ teaspoon black pepper
1½ cups long grain rice

In heavy skillet, brown pork in oil and butter; add onion and ham. Cook, stirring, until onion is soft (about 2 minutes). Remove meat and onion to large casserole. Combine water, Sherry and seasonings in saucepan; bring to boiling. Add rice to liquid, stir and remove from heat. Pour mixture over meat. Cover casserole; bake in moderate oven (350°) for 40 minutes. Stir once after 20 minutes.

Our choice of wine to accompany this dish:
CALIFORNIA CHABLIS OR ROSÉ

PEAS AND PORK ORIENTAL

(6 to 8 servings)

Mrs. William Perelli-Minetti, A. Perelli-Minetti & Sons, Delano

2 lbs. lean pork, cut in thin strips,
about 2 x ¼ x ¼"
1 or 2 tablespoons oil
2 teaspoons salt
⅛ teaspoon pepper
3 tablespoons soy sauce
½ cup California Sherry
3 cups cold water
1 cup sliced onion
1 cup sliced celery
4 tablespoons cornstarch
2 vegetable bouillon cubes (optional)
2 (10-oz.) packages frozen peas,
partially defrosted
1 (6-oz.) can sliced broiled-in-butter
mushrooms, drained

Brown pork in oil. Add 1 teaspoon salt, pepper, 2 tablespoons soy sauce, ¼ cup Sherry and ½ cup water. Cover tightly; simmer 45 minutes to 1 hour, or until meat is tender. If needed, add more water, a tablespoon at a time. When tender, remove from pan. Blend remaining water with cornstarch, stirring until free of lumps. Stir into meat drippings. Add bouillon cubes, peas, and remaining teaspoon salt, ¼ cup Sherry and tablespoon soy sauce. Cook, stirring constantly, until sauce is thickened and peas are barely tender. Meanwhile, in second skillet, sauté onion and celery in a little hot oil until clear. Then add onions and celery to thickened sauce along with meat and mushrooms. Heat thoroughly. Good with rice or mashed potatoes, fruit salad or a rather bland molded salad, or fresh sliced tomatoes (no dressing) and cold, sliced marinated cucumbers.

My choice of wine to accompany this dish:
CALIFORNIA CLARET OR ZINFANDEL

MORGAN HILL PORK SAUSAGES

(4 servings)

Walter S. Richert, Richert & Sons, Morgan Hill

I invented this to leach out all those excessive spices used in sausage formulas. Place 1 pound link sausage in frying pan. Barely cover with California Sauterne, Chablis or other white dinner wine. Cover pan and simmer about 10 minutes. Remove cover; continue cooking over low heat until wine is evaporated and sausages are a delicate brown. Turn sausages over and lightly brown other side. Serve with hash-brown potatoes for brunch.

My choice of wine to accompany this dish:
CALIFORNIA RIESLING OR PINOT CHARDONNAY

GERMAN MEAT PIE

(8 servings)

Justine Mirassou, Mirassou Vineyards, San Jose

This recipe has been handed down for generations in the family, to the present-day children and grandchildren. It is also a good way to cook rabbit.

   1 (6-lb.) pork shoulder roast
   2 pkgs. whole pickling spice
   2 onions, chopped
   2 cloves garlic, chopped
    Large bunch parsley
    Salt and pepper
  ¾ cup California wine vinegar
    California white dinner wine
   5 cups sifted all-purpose flour
 1¼ teaspoons baking powder
   1 teaspoon salt
  ½ cup rendered fat from meat
 1½ cups milk
   1 egg

Cut fat from roast; render fat and set aside. Cut meat in 1″ cubes. Combine pickling spice, onions, garlic, parsley, salt, pepper and wine vinegar. Pour over meat in a large glass or porcelain dish; add enough wine to cover meat. Marinate in refrigerator 3 days. Drain meat well, removing any whole spices left on meat. Sift together flour, baking powder and salt. Mix in rendered fat. Combine milk and egg; add to flour mixture. Roll out part of dough to fit a 13 x 9″ baking pan (don't roll too thin). Line pan; dough should lap well over sides. Fill with drained meat. Cover with pricked top crust, sealing with overlapping bottom crust. Bake in moderately hot oven (375°) for 1 hour, or until crust is rich brown. As the pie is quite rich, a crisp curly endive salad is all that is necessary to serve with it.

Our choice of wine to accompany this dish:
CHILLED CALIFORNIA WHITE RIESLING

SHERRY-GLAZED SPARERIBS

(4 to 6 servings)

Mrs. Bruno T. Bisceglia, Bisceglia Bros. Wine Co., Fresno

   1 side meaty spareribs
    Salt and pepper
   1 (8-oz.) can tomato sauce
  ½ cup California Sherry
  ½ cup honey
   2 tablespoons California wine vinegar
   2 tablespoons minced onion
   1 clove garlic, minced (optional)
  ¼ teaspoon Worcestershire sauce

Sprinkle spareribs with salt and pepper. Place in shallow baking pan and bake in hot oven (400°) for 40 minutes. Drain off fat. Combine remaining ingredients; pour over spareribs. Bake 1 hour longer in moderate oven (350°) or until tender. If desired, spareribs can be barbecued over low coals, brushing on the same sauce to glaze.

My choice of wine to accompany this dish:
A DRY RED CALIFORNIA DINNER WINE

LAMB STEW SANTA CLARA

(6 servings)

Mrs. H. Peter Jurgens, Almaden Vineyards, Los Gatos

   3 lbs. lean boneless lamb stew meat,
    cut in 1-inch cubes
   3 tablespoons butter or margarine
   2 level tablespoons flour
   2 cups California Mountain White, or
    Chablis or other white dinner wine
    Herb bouquet (tie together 3 or 4 sprigs
    parsley, sprig thyme and small bay leaf)
   1 large onion, sliced
   1 clove garlic, minced
    Salt and pepper

In large heavy skillet or Dutch oven, lightly brown lamb in butter. Stir in flour. Add wine and enough water to just cover meat. Add herb bouquet. Cover; simmer 1 hour, or until almost tender. Add onion, garlic, salt and pepper; continue cooking until meat is tender. Remove herb bouquet.

NOTE: *Since many stews are even better when some wine is added at the last minute, about ¼ cup of the wine called for can be saved for this purpose. The same kind of wine would also be delightful served with this succulent dish — or, perhaps, a California Rosé. Either one well chilled, of course.*

BRAISED LAMB BURGUNDY

(5 to 6 servings)

Mrs. Ferrer Filipello, California Wine Association, Lodi

   2 tablespoons bacon drippings or other fat
   2 lbs. boned lamb shoulder, cubed
   3 tablespoons flour
   1 cup California Burgundy or other
    red dinner wine
   1 cup beef stock (canned or
    bouillon-cube broth may be used)
   1 (8-oz.) can tomato sauce
    Pinch of rosemary
  ½ teaspoon salt
  ⅛ teaspoon pepper
   1 cup diced celery
  ½ cup chopped onion
   1 (4-oz.) can mushroom stems and
    pieces, drained
   2 tablespoons chopped parsley
   1 (10-oz.) pkg. frozen peas and
    carrots (optional)

Heat bacon drippings in Dutch oven or other heavy kettle; brown lamb slowly on all sides. Sprinkle flour over meat; stir well. Add ¾ cup of the wine, stock and tomato sauce; cook, stirring constantly, until mixture boils and thickens. Add rosemary, salt, pepper, celery and onion. Cover; simmer gently 1 hour, or until meat is tender, stirring occasionally. (Add a little more wine during cooking if necessary.) Shortly before serving, add mushrooms and parsley, and cooked and drained peas and carrots. At very last minute, stir in remaining ¼ cup wine.

My choice of wine to accompany this dish:
CHILLED CALIFORNIA VIN ROSÉ

MINT-STUFFED LEG OF LAMB

(6 to 8 servings)

Mrs. George Marsh, U. of Calif. Dept. of Food Technology

- 1 (5 or 6-lb.) leg of lamb, boned
  - Lemon juice
- ¼ teaspoon salt
  - Pepper
- ⅓ cup golden or dark raisins, chopped
- 1 small clove garlic, minced
- 1 small onion, chopped
- ¼ cup butter or margarine
- 3 tablespoons California Rosé
- 3 cups soft stale bread crumbs, **or**
  - 1 (8-oz.) pkg. stuffing mix
- 2 or 3 tablespoons chopped mint or parsley
  - Pinch of dried rosemary or oregano
  - Wine Lamb Baste (see below)

Rub lamb with lemon juice; sprinkle with salt and pepper. Combine other ingredients; mix well. Stuff lamb, fitting meat around mixture. Tie or hold in place with skewers. Place skewered side down in roasting pan. Roast in moderately hot oven (375°) for 2½ to 3 hours, basting often with Wine Lamb Baste.

WINE LAMB BASTE: Combine 1 cup California Rosé, ¼ cup soy sauce and ½ teaspoon **each** dried rosemary and oregano, in saucepan; simmer a few minutes before using to baste meat.

My choice of wine to accompany this dish:
CHILLED CALIFORNIA PINOT CHARDONNAY

BARBECUED LEG OF LAMB

(8 to 10 servings)

John Cadenhead, Wine Advisory Board, San Diego

- 2 cups California red or white dinner wine
- 2 teaspoons poultry seasoning
- 2 teaspoons salt
- 3 cloves garlic, peeled
- 1 leg of lamb, boned and butterflied
  - (spread out flat)

Combine wine, poultry seasoning, salt and garlic; pour over lamb in glass or porcelain dish. Marinate 12 to 24 hours, turning occasionally. Barbecue over charcoal, skin side up, for 30 minutes. Turn; cook 30 minutes more. Baste with remaining marinade while cooking. When done, slice across grain to serve. I prefer this with a pilaf, green salad, and strawberries in Port with brown sugar.

My choice of wine to accompany this dish:
CALIFORNIA BURGUNDY OR CLARET

NOTE: *For strawberry idea mentioned, see Dessert section.*

VINEYARD LAMB SHANKS

(4 servings)

Mrs. Fred Snyde, Woodbridge Vineyard Association, Lodi

- 4 lamb shanks
- 1 lemon, cut
  - Salt and pepper
- 1 tablespoon dry mustard
- 1 medium-size onion, chopped
- 1 clove garlic, chopped
- 1 green pepper, chopped
- 1 cup California Sauterne, Chablis
  - or other white dinner wine

Rub shanks thoroughly with cut lemon; sprinkle with salt and pepper; coat with dry mustard. Put shanks in large casserole so they do not overlap. Add chopped vegetables and wine. Cover; cook in moderately slow oven (325°) for 2 hours. Turn during last hour of cooking. More wine may be added if they become dry. Serve with rice pilaf, green vegetable, tossed salad with oil and wine vinegar dressing, and lemon pie.

My choice of wine to accompany this dish:
THE SAME DRY WHITE WINE USED IN THE RECIPE

CURRIED LAMB SHANKS

(8 servings)

Mrs. E. A. Mirassou, Mirassou Vineyards, San Jose

- ½ cup cooking oil
- 8 medium-size lamb shanks
- ⅓ cup flour
- 1 tablespoon curry powder
- 1 cup water
- 1 cup California Sauterne, Chablis
  - or other white dinner wine
- 2 teaspoons salt
- ¼ teaspoon pepper
- ⅛ teaspoon garlic salt
- 1 onion, thinly sliced

Heat oil in large, heavy skillet. Add shanks; brown well. Remove shanks from pan; blend flour and curry powder into drippings. Add water and wine. Cook, stirring constantly, until mixture is thickened and smooth. Add salt, pepper and garlic salt. Return shanks to pan; add onion slices. Cover tightly; simmer 1½ hours, or until meat is tender. Serve with rice, vegetable of the season, and green salad.

My choice of wine to accompany this dish:
A CHILLED CALIFORNIA WHITE DINNER WINE

NOTE: *California Dry Sherry flavors the lamb shanks cooked by Mrs. Herman Wente of Wente Bros., Livermore. She says Sauterne may also be used, and adds: "If dinner is delayed, add a little more wine, turn off the oven and do not worry."*

SHISH KABOB SAN JOAQUIN

(10 to 12 servings)

Zoe Vartanian, Crest View Winery, Inc., Fresno

- 1 (5 or 6-lb.) leg of lamb, boned
- 2 large onions, each cut in 6 wedges
- 6 to 8 large sprigs parsley, chopped
  Salt and pepper
- ½ cup California Burgundy or other dry red dinner wine
- 4 or 5 tomatoes, quartered
- 4 or 5 green peppers, cut in chunks

Trim part of fat from meat; cut meat in 2″ cubes. In large glass bowl, combine meat, onions, parsley, salt and pepper; pour over wine and mix thoroughly. Refrigerate overnight. When ready to barbecue, mix meat again; spear meat alternately with onions, tomatoes and peppers on long metal rods or small individual wooden skewers. Cook over coals to desired degree of doneness. Menu might include a rice pilaf, green beans and tossed green salad.

My choice of wine to accompany this dish:
CALIFORNIA VIN ROSÉ OR SPARKLING BURGUNDY

NOTE: *The top-quality meat, plus the marinating, makes this a melt-in-your-mouth treat. Can be cooked indoors under the oven broiler in cold weather.*

BREAST OF LAMB MENDOCINO

(4 servings)

Maynard Monaghan, Beaulieu Vineyard, Rutherford

- 3 lbs. breast of lamb, cut in serving-size pieces
- 1 cup California Sauterne or other white dinner wine
- ½ cup chili sauce
- 1 large onion, chopped
- ½ green pepper, chopped
- 1 tablespoon soy sauce
  Salt and pepper

Arrange pieces of lamb, fat side up, in single layer in shallow baking pan. Mix other ingredients; pour over lamb. Cover with pan lid or aluminum foil; let stand at room temperature 1 hour or so. Bake, covered, in moderately hot oven (375°) for 1 hour; uncover, and continue baking 1 hour more, basting often.

My choice of wine to accompany this dish:
CALIFORNIA ZINFANDEL OR GAMAY

LIVER VINO BLANCO

(3 servings)

Lyman M. Cash, E. & J. Gallo Winery, Modesto

- 1 lb. beef or calf liver (lamb liver may also be used)
  Flour
- ¼ cup olive oil
- 1 or 2 cloves garlic
- 1 small onion, minced
  Salt and pepper
- 1 teaspoon basil, minced
- ½ cup California Sauterne, Chablis or other white dinner wine

Scald liver in boiling water; drain; wipe dry. Dredge with flour; brown slowly in hot oil. Remove from pan; keep warm. Split garlic in half lengthwise; place on wooden picks; brown in oil remaining in pan. Add onion; stir and cook 5 minutes. Return liver to pan; spoon over onion and garlic. Add salt, pepper and basil; pour over wine. Cover; simmer slowly ½ hour, basting every 10 minutes with pan liquid. Discard garlic before serving.

My choice of wine to accompany this dish:
CALIFORNIA CLARET, BURGUNDY OR PINOT NOIR

NOTE: *Over 200 years ago, a similar recipe for liver cooked with white wine was a favorite in England. You can't keep a good idea down! At the same winery, Mrs. Lewis Stern also makes a delicious liver-and-onion dish, but uses red wine in cooking.*

KIDNEY SAUTÉ

(4 to 6 servings)

Mrs. William V. La Rosa, Calif. Grape Products Corp., Delano

- 12 lamb kidneys
- ¼ cup California wine vinegar
- 1 medium onion, sliced
- 1 cup celery, sliced
- 3 tablespoons shortening
- 3 tablespoons flour
- 1 cup stock or water
- 1 cup mushrooms, small whole or sliced
- 1½ teaspoons salt
  Pepper
- 1 teaspoon Worcestershire sauce
- ¼ cup California Dry Sherry

To prepare kidneys for cooking, cut each in half; remove fat and tubes from center. Cover with cold water to which ¼ cup wine vinegar has been added; soak ½ hour. Sauté onion and celery in shortening. Add kidneys; simmer 5 minutes. Stir in flour, then stock or water. When smooth, add mushrooms, salt, pepper and Worcestershire sauce. Simmer, covered, 30 minutes. Add Sherry. Serve over rice or cooked noodles. Menu might include celery, olives and carrot sticks; biscuits; crushed pineapple cole slaw; finally cookies.

My choice of wine to accompany this dish:
CALIFORNIA DRY ROSÉ OR SAUTERNE

NOTE: *Mrs. La Rosa says that veal or beef kidneys may also be prepared in this way. The larger beef kidneys should be soaked 1 hour.*

BREADED SWEETBREADS MARSALA

(4 or 5 servings)

Mrs. Marvin B. Jones, Gibson Wine Company, Elk Grove

    2 pairs sweetbreads
    1 tablespoon vinegar or lemon juice
    1 egg, beaten
    ½ cup fine dry bread crumbs
    ½ teaspoon salt
    ⅛ teaspoon pepper
    ¼ cup melted butter or margarine
      Oil
    ½ cup California Marsala or Cream Sherry

Soak sweetbreads in cold water ½ hour, changing water twice during that time. Drain; plunge into boiling water to which vinegar or lemon juice has been added. Cook 5 minutes. Put into ice water for 10 minutes. Wipe dry, remove membranes. Cut into thick slices. Dip in beaten egg; then in bread crumbs seasoned with salt and pepper; then in melted butter. Dip again in egg; then bread crumbs. Cook to golden brown in small amount of heated oil. About 10 minutes before done, pour over wine; cover; continue cooking. A well-chilled white wine alongside brings out the delicate, delicious flavor.

My choice of wine to accompany this dish:
CALIFORNIA RIESLING OR HAUT SAUTERNE

SWEETBREADS Á LA KING

(6 to 8 servings)

Mrs. Hans Hyba, Paul Masson Vineyards, Saratoga

    2 lbs. sweetbreads
      Salt
    ⅓ cup onion rings
    1 green pepper, cut in rings
    2 tablespoons butter or margarine
    1 pimiento, cut in rings
    1 lb. fresh mushrooms, sliced
    4 teaspoons flour
    1½ cups hot milk or cream
    1 cup California Dry Sherry

Wash sweetbreads in cold water. Cover with salted water in a saucepan; bring to boiling. Reduce heat; simmer 5 minutes. Cool in broth. Meanwhile, sauté onions and green pepper in 2 teaspoons butter a few minutes; add pimiento. Remove cooled sweetbreads, reserving broth; cut in strips about 2″ long and ½″ thick. Add sweetbreads and mushrooms to onion mixture; stir very gently over low heat until hot (do not stir out of shape). Remove from heat. Melt remaining butter in saucepan; blend in flour. Stir in hot milk and 1 cup sweetbread broth; cook, stirring, until smooth and slightly thick. Add Sherry. Fold sauce into sweetbread mixture. Serve on toast; garnish with pieces of green pepper, mushrooms and pimiento.

NOTE: *Such a delectably rich dish deserves a kingly toast in California Champagne. If the budget interferes, serve a white dinner wine or Rosé.*

VEAL SWEETBREADS LOS GATOS

(8 servings)

Louis A. Benoist, Almaden Vineyards, Los Gatos

    2 lbs. veal sweetbreads
      Salt
    ½ lemon
    ¼ cup butter or margarine
    ¼ cup California Dry Sherry
    ½ cup beef stock (canned or
        bouillon-cube broth may be used)
    1 truffle, diced (optional)
    1 cup sliced sautéed mushrooms
    ½ cup pitted sliced green olives
      Rooster combs (optional)

Simmer sweetbreads 15 minutes in water to which salt and lemon have been added (or in Court Bouillon). Drain; plunge into ice water; clean and slice. Sauté in butter until slightly browned. Add Sherry and beef stock; reduce about ¼. Add truffle (if desired), mushrooms and olives. (Parboiled rooster combs may also be added, if you want to be very récherché.) Season to taste; serve with white rice.

My choice of wine to accompany this dish:
CALIFORNIA JOHANNISBERG RIESLING

OXTAIL STEW WITH RED WINE

(6 to 8 servings)

H. Peter Jurgens, Almaden Vineyards, Los Gatos

    3 lbs. oxtails, cut in 2″ pieces
    2 qts. water
    1 bay leaf
    1 large onion with 2 cloves inserted
    4 carrots, sliced
    4 stalks celery, sliced
    2 sprigs parsley
    1 tablespoon salt
    ¼ teaspoon pepper
    6 white onions
    ¼ cup butter or margarine
    3 level tablespoons flour
    1 cup California Cabernet, Burgundy
        or other red dinner wine
    1 teaspoon kitchen bouquet
    2 tablespoons finely-chopped parsley

Simmer oxtails in water with bay leaf, spiced onion, carrot and celery slices, parsley, salt and pepper. Cook until tender (about 2 hours). Meanwhile, cook onions until tender; set aside. When oxtails are tender, melt butter in saucepan; stir in flour. Slowly add 2 cups of strained hot broth from oxtails and wine; stir constantly until smooth. Add kitchen bouquet. Taste; correct seasoning. Add pieces of oxtail, carrot slices and cooked onions. Simmer 10 minutes; sprinkle chopped parsley over stew before serving.

NOTE: *Utterly delicious. Liquid could be thickened slightly, if desired, or served in a bowl over French bread. Would be even more enjoyable with the same red wine served with the meal. Another who makes a good oxtail stew is Mrs. Lewis A. Stern of E. & J. Gallo Winery, Modesto, who adds this idea: "If we have company, I serve the stew from my silver chafing dish, and I heat 3 tablespoons California brandy, ignite it and pour the flaming spirits over the oxtails at the table. This bit of ceremony adds charm and delightful interest to such a dish as stew. I serve rice or mashed potatoes with this oxtail recipe, as everyone loves the gravy."*

LAMB TONGUES BON VIN

(8 servings)

Mrs. E. A. Mirassou, Mirassou Vineyards, San Jose

This recipe has been handed down through the family for generations, through Ed's mother and grandmother.

    12 lamb tongues
    ½ cup California wine vinegar
     2 onions, chopped
     6 stalks celery, chopped
     1 clove garlic
    ¼ cup oil
    ¼ cup flour
     2 cups beef or chicken broth
       Salt and pepper
       Chopped parsley
    ½ cup California Sauterne or other
       white dinner wine

Place tongues in saucepan; add wine vinegar and enough water to cover. Let stand 2 hours; bring to boiling and simmer 2 hours. Remove tongues, reserving broth. Remove skin from tongues; cut into 1" pieces. Sauté onion, celery and garlic in oil until almost soft. Add flour, blending well. Stir in broth; cook slowly until thickened, stirring constantly. Add other ingredients and pieces of tongue; heat through. Serve over rice, with fresh vegetable of the season and green salad.

My choice of wine to accompany this dish:
A CHILLED CALIFORNIA WHITE DINNER WINE

TONGUE NAPA VALLEY

(3 or 4 servings)

Mrs. Robert Mondavi, Charles Krug Winery, St. Helena

     1 fresh tongue (calf or veal)
       Butter or margarine
     1 onion, chopped
     2 carrots, cut in small cubes
     1 cup California Sauterne, Chablis
       or other white dinner wine
     1 cup tomato sauce
       Salt and pepper
     2 tablespoons chopped pickles or relish
    ½ teaspoon chopped oregano
     1 tablespoon fresh chopped parsley

Cover tongue with water; bring to boiling. Reduce heat; simmer 20 minutes. Cool until easy to handle; remove skin. Brown meat in butter to which onion and carrots have been added. When brown, add wine, tomato sauce, salt and pepper. Simmer, covered, 45 minutes. Skim off excess fat. Remove tongue, keeping warm. Add chopped pickles and herbs to pan liquid. Cut tongue in thin slices, arrange on serving platter and pour sauce over all.

NOTE: *Either red or white dinner wine would be a pleasurable accompaniment — and especially a chilled Rosé.*

SWEET-SOUR TONGUE

(6 servings)

Mrs. Eugene Morosoli, Wine Advisory Board, San Francisco

    ¼ cup butter or olive oil
     1 small onion, sliced
     1 tablespoon flour
    ¼ cup California Burgundy or
       other red dinner wine
     2 tablespoons California red
       wine vinegar
    ½ cup sweet pickle, chopped
    ½ cup sweet pickle juice
     1 bouillon cube dissolved in
       1 cup hot water, or 1 cup broth
     2 tablespoons catsup
    ⅛ teaspoon *each:* rosemary, thyme, sage
     1 clove garlic, finely chopped
     2 tablespoons chopped parsley
    18 slices boiled beef tongue

Heat butter or oil in saucepan; sauté onion until slightly brown. Stir in flour to make a paste; add all remaining ingredients, except tongue. Simmer ½ hour, stirring occasionally. Add tongue; heat through 5 to 10 minutes.

My choice of wine to accompany this dish:
CALIFORNIA BURGUNDY OR A RED "VINO" TYPE

TRIPE PARISIENNE

(6 to 8 servings)

Mrs. Rene Baillif, Buena Vista Vineyards, Sonoma

This old recipe originated in France in the province of Normandy, but it is served "par excellence" in Paris, where some restaurants have for many generations specialized in this dish.

     4 to 4½ lbs. honeycomb tripe,
       cut in 2" squares
     1 bottle California Sauterne or
       other white dinner wine
     1 (14-oz.) can condensed chicken broth
       Salt and pepper
     1 bay leaf
       Dash thyme
     1 onion, chopped
     3 or 4 green onions, chopped
    ½ cup chopped parsley
     1 (1-lb.) veal shank, cut in 2" cubes
    12 whole peppercorns
     3 or 4 tablespoons California brandy

Cover tripe with slightly salted water; bring to boiling; cook 30 minutes. Drain thoroughly; place in large heavy kettle. Cover with boiling water, wine and chicken broth. Season with salt and pepper. Add bay leaf, thyme, chopped onion, green onions and parsley. Bring to medium boil. Cook about ½ hour, skimming foam thoroughly. Add veal. Cover and bake in slow oven (250°) for 4 or 5 hours. Add more hot water and wine during cooking, if necessary. During last 15 minutes, add peppercorns and brandy. Carefully remove bones from veal. Serve very hot in individual oven-proof casseroles. Almost a meal in itself, it can be served with steamed potatoes and followed by green salad and cheese.

My choice of wine to accompany this dish:
CALIFORNIA GREEN HUNGARIAN OR GREY RIESLING

POULTRY

Chicken, Turkey, Duck, Goose, Squab

"A hot bird and a cold bottle" sums up one of man's happiest conditions at the dining table. And as in the case of meats, the bird is juicier, tenderer than ever, when cooked as well as served with a fragrant wine from California's vineyards. Wine is indispensable for perfect poultry. You'll enjoy these time-tried recipes. (For suitable sauces, see the section starting on Page 57.)

CHICKEN ZELLERBACH

(7 or 8 servings)

J. D. Zellerbach, Hanzell Winery, Sonoma

> 2 (3-lb.) frying chickens or
> 1 (6-lb.) roasting chicken
>   Flour, seasoned with salt and pepper
> 1 cup butter or margarine
> ½ cup chopped onion
> 1 chicken bouillon cube dissolved in
>   1 cup hot water; or 1 cup chicken broth
> 1½ cups California Pinot Chardonnay
>   or other white dinner wine
> ½ cup California Marsala or Cream Sherry
> 1 teaspoon marjoram
> 1 teaspoon thyme
> ½ bay leaf
> ¼ teaspoon curry powder
> ½ teaspoon paprika

Cut chicken in serving size pieces; dredge in seasoned flour. Melt ½ cup butter in skillet; fry chicken on all sides over moderate heat until tender. Meanwhile, melt remaining ½ cup butter in saucepan; sauté onions until yellow. Add other ingredients. A few minutes before serving, add chicken to sauce; heat thoroughly. If more sauce is desired, simply add a little more wine or chicken broth.

NOTE: *A rich, sound chicken of excellent flavor. Would be especially good served with chilled glasses of the same white dinner wine, or a Chablis.*

QUICK FEAST FOR THE HURRIED: Pick up a barbecued chicken at the butcher's or delicatessen on your way home. Have it cut in half. In shallow baking pan, melt ¼ cup butter; add about ¼ cup California Light Muscat, Cream Sherry or Muscatel. Roll chicken halves in this mixture, then sprinkle with instant minced onion, salt and monosodium glutamate. Heat thoroughly in same pan in moderately hot oven (350 to 375°), about 20 minutes. Baste once or twice with wine-butter from pan bottom. Pour any remaining sauce over hot chicken just before serving to two hungry persons, with glasses of cold California Rhine or Rosé alongside.

ROASTED CHICKEN CALABRIAN

(8 servings)

M. J. Filice, San Martin Vineyards Co., San Martin

Delicious, exotic—one of Italy's famous, classic fryer dishes (Pollo alla Calabrese). In proper platter, has tremendous eye appeal. When garnished attractively with figs, orange slices and parsley, this dish is a composition of epicurean art.

> 2 (2½ or 3-lb.) frying chickens, quartered
>   Olive oil
> 1 teaspoon dried oregano, crumbled
> 2 teaspoons minced fresh parsley
> 2 cloves garlic, minced
>   Salt
>   Monosodium glutamate
> 1 cup California Malvasia Bianca, Light Muscat,
>   Sauterne or other white dinner wine
> 1 lemon
> 1 (1-lb. 1-oz.) can Kadota figs, drained
> 1 medium-size thin-skinned orange,
>   sliced ¼" thick
>   California Sherry

Brush chicken with oil. Sprinkle with seasonings. Place in shallow baking pan, skin side up. Bake, uncovered, in hot oven (400°) for 20 to 25 minutes, or until brown. Combine wine and juice of lemon; baste chicken often during cooking. Meanwhile, prick figs with fork; marinate figs and orange slices in Sherry. Turn chicken; brown other side 15 to 20 minutes. Taste; correct salt (should have slightly salty taste). Add figs and orange slices; continue cooking 5 to 10 minutes, or until golden. (If chicken seems dry, finish basting with Sherry marinade from fruit.) Menu may include soup, tossed green salad, spaghettini, fresh fruit, good music, and a good book or good friends in conversation.

My choice of wine to accompany this dish:
CALIFORNIA MALVASIA BIANCA
OR CHABLIS OR SAUTERNE

BAKED CHICKEN ROSÉ

(3 or 4 servings)

Mrs. Joseph S. Concannon, Jr., Concannon Vineyard, Livermore

While a dry white wine is quite appropriate in this recipe, we prefer the flavor from cooking it with a dry Rosé. With it, however, we like to serve a chilled white.

        1 (2½ or 3-lb.) chicken, quartered or
           cut in large serving-pieces
           Flour seasoned with salt and pepper
        6 tablespoons butter or margarine
        2 tablespoons flour
      ¾ cup chicken bouillon (canned or
           bouillon-cube broth may be used)
      ½ cup California Rosé or a white dinner wine
      ¼ cup thinly sliced green onions
           (including tops)
        1 (4-oz.) can mushrooms, or
      ½ cup fresh mushrooms sautéed in butter
        1 (9-oz.) pkg. frozen artichoke hearts
           (cooked according to pkg. directions)

Dust chicken with seasoned flour. Melt 4 tablespoons butter in shallow baking pan. Place chicken in pan, skin side down; bake, uncovered, in moderate oven (350 to 375°) 45 minutes to 1 hour, or until almost tender. Meanwhile, melt other 2 tablespoons butter in saucepan. Stir in flour. Add bouillon and wine; cook, stirring constantly, until thickened and smooth. Remove chicken from oven. Turn pieces over; sprinkle with onions, mushrooms and cooked artichokes. (Water chestnuts or thinly sliced fresh tomatoes may be substituted for artichoke hearts.) Pour over sauce. Return to oven; reduce heat to 325°; bake 25 to 30 minutes longer. We serve this usually with a rice Milanese, with chicken sauce on top, and fresh asparagus if in season.

My choice of wine to accompany this dish:
CHILLED CALIFORNIA CHABLIS OR MOSELLE

BAKED CHICKEN CALIFORNIAN

(3 or 4 servings)

Jack Pandol, Delano Growers Co-Op. Winery, Delano

        1 (3 or 4-lb.) frying chicken, quartered
           or cut in large serving pieces
           Salt and pepper
        1 onion, sliced
        2 slices bacon, diced
      ¼ cup water
      ¼ cup California Sherry

In a shallow baking pan, place chicken pieces snugly in a single layer, skin side up. Sprinkle generously with salt, pepper; add onion and bacon. Sprinkle with water and Sherry. Cover; bake in moderate oven (350°) ½ hour. Remove cover; bake 20 to 30 minutes longer or until chicken is tender. Serve with pilaf or steamed rice, vegetable and green salad.

My choice of wine to accompany this dish:
ANY CALIFORNIA WHITE DINNER WINE

EASY ROAST CHICKEN

(8 servings)

Mrs. Herman Ehlers, East-Side Winery, Lodi

        2 (2 or 2¼-lb.) frying chickens, quartered
      ¼ cup butter or margarine
           Salt and pepper
        2 cups California Sauterne or other
           white dinner wine
      ½ cup chicken stock (canned or
           bouillon-cube broth may be used)
      ½ cup thinly sliced green onions
      ½ cup chopped celery
      ¼ cup finely-chopped parsley

Rub skin side of chicken with butter; sprinkle with salt and pepper. Place skin side down in shallow baking pan; bake in hot oven (425°) for 15 minutes. Combine remaining ingredients; pour over chicken. Bake 30 minutes longer, basting several times. Reduce heat to 350°, turn chicken skin side up; continue baking and basting until chicken is done and as brown as desired. Pan drippings make a good gravy.

NOTE: A most pleasing flavor, and quite simple to prepare. Serve the same wine, chilled, on the side.

CHICKEN IN THE POT

(4 servings)

Mrs. Stanford J. Wolf, Paul Masson Vineyards, Saratoga

This is even more flavorful if made the day before and reheated.

        1 roasting chicken
        1 lemon, cut in half
           Salt and pepper
        2 tablespoons butter or margarine
        2 cups chicken broth
           (chicken stock base broth may be used)
        1 stalk celery
        2 tomatoes
        2 onions
        2 carrots
      ¼ lb. green beans
           Small bunch parsley, chopped
        2 cups California Sauterne or other
           white dinner wine

Rub chicken inside and out with cut lemon, salt and pepper. Melt butter in Dutch oven; brown chicken on all sides. Add broth; simmer 45 minutes. Meanwhile, cut vegetables in chunks. Add to chicken with wine; simmer 1 hour longer, or until chicken and vegetables are tender. Taste and correct seasoning. Preferred menu with the chicken: rice, large stuffed mushrooms, and salad of watercress and bean sprouts.

My choice of wine to accompany this dish:
CHILLED CALIFORNIA ROSÉ OR RIESLING

NOTE: Those who enjoy a particularly winey flavor can pour a little more wine into the pot immediately before serving. There are many variations on this great classic treatment for chicken (cooked in wine, with vegetables). The dish has a long history, and was a favorite of Henri IV of Navarre.

CLASSIC CHICKEN IN WINE

(4 to 6 servings)

Mrs. Frank H. Bartholomew, Buena Vista Vineyards, Sonoma

In a flower-filled garden high above the ancient old-world village of Tramin, this savory Coq au Vin was served to us in a silver bowl, on a tray garlanded with spring flowers. Cuttings from steep hillside vineyards above the town have been growing in California more than 100 years, producing one of the finest of dry white wines.

    1 (5 or 6-lb.) roasting or fricassee chicken,
        cut in large pieces
        Salt and pepper
    ¼ cup chicken fat
    ¾ cup butter or margarine
    ⅓ cup California brandy
    3 cups California Gewurz Traminer,
        Rhine or other white dinner wine
    1 cup chicken broth (canned or
        bouillon-cube broth may be used)
    1 teaspoon marjoram
  12 small white onions
  12 tiny new carrots
  12 small new potatoes
      Chopped parsley

Wipe chicken with damp cloth; sprinkle with salt and pepper. Melt chicken fat and ¼ cup butter in large, heavy skillet or Dutch oven; brown chicken slowly on all sides (about 10 minutes). Pour over brandy; ignite. When flames die down, add wine, broth and marjoram. Cover; place in slow oven (250 to 300°) about 3 hours or until chicken is nearly tender. (Add a little more wine during cooking, if necessary.) Meanwhile, brown onions, carrots and potatoes in remaining ½ cup butter. Add to chicken; continue cooking about 30 minutes or until vegetables are tender. Sprinkle with chopped parsley. Serve with green salad and hot, crusty, sour-dough French bread.

My choice of wine to accompany this dish:
CHILLED CALIFORNIA GEWURZ TRAMINER

NOTE: *The flaming brandy treatment for chicken is also favored by Mrs. Marvin B. Jones of Gibson Wine Company, Elk Grove. Mrs. Jones' Chicken au Vin is simmered in a combination of red and white dinner wines (after first browning, then flaming). Egg yolks, cream and flour are finally added, to make a marvelous gravy. She prefers California Rosé with the dish— "a pleasing and striking accompaniment."*

STILL ANOTHER luscious brandy-and-wine treatment for chicken (unflamed) features California Dry Vermouth. Brown chicken parts in ¼ lb. butter, add salt and bare hint of chopped green onions, shallots or garlic, if desired. Pour over 1 cup Dry Vermouth and 2 or 3 tablespoons California brandy; simmer 20 minutes, covered. Result is rich and moist; good treatment also for pheasant. Leftover clear sauce can be refrigerated for later flavoring of other dishes, even vegetables.

BRANDIED FRICASSEE CHICKEN

(6 servings)

H. Peter Jurgens, Almaden Vineyards, Los Gatos

    1 (4-lb.) roasting or fricassee chicken,
        cut in serving pieces
    ¼ cup sifted flour
    ½ cup butter or margarine
    1 thin slice raw ham, diced
  10 small onions, peeled
    2 tablespoons California brandy
        Herb bouquet (tie together 3 or 4 sprigs
        parsley, sprig thyme and small bay leaf)
        Salt and pepper
    1 cup mushrooms (optional)
    1 cup California Pinot Noir, Burgundy
        or other red dinner wine

Dredge chicken in flour; sauté in melted butter until nicely browned. Add ham and onions; cook until lightly browned. Pour over brandy; ignite. When flames die down, add herb bouquet, salt, pepper, mushrooms and wine. Cover tightly; simmer until chicken is very tender, about 2½ hours. Discard herb bouquet. If desired, thicken gravy with a little cornstarch mixed with cold water.

My choice of wine to accompany this dish:
CALIFORNIA PINOT NOIR

NOTE: *The brandy in cooking adds a wonderfully subtle flavor. Another using this method in a similar recipe is Mrs. Walter Staley of Western Grape Products, Kingsburg. Mrs. Staley says a package of frozen peas may be added during the last half-hour, which would add attractive color. She prefers to serve a dry white wine with her chicken, although she uses red wine in the cooking.*

SUPERB BARBECUED CHICKEN

(Any amount)

Nino Muzio, California Growers Wineries, Cutler

Remove wing tips, ends of leg bones and excess fat from chicken (quartered, halved or whole). Place chicken in wooden bowl, tub or glass container. Cover with ½ California white dinner wine and ½ California Dry Sherry (or **all** white wine or Sherry); marinate 12 hours in refrigerator. Drain off wine; dry with paper towels, brush with thin layer of olive oil, and season with salt, pepper, savory salt, onion salt and poultry seasoning. Layer chicken in bowl, with additional olive oil, salt, pepper, parsley, rosemary and a few garlic chips on each layer. Cover bowl; refrigerate 12 to 15 hours. Barbecue over medium-hot coals. When almost done, baste with a mixture of ½ soy sauce and ½ melted butter or margarine.

NOTE: *Chilled California white dinner wine or Rosé would be perfect with this—or a red dinner wine, since the chicken is highly seasoned.*

CHICKEN PARISIENNE

(4 servings)

Mrs. A. H. Burton, Roma Wine Co., Fresno

This is a good way to use leftover chicken, or stewing chicken.

   1 (10-oz.) pkg. frozen broccoli
   2 tablespoons butter, melted
   2 tablespoons flour
   1 cup milk
   ½ teaspoon salt
   ¼ cup California Sherry
   4 to 8 slices cooked chicken
     (or, turkey may be used)
   1 cup grated Cheddar cheese

Cook broccoli according to package directions. Meanwhile, in small saucepan, blend butter and flour; slowly stir in milk. Cook, stirring constantly, until mixture is smooth and thick. Add salt; stir in Sherry. Drain broccoli; place in 4 individual casseroles. Top with chicken or turkey slices. Pour over wine sauce; top with grated cheese. Broil until cheese is melted and delicately browned. With this dish we like a tossed green salad with tomatoes, rolls, and ice cream or sherbet for dessert.

My choice of wine to accompany this dish:
CHILLED CALIFORNIA GREY RIESLING

CHICKEN CACCIATORE

(4 to 6 servings)

Mrs. L. J. Berg, Mont La Salle Vineyards, Napa

   ¼ cup olive oil
   2 (3 or 4-lb.) frying chickens, cut
     in serving pieces
   2 cloves garlic, minced
   1 teaspoon salt
   ¼ teaspoon pepper
   ½ teaspoon crumbled oregano
   ½ teaspoon crumbled basil
   1 (1-lb. 4-oz.) can tomatoes
   1 (3-oz.) can mushrooms, drained
   ¼ cup California Sherry
     Parsley

Heat oil in chicken fryer or heavy skillet. Brown chicken until golden-brown. Add garlic, salt, pepper, oregano, basil, tomatoes and mushrooms. Cover; simmer about 25 minutes or until tender. Add Sherry; cook 10 minutes longer. Sprinkle with parsley.

My choice of wine to accompany this dish:
CALIFORNIA DRY SAUVIGNON BLANC
OR JOHANNISBERG RIESLING

NOTE: *Another delicious recipe with similar combination of ingredients is used by Mrs. John G. Laucci of Franzia Brothers Winery, Ripon. Her version is called CHICKEN HUNTER STYLE, and includes sage leaves and potatoes (deep-fried first, then cooked 10 minutes with chicken). Excellent Cacciatores are also made by Mrs. Frank G. Cadenasso of Cadenasso Winery, Fairfield; and Mrs. August Sebastiani of Samuele Sebastiani, Sonoma.*

CHICKEN RAPHAEL WEILL

(4 servings)

Louis A. Benoist, Almaden Vineyards, Los Gatos

This delicate chicken dish, with its melting celestial sauce, was named after the gourmet uncle of the owner of one of San Francisco's oldest department stores. It is interesting to note that a famous Paris restaurant includes this dish on its menu. Quite a feather in the culinary cap of California!

   2 (2-lb.) broiling chickens
   ½ lemon
     Salt and pepper
     Flour
   ¼ cup butter or margarine
   3 medium-size green onions, chopped
   ½ cup California Pinot Blanc, Sauterne
     or other white dinner wine
   2 tablespoons rich chicken broth
   4 egg yolks
   1 cup heavy cream
     Freshly-grated nutmeg
     Cayenne pepper
     Minced chives
     Parsley
     Chervil and tarragon (optional)
     Few drops lemon juice

Cut chickens into serving size pieces. Rub with lemon; sprinkle with salt and pepper; dust with flour. Heat butter in heavy skillet; sauté chicken until golden on all sides. Cover; simmer 10 minutes. Add onions; cook 5 minutes longer, shaking pan frequently. Pour over wine; simmer 2 minutes. Add rich chicken broth (can be made by reducing ¼ cup chicken broth by half). Cook, covered, over low heat 10 minutes or until chicken is fork-tender, shaking pan frequently (be careful not to boil). Meanwhile, beat egg yolks with heavy cream; season to taste with nutmeg, cayenne, chives, parsley and, if desired, chervil and tarragon. Just before serving, pour cream mixture over chicken in pan. Cook over very low heat, stirring or shaking pan constantly, until sauce thickens. Add a few drops lemon juice. Arrange chicken on warm platter; pour over sauce; serve at once.

My choice of wine to accompany this dish:
CALIFORNIA PINOT CHARDONNAY

LODI CHICKEN

(4 servings)

Mrs. Hubert Mettler, Guild Wine Co., Lodi

- 1 (10½-oz.) can cream of mushroom soup
- 1 cup sour cream
- 1 (4-oz.) can button or sliced mushrooms, undrained
- ½ cup California Sherry
- 1 frying chicken, quartered
  Paprika

Combine soup, sour cream, mushrooms and Sherry. Pour over chicken in baking pan. Sprinkle with paprika. Bake, covered, in a moderate oven (350°) for 1 or 1¼ hours, or until tender. Serve with baked potatoes, a hot vegetable such as peas and carrots, green tossed salad, rolls, and cookies for dessert.

My choice of wine to accompany this dish:
ANY FAVORITE CALIFORNIA WHITE DINNER WINE

NOTE: *This is an exceptionally easy recipe, providing lots of tantalizing gravy for the potatoes (or perhaps noodles or rice). Many good cooks like the combination of sour cream, mushrooms and California Sherry with baked chicken. It's an ever-pleasing blend, recommended also by Mrs. A. Jensen of Gemello Winery, Mountain View; and Mrs. Alvin Ehrhardt of United Vintners, Inc., Lodi.*

CHICKEN ALMOND

(6 to 8 servings)

Mrs. Joseph S. Concannon, Jr., Concannon Vineyard, Livermore

I've found this to be one of the simplest chicken recipes, especially handy when supervising our three pre-school children.

- 1 (10½-oz.) can cream of mushroom soup
- 1 (10½-oz.) can cream of celery soup
- 1 cup grated Cheddar cheese
- ¾ cup California Sauvignon Blanc, Chablis or other white dinner wine
- 2 (3-lb.) frying chickens, quartered or cut in large serving pieces
- ⅓ cup sliced almonds

Combine soups, cheese and wine in large shallow baking pan. Add chicken, bone side down. Cover pan with foil; bake in moderately slow oven (325°) 2½ hours. Remove foil; add sliced almonds. Bake 30 minutes longer. The recipe sauce is good as a gravy on rice or mashed potatoes.

My choice of wine to accompany this dish:
CALIFORNIA SAUVIGNON BLANC OR WHITE RIESLING

CHICKEN AND RICE CREOLE

(6 servings)

Mrs. William Perelli-Minetti, A. Perelli-Minetti & Sons, Delano

- 1 (4-lb.) fricassee chicken, cut in serving-size pieces
- ½ cup flour
- 2 teaspoons salt
- ¼ teaspoon white pepper
  Heated shortening or cooking oil
- 2 cups canned tomatoes
- ¼ cup instant minced onion
- ¼ cup dried sweet pepper flakes
- 1½ cups water
- ½ cup California Chablis or other white dinner wine
- ½ bay leaf
- 1 tablespoon dried parsley flakes
- ½ teaspoon thyme
- 1 teaspoon salt
  Hot cooked rice

Coat chicken with flour seasoned with salt and pepper. Brown in hot shortening. Add tomatoes, onion, sweet pepper, water, wine and bay leaf; cover tightly; simmer 1 hour. Add parsley, thyme and salt; simmer 15 to 20 minutes longer, or until chicken is fork-tender. Serve over hot cooked rice, with menu including green peas and tossed salad.

My choice of wine to accompany this dish:
CALIFORNIA SAUTERNE OR CHABLIS

SMOTHERED CHICKEN

(4 servings)

Mrs. Harold E. Roush, Guild Wine Co., Lodi

You can also use this same easy mushroom sauce to enhance the flavor of Swiss steak or pork chops as they bake.

- 1 (4-lb.) frying chicken, cut in serving pieces
- ¼ cup flour
  Salt
- 3 tablespoons oil
- 1 cup diced celery
- ½ cup diced onion
- 1 (10½-oz.) can cream of mushroom soup
- ¼ cup California Cream Sherry

Coat chicken with flour seasoned with salt. Heat oil in heavy skillet; brown chicken. Combine remaining ingredients; pour over chicken. Cover; bake in a moderate oven (350°) for 30 minutes. Uncover; bake 15 minutes longer. The menu with this might include baked rice (using broth from neck, wing tips, etc., for liquid); buttered green beans; crisp apple-celery-pineapple salad and toasted French rolls.

My choice of wine to accompany this dish:
CALIFORNIA WHITE DINNER WINE

CHICKEN MARSALA

(2 to 4 servings)

Harry Baccigaluppi, Calif. Grape Products Corp., Delano

4 chicken breasts
3 tablespoons flour
½ teaspoon seasoned salt
Dash of pepper
Pinch of oregano
3 tablespoons olive oil
3 tablespoons butter or margarine
½ cup California Marsala or Cream Sherry

Remove skin from chicken breasts. Dredge in flour seasoned with salt and pepper. Sprinkle oregano over breasts. Heat oil and butter in heavy skillet. Brown chicken, cavity side first. When browned on both sides, add wine. Cover and simmer about ½ hour or until tender. Serve with risotto or buttered rice.

My choice of wine to accompany this dish:
CALIFORNIA NEBBIOLO, OR ROSÉ OR CHABLIS

CHICKEN IN THE VINE

(4 to 6 servings)

J. B. Cella, II, Cella Wineries, Fresno

12 halved chicken breasts
Flour seasoned with salt and pepper
6 tablespoons butter or margarine
1 (6-oz.) can sliced mushrooms, undrained
2 tablespoons flour
½ teaspoon salt
¼ teaspoon pepper
2 tablespoons grape juice
1 cup chicken stock (canned or bouillon-cube broth may be used)
1 cup seedless grapes
Paprika
1 cup California Cream Sherry

Remove skin from chicken breasts. Dust chicken with seasoned flour. Sauté in melted butter, turning occasionally until tender and slightly browned. Place in casserole. Stir undrained mushrooms into rich brown drippings left in pan. Combine flour, salt and pepper; mix with grape juice to form smooth paste. Stir into mushrooms and drippings; add chicken stock, grapes and paprika. Simmer gently 10 minutes, stirring occasionally. Pour in wine; let sauce simmer 1 minute. Pour sauce over chicken; bake in moderate oven (350°) for 30 minutes.

My choice of wine to accompany this dish:
CALIFORNIA RIESLING OR DRY SAUTERNE

NOTE: *If a less-sweet chicken flavor is desired, California Dry or Medium Sherry can be used in the cooking instead of Cream Sherry. Either way, it's a flavorful and interesting dish.*

SAUTÉED CHICKEN IN CREAM

(6 servings)

Mrs. Klayton Nelson, U. of Calif. Dept. Viticulture & Enology

This is an excellent choice for a buffet luncheon or even a hearty dinner. Sauce is rich and good, but not complicated, and economical to prepare.

12 chicken breasts or thighs, boned
½ cup butter or margarine
12 medium-size fresh mushroom caps
3 tablespoons butter or margarine
7 tablespoons flour
2⅓ cups chicken broth (canned or bouillon-cube broth may be used)
¼ cup California Dry Sherry
1 cup light cream

Sauté chicken gently in ½ cup butter until slightly brown, turning occasionally, until almost tender. Add mushroom caps; cook, covered, until done. Meanwhile, melt 3 tablespoons butter in saucepan; stir in flour and chicken broth; cook, stirring constantly, until very thick. Remove chicken and mushrooms to warm serving dish. Add Sherry to pan in which chicken was cooked; scrape up browned bits in bottom and on sides of pan; stir in cream. Blend wine-cream sauce into thickened white sauce. Strain sauce; spoon over chicken and mushrooms. Nice with frozen peas or beans, or any other bright green vegetable, and buttery baked potatoes.

My choice of wine to accompany this dish:
ANY CALIFORNIA DRY WHITE OR DRY ROSÉ

CHICKEN JUBILEE

(6 to 8 servings)

Esther Gowans, Glen Ellen Winery & Distillery, Glen Ellen

6 to 8 chicken breasts
½ cup flour
¼ teaspoon garlic salt
½ teaspoon paprika
1½ teaspoons salt
¼ cup butter or oil
1 cup California Sauterne, Chablis or other white dinner wine
2 cups canned pitted Bing cherries
½ cup California brandy

Shake chicken breasts in bag with flour, garlic salt, paprika and salt. Sauté slowly in butter or oil to rich golden-brown. Arrange in casserole or baking pan; pour over wine. Cover; bake in moderately hot oven (375°) 20 minutes. Remove cover; add cherries. Return to oven; bake, uncovered, 15 to 20 minutes longer or until chicken is tender. Place on top of stove over very low heat. Pour over brandy; do NOT allow to boil. Set aflame; when flames die down, serve chicken with cherries and sauce. I usually serve this with buttered noodles; green peas; tossed salad with olive oil and wine vinegar dressing, and beets pickled in wine vinegar; and finally cheese cake.

My choice of wine to accompany this dish:
CHILLED CALIFORNIA RIESLING

BREASTS OF CHICKEN AU PORTO

(6 servings)

Mrs. Joseph Heitz, Heitz Wine Cellar, St. Helena

        6 boned chicken breasts
        4 blades tarragon
        2 tablespoons butter or margarine
        6 small white onions, thinly sliced
        1 cup sour cream
      ½ cup California Port
        3 tablespoons California Sherry
      ½ cup very rich chicken broth
            (2 cups broth over high heat
            reduced to ½ cup)
            Salt and freshly ground pepper
            Dash nutmeg

In a skillet, sauté chicken breasts lightly in butter until tender. Meanwhile, prepare sauce, as follows: Parboil tarragon in water; drain; pound to a paste with 2 tablespoons butter. Melt flavored butter; add onions; cook until delicately colored, stirring constantly. Put pan over hot water; stir in sour cream; heat 5 minutes. Stir in wines and broth; simmer 5 minutes more. Place chicken breasts in sauce, cover and simmer gently 5 to 10 minutes, or until sauce is thick. Season with salt, pepper and nutmeg.

My choice of wine to accompany this dish:
CALIFORNIA JOHANNISBERG RIESLING
OR CABERNET SAUVIGNON

NOTE: *This unusual, flavorful recipe, also known as Supremes de Volaille au Porto, is ideal for a chafing dish.*

SUPREME DEVILED CHICKEN

(4 to 6 servings)

Earle M. Cobb, California Growers Wineries, Cutler

        1 (3-lb.) broiling or frying chicken,
            cut in serving-size pieces
            Paprika
            Salt and pepper
      ½ cup oil or melted shortening
        2 tablespoons flour
    1½ teaspoons dry mustard
        1 cup soup stock or chicken broth
            (canned or bouillon-cube broth may be used)
        2 teaspoons Worcestershire sauce
        2 teaspoons catsup
      ½ cup California Sherry

Sprinkle chicken with paprika, salt and pepper. Brown in heated oil; remove from pan. Stir flour and mustard into fat remaining in pan. Slowly stir in stock. Cook, stirring constantly, until thick. Add remaining ingredients. Return chicken to pan. Simmer, covered, 1 hour.

NOTE: *This would be spicy enough for any type of dinner wine to accompany it — white, Rosé or red.*

GOLD RUSH CHICKEN LIVERS

(4 to 6 servings)

Mrs. Gerta Wingerd, U. of Calif. Med. Center, San Francisco

        1 lb. chicken livers
      ½ teaspoon salt
      ⅛ teaspoon pepper
      ½ cup sifted flour
      ¼ cup bacon fat
      ½ cup California Sauterne, Riesling,
            or other white dinner wine
        6 slices crisply-fried bacon, crumbled
            Finely-chopped fresh parsley

Dredge chicken livers in mixed salt, pepper, flour; brown lightly in hot bacon fat. Turn heat low, add wine; cover and steam 5 minutes, or until cooked. Sprinkle with bacon and parsley. Serve atop hot rice or noodles, with watercress or tomato garnish.

NOTE: *Either red or white wine would be highly satisfactory served along with this piquant dish: the same used in cooking, or perhaps a Claret.*

CHICKEN LIVERS IN PORT

(2 or 3 servings)

Mrs. David B. Ficklin, Ficklin Vineyards, Madera

This is a particular favorite of ours for chafing dish cookery, but equally good when done "top of the stove." We like it for a cool winter evening, cooked and served before the fireplace.

        2 small green onions, finely chopped
      ¼ cup butter or margarine
      ½ lb. chicken livers
      ¼ teaspoon fresh sage, or
            ⅛ teaspoon ground sage
      ¼ teaspoon salt
        1 tablespoon lemon juice
      ⅓ cup California Port
      ⅛ teaspoon freshly ground pepper

Sauté onions in melted butter a few minutes. Add livers; sauté 3 to 5 minutes, depending on size of livers. Bruise sage; add along with salt, lemon juice, Port and pepper. Cook slowly about 8 minutes, stirring occasionally. Correct seasoning and serve it forth on toast! Menu might include a tossed green salad with oil and wine vinegar dressing; toasted French bread; and dessert of Port, apple wedges and a few walnuts.

My choice of wine to accompany this dish:
CALIFORNIA PINOT NOIR

SQUABS IN RED WINE

(2 servings)

Mrs. Joseph J. Franzia, Franzia Brothers Winery, Ripon

          4 slices bacon, diced
          2 (1-lb.) squabs, prepared for roasting
          3 tablespoons flour
          1 teaspoon salt
          ¼ teaspoon pepper
          1 cup California Burgundy, Claret
            or other red dinner wine
          ½ cup chicken stock (canned or
            bouillon-cube broth may be used)
          8 small white onions, peeled
          2 carrots, peeled and sliced
          ½ bay leaf
          2 tablespoons chopped parsley
          2 squab livers, chopped
          ¼ lb. fresh mushrooms, sliced, or
          1 cup shelled fresh peas

In heavy skillet, fry bacon until golden brown, then put in large casserole or covered roaster. Sprinkle birds with flour seasoned with salt and pepper. Brown all over in bacon drippings remaining in skillet. Add any remaining flour; blend well. Put birds in casserole. Add ½ to ¾ cup wine and all the stock to drippings in skillet. Bring to boiling; reduce heat; simmer, stirring to scrape up all browned bits in bottom and on sides of pan. Cook 5 minutes, stirring constantly. Pour over squabs. Add onions, carrots, bay leaf, parsley, livers and remaining wine. Cover; bake in moderate oven (325 to 350°) for ½ hour. Add mushrooms (or peas); cook, covered, 40 to 45 minutes longer, or until squabs are tender. If mushrooms are used, then menu might include steamed buttered rice or baked potatoes; and tossed green salad with wine vinegar and olive oil dressing.

My choice of wine to accompany this dish:
CALIFORNIA BURGUNDY OR SPARKLING BURGUNDY

QUICK ROAST TURKEY CHABLIS

Mrs. Frank G. Cadenasso, Cadenasso Winery, Fairfield

This method shortens the cooking time of your bird. After cooking many turkeys, we find this wine-and-butter treatment gives a moist white meat and a rich, really elegant gravy that needs only slight thickening with flour.

          Roasting turkey, stuffed with
            favorite dressing
          Oil
          Salt
          California Sauterne, Chablis or
            other white dinner wine
          ½ cup butter or margarine

Place turkey, oiled and salted, breast side up on rack in large roasting pan in moderately hot oven (400°); brown. Turn turkey breast side down; cover with cheesecloth dampened thoroughly with wine. Reduce heat to 300 to 325°. Melt butter; brush cheesecloth with butter and wine frequently as turkey cooks. An 18 to 20-lb. bird takes only about 3½ hours. Serve with any traditional turkey dinner menu.

My choice of wine to accompany this dish:
CHILLED CALIFORNIA RHINE WINE OR CHABLIS

STUFFED ROASTED SQUABS

(8 servings)

Mrs. Eugene P. Seghesio, Seghesio Winery, Cloverdale

My father has always raised squabs for as long as I can remember. He gives them special attention; and we, as children, helped in their care. For Sunday dinner and on many special occasions, we enjoyed squab prepared in a variety of ways by my parents, and always with wine in the recipe.

          8 (1-lb.) squabs (cavities salted)
            Wild Rice Stuffing
            Butter
            Salt and pepper
          ½ cup California Sauterne, Chablis
            or other white dinner wine, or
          ⅓ cup California Dry Sherry

Stuff each squab with Wild Rice Stuffing (see below). Rub birds generously with butter or margarine; season with salt and pepper. Place in roasting pan in hot oven (400°) 10 minutes. Reduce heat to 325°; cook 50 minutes longer, basting frequently with pan juices. During last 15 minutes, pour over wine. This is one dish I especially enjoy serving to guests. The following menu would be for a **special** dinner party: Hors d'oeuvre such as Camembert cheese and crackers, and small cantaloupe wedges wrapped in prosciutto slices, with California Champagne. Then as first course, homemade antipasto (made with red wine vinegar) and California Chablis or Johannisberg Riesling. Next, tortellini with a meat sauce made with ½ cup red or white dinner wine. Then the squab with wild rice, fresh asparagus, sautéed mushrooms and mixed green salad. With this main course a California Pinot Noir. For dessert, fresh strawberries in Burgundy, flamed with brandy and spooned over coffee ice cream. Finally, coffee with California brandy.

WILD RICE STUFFING: Chop ½ medium onion, ½ clove garlic and 2 stalks celery; saute in ¼ cup butter or margarine until onion is clear. Combine with 2 cups cooked wild rice, ⅓ cup California Sauterne or other white dinner wine, salt and pepper.

NOTE: Such an epicurean menu, for a special occasion, would certainly deserve California Champagne at the beginning. One kind of wine (such as a Burgundy) throughout the dinner would still be correct, if desired. For those on budgets, delicious brown rice stuffing might be made same way.

BREASTS OF CORNISH GAME HEN

(6 servings)

Brother Timothy, Mont La Salle Vineyards, Napa

We served this menu several years ago to a group of visiting food editors, and it met with such enthusiasm that we serve it, with small variations, at many of our luncheons for distinguished visitors. It never fails to call forth much praise.

        6 boned breasts of Cornish game hens
          (chicken breasts may be used)
          Monosodium glutamate
     ¼ cup flour
          Salt and pepper
     ¼ cup butter or margarine
     ¼ cup finely-chopped green onions
     ½ cup California Light Muscat or
          other light sweet white wine
     1 cup chopped fresh mushrooms
     2 cups chicken broth
          (chicken stock base broth may be used)
     ¾ cup light cream
          Chopped parsley

Sprinkle game hen breasts with monosodium glutamate; dredge in flour seasoned with salt and pepper. Sauté in melted butter until lightly browned. Add onions; cook until onions are tender but not browned. Add wine and mushrooms. Simmer gently, covered, 15 minutes. Add chicken broth; simmer 20 minutes longer, or until tender. Remove breasts to warm platter. Stir cream into pan juices; heat thoroughly. Pour sauce over breasts; sprinkle with parsley. Serve with rice pilaf; hearts of artichokes Parmesan; a simple green salad with wine dressing; hot rolls; fresh strawberries or pineapple flavored with a Light Muscat; and thin wafers.

My choice of wine to accompany this dish:
CALIFORNIA DRY SAUVIGNON BLANC
OR JOHANNISBERG RIESLING

CHESTNUT TURKEY STUFFING

(For 10 to 15-lb. turkey)

Mrs. Tulio D'Agostini, D'Agostini Winery, Plymouth

     1 lb. large chestnuts
     ¼ cup shortening
     1 teaspoon salt
     1 egg, beaten
     1 cup ground pork sausage, lightly browned
     1 cup soft stale bread crumbs
     1 teaspoon chopped parsley
     ½ teaspoon basil, chopped or powdered
     ½ teaspoon oregano
     1 small onion, chopped
     ½ cup California Light Muscat or
          other light sweet white wine

Boil chestnuts about 20 minutes; remove shells and skins. Re-boil shelled chestnuts in salted water until tender; drain and put through ricer or sieve. Combine with other ingredients; mix well. Use to stuff cavity of 10 to 15-lb. turkey.

My choice of wine to accompany this dish:
A CALIFORNIA BURGUNDY

ROAST TURKEY ROSÉ

Mrs. Joseph Roullard, Petri Wineries, Escalon

Prepare favorite stuffing using California Rosé wine as part of the liquid. Rub inside of bird with ⅛ teaspoon salt per pound. Fill neck cavity with stuffing; fasten neck skin to back with skewer. Stuff rest of bird well, but do not pack. Fasten opening with skewers, lacing if necessary. Rub entire bird with soft butter or margarine. Place on rack in large roasting pan, breast side up. Prepare basting liquid of half California Rosé and half chicken bouillon (begin with ½ cup of each, preparing more as necessary). Pour over turkey; cover with foil. Place in a moderate oven (325 to 350°). Baste several times during cooking. Remove foil last 20 minutes to brown. A 10 to 14-lb. bird requires 3½ to 4 hours. Serve with crab cocktail; mashed potatoes with giblet gravy; hot buttered rolls; peas with mushrooms; cabbage-apple-raisin salad and pumpkin pie. Makes a wonderful Thanksgiving dinner, though I serve turkey other times, too.

My choice of wine to accompany this dish:
CHILLED CALIFORNIA ROSÉ OR RIESLING

NOTE: *Mrs. Alvin Ehrhardt of United Vintners, Inc., Lodi, also has a special fillip for roasting fowl: turkey, chicken, squab, pheasant, etc. Before stuffing the bird, she places California brandy in the cavity: from ¼ cup up, depending on bird size. Simply swish brandy around a little, then add stuffing and roast in usual manner. "This enhances the flavor," she says.*

BARBECUED TURKEY

(10 to 15 servings)

Mrs. Don Rudolph, Cresta Blanca Wine Co., Livermore

     1 (15-lb.) turkey
     2 cups California Sherry
     2 cups California Sauterne or
          other white dinner wine
     3 medium onions, cut in eighths
     1 cup olive oil
     5 cloves garlic, finely chopped
     2 green peppers, cubed
     1 tablespoon oregano
     1 teaspoon poultry seasoning
          Salt and pepper

Disjoint turkey. Combine other ingredients; pour over turkey in large glass or porcelain dish. Marinate in refrigerator 2 to 5 days, turning meat twice a day. Barbecue on a spit, basting with strained marinade. Preferred menu with this would be rice, buttered carrots, green salad and hot rolls.

My choice of wine to accompany this dish:
CALIFORNIA GREY RIESLING OR SAUTERNE

NOTE: *The remaining strained marinade can also be made into a good accompanying sauce, to spoon over the rice. Thicken slightly, if desired, and heat thoroughly.*

RAISIN TURKEY STUFFING

(For turkey 14 to 18 lb. size)

Harry Baccigaluppi, Calif. Grape Products Corp., Delano

        ½ cup chopped onion
        2 cups chopped celery
        1½ cups butter or margarine
            (part turkey fat may be used)
        4 qts. (16 cups) bread crumbs
            (use 2 or 3-day-old bread)
        2 cups seedless raisins, plumped in
            boiling water
        ½ cup chopped parsley
        1 tablespoon salt
        2 teaspoons poultry seasoning
        1 cup California Burgundy or other
            red dinner wine (approximately)

Sauté onion and celery gently in melted butter, stirring occasionally, just until onion is soft. Add to crumbs. Add raisins, parsley and seasonings; mix lightly but thoroughly. Gradually add just enough wine to moisten stuffing slightly. Stuff turkey and roast in usual way, preferably covered with oiled cheesecloth, and basted with mixture of additional Burgundy with melted butter.

My choice of wine to accompany this dish:
CALIFORNIA BURGUNDY, NEBBIOLO OR PINOT NOIR

TURKEY STUFFING MUY BUENO

(For turkey about 16-lb. size)

Inez Bueno Wargo, Wine Advisory Board, San Francisco

This is a very old family recipe from Mexico, richly flavored and interestingly different.

        Gizzard, heart and liver of turkey
        4 cups water
        1 teaspoon salt
        1 clove garlic
        3 tablespoons oil
        ½ pound ground pork
        ½ cup blanched almonds, halved and toasted
        ½ cup raisins, plumped in hot water
        ½ cup pitted chopped green olives
        1 tablespoon chopped green pepper
        1 tablespoon chopped onion
        1 tablespoon chopped parsley
        1 tablespoon chopped celery
        ¼ teaspoon oregano
        ½ cup tomato sauce
        1 cup California Sherry
        1 teaspoon California wine vinegar
        Strained broth from giblets
        Salt (additional)
        ¼ teaspoon black pepper
        Garlic (additional)
        1 large pkg. bread cubes for stuffing

Simmer turkey gizzard, heart and liver in water seasoned with salt and garlic, until tender. Remove giblets; chop well; strain and reserve broth. Heat oil in heavy skillet; brown ground pork with giblets. Combine with other ingredients. Rub turkey cavity with mixture of salt, pepper and garlic; stuff loosely. Roast turkey in usual way, timed according to size, and basted with additional Sherry if desired.

Our choice of wine to accompany this dish:
ANY CALIFORNIA RED DINNER WINE

DUCK AU VIN

(Allow 1 lb. per person)

Mrs. Robert Mondavi, Charles Krug Winery, St. Helena

        1 duck (domestic)
            Salt and pepper
        2 tablespoons olive oil
        1 cup orange juice
        1 cup California Burgundy, Claret
            or other red dinner wine
        1 tablespoon lemon juice
        1 large onion, thinly sliced
        1 tablespoon grated lemon or orange rind
        ½ teaspoon *each*: marjoram and rosemary
            Pinch of oregano
        2 tablespoons orange curacao

Cut duck into serving-size pieces; season with salt and pepper. Brown in hot olive oil. Remove to a hot casserole with tight-fitting lid. In same skillet, add orange juice, wine, lemon juice, onion, rind and herbs. Bring to boiling, scraping up browned bits in bottom and on sides of pan. Pour mixture over duck; bake, covered, in a slow oven (275°) for 2½ to 3 hours, or until tender. Remove duck to heated platter. Strain and measure remaining pan juices; taste and correct seasoning. Add orange curacao and enough red wine to bring liquid to 2 cups. Thicken to desired consistency with flour stirred smooth in a little wine. Add to measured liquid; cook, stirring constantly, until thickened. Pour over duck. Serve with rice.

NOTE: Mrs. Mondavi says domestic goose is good this way, too — also wild duck or goose. Wild rice may be used if desired. Your favorite California Burgundy or Claret would be most fitting with such a memorable dinner.

ROAST GOOSE

(8 servings)

Charles van Kriedt, California Wineletter, San Francisco

        1 (10-lb.) frozen goose
            California brandy
            Salt
        2 cups small cubes or pieces white toast
        1 medium onion, diced
        2 stalks celery with leaves, finely cut
        1 cup *each*: dried prunes & dried apricots
        ½ cup melted butter
            Salt, pepper, thyme and oregano
            California Sherry
        2 cups California Burgundy, Claret
            or other red dinner wine
        2 cups stock (canned or
            bouillon-cube broth may be used)

Thaw goose; rub with brandy and sprinkle with salt. Combine toast cubes, onion, celery, prunes, apricots, butter, salt, pepper, thyme and oregano. Moisten with Sherry. Stuff goose, reserving a little dressing for use in gravy. Prick skin all over with sharp fork to let out melting fat. Roast uncovered on rack in slow oven (300°), allowing 25 to 30 minutes per lb. Combine wine and stock; use to baste bird frequently. As fat and liquid accumulate in bottom of roasting pan, draw off with basting syringe. Place in jar and cool; skim off fat. Use liquid for gravy, combining with reserved dressing and simmering about 1 hour.

NOTE: Such a richly-flavored masterpiece deserves a fine California Claret or Burgundy alongside.

FISH

And Shellfish

The green vineyards of California are never very far away from rivers, lakes, bays or the sea; hence the wide interest among winemakers in the ancient sport of angling. And they love to cook their catch with their own good California wines, for in this field of cookery wine is particularly helpful. The sometimes "fishy" oils or tastes are eliminated by the addition of a white dinner wine or Sherry. At the same time, bland flavors are delicately enriched. To make the dining pleasure complete, put California wine on the table, as well.

BAKED FISH CUCAMONGA

(6 servings)

Cesare Vai, Cucamonga Vineyard Company, Cucamonga

- 4 lbs. whole fresh fish (sea bass, barracuda, corbina, bonita, etc.)
  Lemon juice
  Salt and pepper
  A few *each:* parsley leaves, celery leaves, onion slices
- ½ lb. fresh mushrooms, thinly sliced
- 2 tablespoons *each:* butter and olive oil
- 1 medium onion, minced
- 2 stalks celery, minced
- 1 cup California Chablis or other white dinner wine
- 2 tablespoons chopped parsley

Wash, dry and split fish. Rub inside and out with lemon juice, salt and pepper. Place parsley and celery leaves and onion slices in cavity. Place a few more slices onion on bottom of oiled baking dish; cover with a few of the mushroom slices; top with fish. Bake, uncovered, in moderate oven (350°) for 15-20 minutes. Meanwhile, heat butter and oil; slowly brown minced onion and celery; add mushrooms, wine and parsley. Pour over fish; bake 30 to 45 minutes longer, basting fish frequently. Add more melted butter and wine during cooking, if necessary. Serve garnished with fresh chopped parsley and lemon wedges. Menu might include new potatoes in parsleyed butter, asparagus vinaigrette, broiled tomatoes au gratin, and a lemon-gelatin cake.

My choice of wine to accompany this dish:
CALIFORNIA DRY WHITE, PREFERABLY CHABLIS

NOTE: *This is a really simple treatment, with a fresh pleasing flavor. Mr. Vai says that dried mushrooms may be substituted for the fresh ones, if they are soaked in warm water 30 minutes before adding to the dish.*

POACHED SOLE WITH GRAPES

(6 servings)

Mrs. Kerby T. Anderson, Guild Wine Co., Lodi

- 1½ lbs. fillet of sole
- 1½ cups milk
- 3 tablespoons butter
- 4 tablespoons flour
- ½ lb. sharp Cheddar cheese, grated or cubed
- ½ teaspoon salt
  Dash *each:* pepper and paprika
- ½ cup California Sauterne or other white dinner wine
- 1 cup fresh or canned seedless grapes (drained if canned)

Roll fillets; secure with wooden picks. Poach in hot milk a few minutes. Remove fish to a buttered casserole, reserving liquid. Melt butter in saucepan; mix in flour. Slowly add milk used to poach fish; cook, stirring constantly, until mixture is slightly thickened. Add cheese; stir until melted. Add salt, pepper, paprika and wine. Pour sauce over fillets; sprinkle with paprika. Bake in moderately slow oven (325°) for 25 minutes. Just before serving, pour grapes over fish. This can be served with rice pilaf or baked potatoes, green vegetable for color contrast, tossed green salad with tart herbed dressing, and pineapple sherbet for dessert.

My choice of wine to accompany this dish:
CALIFORNIA RIESLING

NOTE: *A most enjoyable variation on the classic combination of sole with grapes (Sole Veronique). Still another is recommended by Brother Gregory of Mont La Salle Vineyards, Napa. He likes the grapes browned in butter, with a California Light Muscat added, plus a touch of curry powder. This is boiled until reduced one-half (but left unthickened), then poured over cooked fish.*

ST. HELENA SOLE

(6 servings)

Mrs. Joseph Heitz, Heitz Wine Cellar, St. Helena

- 6 tablespoons butter or margarine
- 2 tablespoons flour
- 1½ cups milk, heated
- 2 fresh sole
- 2 cups California Chablis or other white dinner wine
- ½ lb. fresh mushrooms
- 6 tablespoons heavy cream
  Salt and pepper

Melt 3 tablespoons of the butter in a saucepan; stir in flour; gradually add heated milk. Cook, stirring constantly, until thickened. Remove from heat; cool, stirring occasionally to prevent a skin from forming. Meanwhile, clean and fillet fish. Place in fairly deep baking dish; cover with wine. Bake in moderate oven (350°) for 30 minutes. Wipe mushrooms with damp cloth; cut off earthy part of stems. Chop mushrooms finely. Combine with ½ of the white sauce; pour into serving dish and keep warm. Carefully remove fillets and place on top of mushroom sauce. To remaining white sauce, add the cream, remaining 3 tablespoons butter, salt and pepper. Heat, but do not boil. Pour sauce over fish.

My choice of wine to accompany this dish:
CALIFORNIA JOHANNISBERG RIESLING

SHERRY-ALMOND SOLE

(4 servings)

Mrs. Joe Cooper, Wine Advisory Board, San Francisco

- 4 large fillets of sole, about ¾" thick
- 2 green onions (including part of tops), chopped
- ½ cup fresh mushrooms, cleaned and chopped
- ¼ teaspoon salt
  Pinch dried rosemary
- ⅔ cup California Dry Sherry or Sauterne or other white dinner wine
- ½ cup heavy cream
- 1 tablespoon butter or margarine
- ⅓ cup chopped almonds

Combine fish, onions, mushrooms, salt, rosemary and wine in small frying pan. Simmer over low heat 10 minutes. Place fillets in shallow casserole. Reduce liquid remaining in pan by half, over high heat. Lower heat; add cream and butter; bring to boiling. Pour over fish, distributing onions and mushrooms evenly. Sprinkle almonds over top. Broil under medium heat for about 10 minutes, watching carefully to avoid burning.

My choice of wine to accompany this dish:
CALIFORNIA CHABLIS OR SAUTERNE

FILLET OF SOLE MONTEREY

(4 servings)

Mrs. Stanford J. Wolf, Paul Masson Vineyards, Saratoga

The leftover sauce from this dish can be used to make a gourmet soup the following day.

- 1 medium-size onion, sliced
- 1 bunch parsley, chopped
- 1 teaspoon salt
  Few whole white peppercorns
- 2 lbs. fillet of sole
- ¼ lb. fresh mushrooms (caps only)
- 2 tablespoons chopped shallots or chopped green onions
- ¼ cup butter or margarine
- 1 cup small oysters
- 1 cup heavy cream
- ½ cup chicken broth
- ½ cup California Sauterne or other white dinner wine
- 1 cup fresh cooked or canned shrimp

Fill large heavy skillet ¼ with water; add onion slices, parsley, salt and peppercorns. Simmer ½ hour. Carefully place fillets in pan; simmer 10 minutes. Carefully remove fish to ovenproof dish; set aside. Peel (but don't wash) and slice mushroom caps; sauté with shallots or green onions in melted butter for 2 minutes. Add oysters; cook 1 minute longer. In top of double boiler, heat cream over hot water (do not boil). Add chicken broth and wine; heat thoroughly. Place sautéed mushrooms, onions, oysters and shrimp over and around fish. Pour over sauce. Bake in moderate oven (350°) for 20 minutes. Serve **immediately.** This is good with small new potatoes, boiled and parsley-buttered; baby carrots and buttered toasted crackers.

My choice of wine to accompany this dish:
CALIFORNIA RIESLING OR PINOT CHARDONNAY

HERBED FISH SAUTERNE

(6 servings)

S. Martinelli, S. Martinelli & Company, Watsonville

- ½ cup butter or margarine
- ½ cup California Sauterne, Chablis or other white dinner wine
- ⅓ cup lemon juice
- 1 clove garlic, chopped
  Generous pinch of rosemary
  Chopped parsley
  Chopped chives or green onions
- 6 servings halibut, salmon, bass, trout, etc.

In a saucepan, melt butter; add wine and lemon juice; bring to boiling. Add garlic, rosemary, parsley and chives. Use to baste fish frequently while frying, baking, broiling or barbecuing. (If desired, marinate fish in the wine ½ hour; drain off; combine as above.)

My choice of wine to accompany this dish:
CALIFORNIA SAUTERNE, OR A VERY DRY SHERRY

FROZEN FISH STICKS are special when marinated 15 minutes in ½ cup California Rhine or other white dinner wine, ¼ cup California wine vinegar, ¼ cup water, plus salt. Drain fish sticks well; dip in crumbs if not already breaded. Arrange in oiled shallow baking dish; cover with mixed sour cream, mayonnaise and chopped onion. Dust with paprika; bake in hot oven (500°) for 10 minutes. Serve with lemon wedges.

SOLE WITH SHELLFISH

(10 servings)

Mrs. Frederick H. McCrea, Stony Hill Vineyard, St. Helena

This makes an ideal Saturday or Sunday luncheon in the country, especially since it can be prepared the day before (except for final heating) and refrigerated. In this case, let stand at room temperature a couple of hours before baking. If you are lucky enough to have any left over, freeze it for another day. (Seafood used can be fresh, frozen or canned.)

        4½ lbs. fillets of sole, uncooked
            Salt and pepper
        ⅔   cup butter or margarine
        5   tablespoons sifted flour
        1   cup cream or chicken broth
        ½   cup California Chablis or other
            white dinner wine
        ½   lb. small cooked shrimp
        ½   lb. cooked crabmeat
            Dash cayenne pepper
        2   tablespoons Worcestershire sauce
            Paprika

Cut fillets in 20 serving-size pieces; sprinkle with salt and pepper. In large casserole, oiled, arrange fish one piece on top of another (so that there are 10 nice double pieces for serving). Bake in moderate oven (350°) for 35 to 40 minutes. Meanwhile, melt ½ cup of the butter, browning slightly. Add flour, stirring until smooth. Drain fish liquid from casserole; add enough cream or broth to make 2½ cups liquid. Stir liquid into butter-flour mixture. Cook over low heat, stirring constantly, until thickened and smooth. Add wine, shrimp, crab, cayenne and Worcestershire sauce. Sprinkle fillets with paprika; dot with remaining butter; spoon sauce over fish. Bake, covered, in moderate oven (350°) until bubbling hot. Serve with rice or narrow noodles, a good green salad and a loaf of French bread.

My choice of wine to accompany this dish:
CALIFORNIA GEWURZ TRAMINER OR PINOT CHARDONNAY

NOTE: *There are many variations on baked sole with seafood-and-wine sauce, most of them rich and sumptuous. Mrs. Herbert Cerwin of Cerwin Vineyards, Sonoma, started making the dish in Rio de Janeiro, where fresh shellfish is plentiful. She likes lobster or mussels as well as shrimp in her sauce, with California Riesling or Traminer accompanying the dish.*

OVEN-FRIED FISH

(6 to 8 servings)

Mrs. Tulio D'Agostini, D'Agostini Winery, Plymouth

This is an original recipe. My family does not like the usual pan-fried fish, so I tried the drier way of oven-frying, and it is a favorite with family and friends. Any white wine may be used, but the Dry Muscat gives a special zest.

        2   lbs. fish fillets
        1   cup California Dry Muscat,
            Sauterne or other white dinner wine
        1   tablespoon salt
        1   cup toasted bread crumbs
        ⅓   cup oil
        1   tablespoon chopped parsley
        4   lemons, quartered

Cut fillets in serving-size pieces. Dip in wine; roll in salted bread crumbs; place on well-oiled baking sheet. Sprinkle with oil and remaining wine. Bake in a hot oven (450°) about 15 minutes, or until fish flakes easily. Serve sprinkled with parsley and garnished with lemon quarters. Good with baked cauliflower, tossed green salad, and peach compote for dessert.

My choice of wine to accompany this dish:
CALIFORNIA DRY MUSCAT OR SAUTERNE

RUSSIAN RIVER STEELHEAD

(2 servings per lb.)

Mrs. Edward Seghesio, Seghesio Winery, Cloverdale

Healdsburg, our home, is of course on the banks of the Russian River. Ed always looks forward to the steelhead run, and is often lucky. We believe the steelhead is an especially good fish, and this recipe is our favorite way of preparing it. The recipe is very flexible as to ingredients, however; I have never made it exactly the same way twice, yet it is always tasty.

        1   large baking-size steelhead (or,
            other fish, such as bass, cod,
            salmon, etc., may be used)
            Salt and pepper
        ⅓   cup olive oil
        1   onion, chopped
        ½   cup chopped parsley
        1   clove garlic, finely chopped
        ½   cup minced canned tomatoes
        ½   cup tomato sauce
        ¾   cup California Sauterne, Chablis
            or other white dinner wine

Place fish in shallow baking dish; season with salt and pepper. Cover with oil. Place in moderate oven (350°) until oil is hot. Add onion, parsley and garlic. When brown, add tomatoes, tomato sauce and wine. Continue baking about 45 minutes, or just until fish flakes easily. We like it served with baked potatoes, tossed green salad and French bread.

My choice of wine to accompany this dish:
CALIFORNIA SAUTERNE OR CHABLIS

STRIPED BASS AU VIN BLANC

(4 servings)

Mrs. James Riddell, Vie-Del Grape Products Co., Fresno

There are many ways to prepare striped bass, but I never fully appreciated the fish until I had this recipe. It was given to me by a close friend, Mrs. Joe Couly, who is an excellent cook of French descent, and an ardent admirer of California wines.

        4 thick slices striped bass
          (about 1 to 1½ lbs.)
        1 teaspoon salt
        ½ teaspoon pepper
        1 tablespoon *each:* very finely chopped
          parsley, celery and green onion
        ½ cup California Sauterne or
          other white dinner wine
        ¼ cup buttered bread crumbs

Remove skin from bass; cut fish into 1-inch cubes. Sprinkle with salt and pepper. Place cubes in a well-buttered casserole in a single layer. Sprinkle with parsley, celery and green onion. Pour in wine (should be about ½-inch deep). Top with buttered bread crumbs. Bake, uncovered, in a moderate oven (350°) for about 20 minutes or until fish flakes easily. Serve with new potatoes and peas, and coleslaw or vegetable salad. Dessert might be a caramel custard, or plain cake with a wedge of Monterey Jack cheese.

My choice of wine to accompany this dish:
CALIFORNIA RIESLING

NOTE: *Exceptionally good eating. Any other firm-fleshed fish, such as halibut or salmon, could be prepared this way.*

BROILED FISH NORTH COAST

(4 to 6 servings)

Don Gregg, Mendocino Grape Growers, Inc., Ukiah

This is a good, easy treatment for almost any kind of fish: salmon, sea bass, trout, etc.

        2 lbs. fish (slices, fillets or
          whole small fish)
          Salt and pepper
        1 tablespoon lemon juice
        1 onion, thinly sliced
        2 tablespoons butter or margarine
        1 cup California Sauterne, Chablis
          or other white dinner wine
        1 tablespoon flour
        3 tablespoons California white
          dinner wine or water, warmed
        6 stuffed olives, sliced
          Few drops onion juice

Place fish slices or fillets in buttered shallow pan. (If whole fish is used, split lengthwise and place skin side down in pan.) Sprinkle with salt, pepper, and lemon juice; spread onion slices over whole surface. Dot with butter; place under broiler. When butter begins to melt, baste with wine. Broil, basting frequently, until fish flakes with a fork. Remove fish to hot platter. Thicken liquid in pan with flour mixed with warm wine or water. Add olive slices and onion juice; pour sauce over fish.

My choice of wine to accompany this dish:
A CALIFORNIA WHITE DINNER WINE

POMPANO EN PAPILLOTTE

(6 servings)

Albert E. Moulin, Jr., Wine Advisory Board, New Orleans

Fish with a rich wine sauce, cooked in a sealed parchment paper, is a very old New Orleans method. One famous restaurant here has featured pompano in this manner for generations.

        3 pompano or medium-size trout
          Salt
        2 cups water
        2 green onions, chopped
        6 or 7 tablespoons butter or margarine
        2 cups California Sauterne, Chablis
          or other white dinner wine
        1 cup crabmeat
        1 cup small or diced cooked shrimp
        1 teaspoon garlic puree
      1½ cups chopped red or white onions
        1 bay leaf
          Pinch thyme
        2 tablespoons flour
        2 egg yolks
          Parchment paper

Clean fish; cut into 6 fillets. Simmer heads and backbones in salted water to make 2 cups fish stock; set aside. Sauté green onions and fillets in 2 or 3 tablespoons butter. Add wine; cover and simmer gently 5 to 8 minutes, or until tender. Drain, saving wine stock. Meanwhile, sauté crab, shrimp and ½ teaspoon garlic in 2 tablespoons butter. Add chopped red onions and remaining ½ teaspoon garlic; cook 10 minutes. Add 1¾ cups fish stock, bay leaf and thyme; cook 10 minutes longer; remove bay leaf. In a large, heavy skillet, blend together 2 tablespoons butter, flour and remaining ¼ cup fish stock. Add crab mixture along with wine stock. Cook, stirring constantly, until thickened. Beat egg yolks with some of the hot sauce; add to skillet, mixing thoroughly. Taste; correct seasoning. Chill sauce until firm. Cut 6 parchment paper hearts (8 x 12"). Oil well. Place a tablespoon sauce on parchment, top with a fillet. Fold over; hand seal. Place on oiled baking sheet; bake in a hot oven (450°) until brown. Serve in paper hearts. (Small paper bags tied close with string may be used in place of parchment hearts.) With this dinner I'd prefer a turtle or onion soup, potatoes (soufflé or French-fried) and green salad with olive oil and wine vinegar dressing.

My choice of wine to accompany this dish:
CALIFORNIA DRY SAUTERNE

BAKED ROCK COD WITH POTATOES

(6 to 8 servings)

Mrs. Frank Franzia, Franzia Brothers Winery, Ripon

This is almost a meal in itself, and delicious. The recipe has been in our family since 1920, when a friend brought us the fish and cooked it for us. We have been using the recipe ever since, and hope you'll enjoy it, too.

        2 tablespoons olive oil
        5 potatoes
          Salt and pepper
        2 tablespoons finely chopped parsley
        2 cloves garlic, chopped
        ½ onion, chopped
        1 (4 to 5-lb.) rock cod
        1 (8-oz.) can tomato sauce
        ¾ to 1 cup California Sauterne,
          Chablis or other white dinner wine

Pour oil into baking dish (13 x 9″). Peel and slice potatoes lengthwise about ½″ thick; arrange on bottom of dish; season with salt and pepper. Combine parsley, garlic and onion; sprinkle half of mixture over potatoes. Salt the cod; place over potatoes. Sprinkle with remaining half of onion mixture. Pour over tomato sauce, then pour over wine. Bake, uncovered, in moderate oven (375°) for 1½ hours, basting occasionally. Could be served with a tossed green salad made with wine vinegar, and, for dessert, baked apple in California Sauterne.

My choice of wine to accompany this dish:
CHILLED CALIFORNIA SAUTERNE, CHABLIS OR VIN ROSÉ
(My husband prefers a California Claret)

TROUT IN WINE

(Any amount)

Kenneth Knapp, Selma Winery, Inc., Selma

Place each trout (or other favorite fish) in center of large sheet of foil; cup foil up around fish. Sprinkle with salt and pepper; top with 2 tablespoons butter or margarine and 2 thin slices lemon. (Dash of dill or rosemary may be added, if desired.) Pour 2 to 4 tablespoons (depending on size of fish) California Dry Sherry or white dinner wine over **each** fish. Pull foil edges together; seal well, leaving small air space inside. Bake in moderately hot oven (400°) for 30 minutes; or, cook over coals of barbecue or campfire for 30 to 40 minutes. Serve with baked potatoes, green salad using wine vinegar, and dessert.

My choice of wine to accompany this dish:
CALIFORNIA SAUTERNE OR ROSÉ

NOTE: A dependable and easy way of cooking trout. Mr. Knapp says he has tried many types of wine in the cooking (except red, which can discolor the white meat of the fish), always with completely different yet pleasing results in taste. It's fun to experiment.

ANOTHER GREAT FAVORITE is fresh salmon, barbecued outdoors or grilled indoors wrapped in foil. The Marquise de Pins, of Beaulieu Vineyard, Rutherford, specifies Chablis and a bay leaf to be added to salmon cooked this way, with the butter, lemon juice, salt, freshly ground pepper and any other favorite seasoning. (For directions, follow those above for TROUT IN WINE.) She favors California Chablis as accompanying beverage with the salmon.

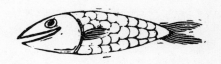

BAKED FISH PIMIENTO

(4 servings)

Mrs. Harold Roush, Guild Wine Co., Lodi

        1 (10½-oz.) can tomato soup
        ⅓ cup California Sauterne, Chablis
          or other white dinner wine
        1 cup shredded process
          pimiento cheese
        2 tablespoons chopped parsley
        1 small onion, minced
        4 fish steaks (salmon,
          halibut or sole)

Combine soup, wine and cheese in saucepan. Stir over low heat until cheese melts and is blended. Add parsley and onion. Arrange fish steaks in shallow baking pan; pour over sauce. Bake in moderately hot oven (375°) about 25 minutes, or until fish flakes with fork. Enjoyable with baked potatoes, tossed green salad and toasted French rolls.

My choice of wine to accompany this dish:
CALIFORNIA VIN ROSÉ

POACHED FROZEN TROUT

(2 servings)

Mrs. Herman L. Wente, Wente Bros., Livermore

        1 cup California Chablis or other
          white dinner wine
        4 frozen trout
        1 lemon
        1 tablespoon butter
          Salt and pepper

In large skillet, bring wine to boiling. Place trout in single layer in boiling wine; cover. Reduce heat; simmer gently 5 to 10 minutes. Turn fish carefully; simmer about 5 minutes longer or just until tender. Remove to hot plates. Add juice of lemon, butter, salt and pepper to liquid in pan. Pour over fish; serve at once. Sprinkle with parsley, if desired.

My choice of wine to accompany this dish:
THE SAME CALIFORNIA CHABLIS OR OTHER WHITE

NOTE: A refreshing change from frying, and very easy.

SALMON COURT-BOUILLON

(4 servings)

Rene Baillif, Buena Vista Vineyards, Sonoma

This is from a fisherman's long experience. If proportions and TIMING are correct, the dish will be perfect.

    1 qt. water
    1 large bottle California Sauterne or
       other white dinner wine
    1 onion
    7 or 8 sprigs parsley
       Thyme
    1 bay leaf
    1 teaspoon seasoned salt
    8 to 10 whole peppercorns
    1 (2-lb.) piece salmon
       (trout may also be used)

Combine water, wine, onion, parsley, thyme, bay leaf and seasoned salt in large saucepan or kettle. Simmer 45 minutes; add peppercorns 10 minutes before end of simmering. Cool broth completely; strain. Place piece of salmon on rack in cold prepared broth (Court-Bouillon). **Very, very slowly** bring liquid to simmering (takes about ½ hour). Simmer 25 minutes. When cooked, peel off skin. Serve hot with white sauce with capers, if desired, using part of the cooking broth as sauce liquid. Or, serve salmon cold, decorated with anchovy fillets, sliced pickles, sliced hard-cooked eggs and a green sauce (thinned mayonnaise with chopped parsley and chopped tarragon leaves added).

My choice of wine to accompany this dish:
CALIFORNIA WHITE JOHANNISBERG RIESLING

NOTE: Mrs. Jack F. M. Taylor of Mayacamas Vineyards, Napa, has a delicious addition for salmon simmered or poached in wine-flavored bouillon. She makes dumplings from prepared biscuit mix with herbs added. She removes cooked salmon from bouillon (easy when it's been cooked in cheesecloth) and keeps it warm in the oven, on a heated platter, then drops dumplings by teaspoonful into simmering bouillon. Dumplings should cook 15 minutes, covered; do not lift lid. Remove and place dumplings around fish. Sprinkle with chopped onion and chopped anchovies which have been sautéed in skillet in butter and added to a little of the bouillon.

SALMON SNACK CHABLIS

J. R. Lazarus, Wine Institute, San Francisco

Drain a can of salmon and turn the fish into a bowl. Pour on a little California Chablis, some salad oil, soy sauce and wine vinegar. Sprinkle with chopped green onion, chopped canned pimiento and seasoned salt. Chill well for several hours. Serve with sliced tomatoes, potato salad, and buttered rye or pumpernickel bread. Very refreshing on a warm day.

My choice of wine to accompany this dish:
CHILLED CALIFORNIA CHABLIS OR ROSÉ

POACHED SALMON FREMONT

(2 servings)

Richard Elwood, Llords & Elwood Wine Cellars, Fremont

    1 lb. salmon steak
       Salt
       White pepper
    4 thin slices cooked tongue
    3 tablespoons butter or margarine
    ¾ cup California Cream Sherry
    ¼ cup boiling water
    8 mushrooms, quartered

Place salmon in shallow saucepan; season with salt and pepper; cover with tongue slices. Dot with 2 tablespoons butter. Add Sherry and boiling water. Cover tightly; simmer until fish is tender. Sauté mushrooms in remaining tablespoon butter. Slide salmon onto hot platter without disturbing tongue; place mushrooms around fish.

NOTE: Very good indeed, and different from the usual poached fish. A chilled California white dinner wine or Rosé would be perfect with it, at the table. Still another interesting salmon method is used by Mrs. Karl L. Wente, Wente Bros., Livermore. She bakes her salmon in white dinner wine, then adds wine sauce including baby clams, shrimp and mushrooms.

FIESTA FISH CASSEROLES

(6 servings)

Mrs. Frank Garbini, Wente Bros., Livermore

This recipe is my own; I just kept adding as I went along.

    ½ cup butter or margarine
    ½ cup sifted all-purpose flour
    1 teaspoon salt
    ⅛ teaspoon pepper
       Dash paprika
    2 cups rich milk
    1 tablespoon soy sauce
    2 tablespoons finely chopped parsley
    ½ cup California Dry Sherry
    1½ cups grated Parmesan cheese
    1 (4-oz.) can sliced mushrooms,
       drained
    6 small slices salmon, halibut or
       striped bass, or 3 large slices halved
    ¾ lb. uncooked prawns or
       large shrimp, shelled and cleaned
    1 (10-oz.) can baby clams

Melt butter in saucepan; stir in flour, seasonings and milk. Cook, stirring constantly, until thickened and smooth. Add soy sauce, parsley, Sherry, 1 cup cheese and mushrooms. Place small slice of fish in each of 6 greased individual casseroles. Top with prawns and clams, divided equally. Cover fish with sauce; sprinkle with remaining cheese and paprika. Bake in moderate oven (350°) for ½ hour. Serve with a tossed green salad, sour French bread and dessert.

My choice of wine to accompany this dish:
CALIFORNIA GREY RIESLING

NOTE: A really elegant combination, unusually good. Sauce can also be used for pasta, substituting ¾ cup California Claret or Burgundy for the Sherry called for above.

SHRIMP NEWBURG

(4 servings)

Mrs. James L. Riddell, Vie-Del Grape Products Co., Fresno

I used this recipe several years ago on a television program. Cooked in a fancy chafing dish and served in individual colorful ramekins, the Newburg sauce makes an appetizing appearance for any shellfish (lobster or crab may also be served with it). If the cream is warmed beforehand, it speeds up the preparation of the dish.

        ¾ cup butter or margarine
        2 tablespoons flour
        3 cups cooked and shelled shrimp,
            cut into bite-size pieces
        ⅛ teaspoon nutmeg
            Dash of paprika
        ½ teaspoon salt
        ½ cup California Sherry
        3 egg yolks
        2 cups cream
            Buttered bread crumbs

Melt butter in top of chafing dish or top of double boiler over hot water. Stir in flour; add shrimp, seasonings and Sherry. Beat egg yolks slightly; add cream; mix well. Stir slowly into shrimp mixture. Cook slowly, stirring until slightly thickened. Spoon into individual ramekins or baking shells; sprinkle with buttered bread crumbs. Brown under broiler a few minutes. Serve with sliced tomatoes and lettuce salad and sour dough bread. Finish with a light dessert, such as a sherbet or sponge cake ring with fresh strawberries.

My choice of wine to accompany this dish:
CALIFORNIA JOHANNISBERG RIESLING

NOTE: *A touch of nutmeg is used in another version of this tempter, by Mrs. Alvin Ehrhardt of United Vintners, Inc., Lodi. Mrs. Ehrhardt says the nutmeg is optional, but "very rakish in flavor." She also recommends the sauce for oysters or sweetbreads.*

WINEMAKER'S SHRIMP

(4 to 6 servings)

Mrs. Harold Berg, U. C. Dept. of Viticulture & Enology

        2 lbs. raw shrimp in shells
        ½ cup tomato sauce
        1 tablespoon chopped parsley
        ¼ teaspoon oregano
            Salt
        ¼ cup butter or margarine
        2 cloves garlic, chopped
        1 (10½-oz.) can consommé
        1 cup California Dry Sherry

Boil shrimp 10 to 20 minutes, or just until tender. Shell and devein. Meanwhile, combine and simmer tomato sauce, parsley, oregano, salt, butter, garlic and soup. Just before serving, add shrimp and Sherry. Heat thoroughly. Serve with plain rice, tossed green salad and sour French bread.

My choice of wine to accompany this dish:
CALIFORNIA SAUVIGNON BLANC

SHERRIED SHRIMP

(6 servings)

Robert S. McKnight, Di Giorgio Wine Company, Di Giorgio

        1 clove garlic
        ⅓ teaspoon tarragon
        ⅓ teaspoon parsley
        ⅓ teaspoon minced shallot
        ⅓ teaspoon minced onion
        ½ cup butter or margarine
        1 cup fine dry bread crumbs
            Salt and pepper
            Dash *each:* nutmeg and thyme (optional)
        ¼ to ⅓ cup California Dry Sherry
        2 lbs. shelled cooked shrimp
            Buttered bread crumbs

Mash garlic to paste; add seasonings. Combine with butter and dry bread crumbs; mix until thoroughly blended, using electric beater or blender. Season with salt and pepper and, if desired, nutmeg and thyme. Blend in Sherry. In 6 buttered shells or individual casseroles, alternate layers of mix with layers of cooked shrimp. Top with buttered crumbs. Bake in moderately hot oven (400°) for 15 to 20 minutes.

My choice of wine to accompany this dish:
CALIFORNIA BRUT CHAMPAGNE OR ROSÉ

NOTE: *A delectable dish, similar to the famous Shrimp de Jonghe.*

RIESLING SEAFOOD SHELLS

(6 to 8 servings)

Mrs. Ze'ev Halperin, Mt. Tivy Winery, Reedley

This is an American adaptation of a dish served by a European airline. All sorts of seafoods may be added, or substituted. It may be served over rice instead of in the pastry shells.

        1 pkg. frozen puff pastry shells
        1½ to 2 cups cooked lobster meat, **or**
            2 (9-oz.) pkgs. frozen
            lobster tails, cooked
        ¾ lb. boiled shrimps, shelled
            and deveined
        20 canned clams
        1 cup fresh or canned mushrooms
        1 tablespoon flour
        2 tablespoons butter or margarine
        1½ cups California Riesling, Sauterne
            or other white dinner wine
        1 cup light cream
        ½ teaspoon salt
        ⅛ teaspoon pepper
        ½ teaspoon seasoned salt
        ½ cup chopped parsley

Bake puff pastry shells according to package directions; remove centers and save for topping. Break or cut seafood and mushrooms into small pieces; dust with flour; sauté lightly in butter. Add wine; simmer 10 minutes. Add cream and seasonings. Pour into pastry shells; sprinkle with parsley. Top with reserved pastry "covers." Serve with tossed green salad and hot buttered rolls. For dessert, an icebox cake, with chocolate frosting flavored with California brandy.

My choice of wine to accompany this dish:
CALIFORNIA RIESLING

SCAMPI TRECATE

(6 servings)

Mrs. Dino Barengo, Acampo Winery, Acampo

- ¾ cup butter or margarine
- ¾ cup olive oil
- 2 lemons
- 1 large clove garlic, crushed
- 6 green onions, minced
- 1 carrot, minced
- 3 stalks celery, minced
- 1 large tomato, cut in small pieces
- 2 lbs. large raw shrimp, unshelled
- ½ cup California brandy
- 2 cups California Dry Sauterne or other white dinner wine
- 2 tablespoons California red wine vinegar
- ½ teaspoon salt
- ¼ teaspoon black pepper
- 1 teaspoon Tabasco sauce
- ½ (10½-oz.) can consommé
- ½ cup water
- 3 tablespoons flour

In large, heavy saucepan, melt ½ cup of the butter; add oil, peel of 1 lemon, garlic, green onions, carrot, celery and tomato. Sauté 5 minutes. Add shrimp; cook, stirring over medium heat 10 minutes. Add brandy; flame. Remove shrimp; when cool enough to handle, shell and devein; set aside. Strain cooked vegetable mixture into saucepan. Add juice of lemons, wine, wine vinegar, salt, pepper, Tabasco sauce, consommé, water and cleaned shrimp; cook 10 minutes. Remove shrimp to serving bowl. Melt remaining ¼ cup butter in small saucepan; blend in flour. Add some of liquid in which shrimp was cooked, 2 tablespoons at a time, stirring constantly, to make a thin paste. Return to remaining shrimp-cooking liquid; boil a few minutes. Pour over shrimp. Serve with thin slices of sour dough Italian bread.

My choice of wine to accompany this dish:
WELL-CHILLED CALIFORNIA DRY WHITE DINNER WINE

NOTE: *Even to read it makes you want to start cooking — and this shrimp bowl is really much easier than it sounds.*

ABALONE LIVERMORE

(4 servings)

Mrs. Herman L. Wente, Wente Bros., Livermore

Instead of deep fat cooking for abalone try deep wine cooking. Since the sauce should be ready before cooking the abalone, make the sauce first, as follows:

- 2 tablespoons butter
- 1 tablespoon flour
- ½ cup California Sauterne, Chablis or other white dinner wine
- 1 tablespoon lemon juice
- 2 tablespoons finely chopped parsley

Melt butter in saucepan; blend in flour. Pour in wine slowly, stirring constantly. Add lemon juice and parsley. Cook, stirring, until thick and smooth. Pour over poached abalone, which you now cook as follows:

TO POACH ABALONE: In heavy pan, bring 1″ of California white dinner wine to boiling. Add slices of well-pounded abalone, one at a time. Cook each slice 1 minute, keeping wine boiling.

NOTE: *The same type of California white dinner wine, well chilled, would be perfect served at the table.*

LOBSTER NEWBURG

(4 servings)

Mrs. Fred Snyde, Woodbridge Vineyard Association, Lodi

- 2 lobsters, cooked, cleaned and cut in half
- ⅓ cup California Dry Sherry
- ¼ cup butter or margarine
- 3 level tablespoons flour
- 2 cups rich milk or thin cream
- 1 teaspoon seasoned salt
- Dash *each*: pepper, cayenne, nutmeg

Remove lobster from shell, saving shells. Cut meat in bite-size pieces. Pour over Sherry; refrigerate 2 or 3 hours. Meanwhile, melt butter in saucepan; blend in flour. Gradually blend in milk; cook, stirring constantly, until thickened and smooth. Add lobster, Sherry and seasonings; heat thoroughly. Fill lobster shells with mixture; place under broiler until slightly browned. Serve with stuffed baked potatoes, fresh peas and a tomato aspic salad.

My choice of wine to accompany this dish:
CALIFORNIA WHITE DINNER WINE

NOTE: *If a thicker sauce is preferred, add a little more flour, or use heavy cream. For an excellent, easy tomato aspic, see VINTAGE ASPIC in the section on Salads.*

COQUILLES ST. JACQUES

(6 to 8 servings)

Mrs. Kerby T. Anderson, Guild Wine Co., Lodi

- 2 lbs. fresh scallops
- 2 cups California Dry Sherry
- 1 bay leaf
- 1 lb. fresh mushrooms, sliced
- 1 medium onion, diced
- ¾ cup butter or margarine
- 3 tablespoons flour
- 2 tablespoons lemon juice
- 1 teaspoon salt
- ½ teaspoon paprika
- ⅛ teaspoon pepper
- Dash cayenne
- Bread crumbs
- Grated Parmesan cheese

Simmer scallops 10 minutes in Sherry with bay leaf. Drain, saving broth. Sauté mushrooms and onion in butter. Add flour; stir in wine broth and lemon juice. Cook, stirring constantly, until thickened. Season with salt, pepper, paprika and cayenne. Add scallops. Place in buttered casserole or individual baking shells. Sprinkle with bread crumbs, Parmesan cheese and paprika. Bake in moderately slow oven (325°) for 25 minutes. This goes well with rice pilaf or baked potatoes, green vegetable for color contrast, tossed green salad with tart herbed dressing, rolls, and pineapple sherbet dessert.

My choice of wine to accompany this dish:
CALIFORNIA RIESLING

NOTE: *Many original or individual variations appear in the various scallop recipes favored by California winemaking families. Mrs. Stanley Strud, California Wine Association, Lodi, adds chopped green pepper and pimientos to her version, and California Chablis. Mrs. A. D. Webb, U. C. Dept. of Viticulture & Enology, has a simple method, baking scallops in a sauce including grated Swiss cheese and California Flor Sherry.*

CRAB-ARTICHOKE CASSEROLE

(6 to 8 servings)

Mrs. E. L. Ely, Jr., Italian Swiss Colony, Asti

- 2 (7½-oz.) cans crabmeat, drained
- ¼ cup butter or margarine
- ¼ cup flour
- 2 teaspoons salt
- ⅛ teaspoon pepper
- 1 teaspoon paprika
- 1 teaspoon instant minced onion
- 3¼ cups milk
- 1¼ cups uncooked macaroni shells
- 1 (9-oz.) pkg. frozen artichoke hearts, *or*
  1 (8½-oz.) can artichoke hearts
- ⅓ cup California Dry Sherry
- ¼ cup grated sharp Cheddar cheese

Flake crabmeat, removing any cartilage; set aside. Melt butter in medium-size saucepan. Remove from heat; stir in flour, salt, pepper and paprika until smooth. Add onion. Gradually stir in milk; bring to boiling, stirring constantly. Reduce heat; simmer 5 minutes. Remove from heat; set aside. Prepare macaroni according to package directions; drain well. Cook artichoke hearts according to package directions; drain well. Combine crabmeat, Sherry, macaroni and artichoke hearts with sauce; mix well. Turn into 2 to 2½-qt. casserole. Sprinkle with grated cheese. Bake in a moderate oven (350°) about 20 minutes or until bubbly. We prefer this as the hot dish for a buffet supper, with green salad, French bread, and assorted cheeses and crackers.

My choice of wine to accompany this dish:
CALIFORNIA RIESLING OR CHABLIS

NOTE: *Mrs. Albert Cribari of Evergreen Vineyards, San Jose, serves a similar crab-artichoke casserole as a luncheon dish. Her version adds mushrooms. For a heartier meal, she suggests serving the mixture over rice.*

WINE LAND CRABMEAT

(4 servings)

Karl L. Wente, Wente Bros., Livermore

- 1 tablespoon grated onion
- ¼ cup butter or margarine
- ¼ cup sifted flour
- 1 cup milk
- ½ cup California Dry Semillon,
  Chablis or other white dinner wine
- ½ cup California Sherry
- 1 teaspoon salt
  Dash Tabasco sauce
- 2 tablespoons thinly sliced mushrooms
- 1 egg yolk, beaten
- 2 cups cooked or canned crabmeat

Sauté onion in melted butter; blend in flour, but do not brown. Gradually blend in milk and wines, stirring constantly, until thickened. Add salt, Tabasco sauce and mushrooms. Remove from heat when bubbles appear; quickly stir in egg yolk and crabmeat. Serve over toast triangles or fluffy rice. Or, if desired, place in ramekins or baking shells, sprinkle with paprika and brown lightly in oven. Good with a green salad and fruit for dessert.

My choice of wine to accompany this dish:
CALIFORNIA SEMILLON OR PINOT BLANC

CRAB ACAPULCO

(8 servings)

Mrs. Bruno T. Bisceglia, Bisceglia Bros. Wine Co., Fresno

- ¼ cup butter or margarine
- ¼ cup sifted all-purpose flour
- 1⅔ cups milk
- ¾ teaspoon salt
- 1 teaspoon Worcestershire sauce
  Dash cayenne pepper
- 2 tablespoons fresh lime or lemon juice
- 3 tablespoons California Sherry
- ⅓ cup grated sharp American cheese
- 2 cups cooked or canned crabmeat
- 4 avocados
  Salt
  Toasted sesame seeds or toasted coconut

Melt butter in saucepan; blend in flour. Gradually blend in milk; cook, stirring constantly, until thickened and smooth. Add salt, Worcestershire sauce, cayenne, lime juice, Sherry and cheese; mix well. Add crabmeat; cook just until heated. Cut avocados in half; remove seeds and skins. Place in shallow baking dish; sprinkle with salt and heap with crab mixture. Sprinkle with sesame seeds or coconut. Bake in a slow oven (300°) for 15 minutes only, or JUST UNTIL WARM. Serve as luncheon entrée, with hot bread or toasted muffins and whole spiced peaches.

My choice of wine to accompany this dish:
CALIFORNIA RIESLING

EASY DEVILED CRAB

(4 servings)

Mrs. August Sebastiani, Samuele Sebastiani, Sonoma

This recipe was handed down to me from my grandmother. It is a very old one, and especially delicious, either as a main course dish or as a salad.

- 3 tablespoons butter or margarine
- 2 tablespoons flour
- 1 cup milk, heated
- 1 teaspoon salt
  Dash cayenne pepper
- 1 teaspoon Worcestershire sauce
- 2 egg yolks, slightly beaten
- 2 cups crabmeat, fresh cooked,
  frozen or canned
- ¼ teaspoon lemon juice
- ¼ cup California Dry Sherry
- ⅔ cup buttered crumbs
- 4 lemon slices
  Paprika

Melt butter; stir in flour and heated milk. Season with salt, cayenne and Worcestershire sauce; cook, stirring constantly, until thick. Add slightly beaten egg yolks and crab; cook 3 minutes. Stir in lemon juice and Sherry. Spoon mixture into individual baking shells or ramekins; cover with buttered crumbs. Top with a lemon slice and sprinkling of paprika. Bake in a hot oven (450°) about 20-25 minutes or until brown.

My choice of wine to accompany this dish:
ANY CALIFORNIA DRY WHITE OR ROSÉ

TUNA TETRAZZINI

(6 servings)

Mrs. Edmund Accomazzo, Cucamonga Winery, Cucamonga

This recipe is supposed to have been named for the famous opera diva, Tetrazzini. I serve it often for bridge luncheons.

- ½ (8-oz.) pkg. spaghettini
- 3 tablespoons bottled garlic spread (or less, to taste)
- ¼ cup sifted all-purpose flour
- 1 cup milk
- ¼ cup California Dry Sherry
- 2 (4-oz.) cans button mushrooms
- 1 (8-oz.) pkg. process American cheese, grated
- ½ teaspoon seasoned salt
- ¼ teaspoon pepper
- 2 (6½ or 7-oz.) cans chunk-style tuna, drained
- 2 tablespoons grated Parmesan cheese

Cook spaghettini according to package directions; drain and set aside. In top of double boiler, melt garlic spread over boiling water. Stir in flour; gradually add milk. Add Sherry and ½ cup liquid drained from mushrooms. Cook, stirring constantly, until thickened. Add grated American cheese, salt and pepper; stir until cheese is melted. Stir in spaghettini, tuna and mushrooms. Pour into 1½-qt. shallow baking dish; sprinkle with Parmesan cheese. Bake in moderate oven (350°) for 20 minutes or until light golden. Serve with green salad.

My choice of wine to accompany this dish:
CALIFORNIA DRY SAUTERNE OR GRIGNOLINO ROSÉ

QUICK CLAM-CORN DINNER

(4 to 6 servings)

John Lockett, Wine Advisory Board, San Francisco

This is an easy main dish for a bachelor cook. All you need is to keep plenty of wine and canned foods on hand.

- 2 (7-oz.) cans minced clams
- 4 tablespoons butter or margarine
- 6 tablespoons flour
- ½ cup milk
- ⅓ cup California Sauterne, Rhine or other white dinner wine
- Salt, garlic salt, pepper
- 1 cup canned whole-kernel corn, drained
- 2 tablespoons chopped parsley
- Buttered fine bread crumbs
- Paprika

Drain clams, reserving liquid. Melt butter and stir in flour; add ⅔ cup reserved clam liquid and the milk and wine. Cook, stirring constantly, until sauce boils and thickens. Season to taste with salt, garlic salt and pepper. Cool slightly. Stir in clams, corn and parsley. Spoon mixture into 4 or 6 greased baking shells or individual casseroles. Sprinkle with bread crumbs and paprika. Bake in moderately hot oven (400°) about 20 minutes, or until bubbly and browned.

My choice of wine to accompany this dish:
CALIFORNIA SAUTERNE, VERY WELL CHILLED

NOTE: *Mrs. Harold Berg, University of California Dept. of Viticulture & Enology, also has an interesting clam casserole, combining sour cream, noodles, mushrooms and white wine with the clams.*

DEVILED CLAMS MORRO BAY

(8 servings)

Marjorie Riley, Mont La Salle Vineyards, Napa

This recipe can be altered to suit the whim of the cook. It is my own version of a way of preparing clams which I first tasted near Morro Bay, where the old-time residents do a lot of clamming. A wonderful Italian woman showed me how to prepare them. Mine never tasted quite like hers, but I think that's because she sang while she cooked, and that makes a difference. Also, she put in "a little of this, a little of that, never the same," and like many truly delicious things, it was almost impossible to figure out the exact ingredients.

- 2 cups finely ground fresh clams, **or** 3 (7½-oz.) cans clams, drained and ground
- ½ cup ground onion
- ⅓ cup ground green pepper
- ⅓ cup ground celery
- 1⅓ cups dry French bread crumbs, toasted and ground
- 1 cup whipping cream
- 2 eggs, beaten
- 2 tablespoons butter or margarine, **melted**
- 2 teaspoons prepared mustard
- 1½ teaspoons salt
- 1 teaspoon pepper
- ½ cup California Dry Semillon, Sauterne or other white dinner wine
- Grated Parmesan cheese
- 4 slices bacon

Using a meat grinder, grind clams, onion, green pepper, celery and toasted bread crumbs. Measure and combine. Stir in cream, eggs, melted butter, mustard, salt, pepper and wine. (Mixture should be thick, rich and creamy.) Scoop mixture into large clam shells or other individual baking dishes. Bake in moderate oven (350°) for 20 minutes. Remove; sprinkle heavily with grated Parmesan cheese. Top with ½ slice bacon; return to oven until bacon is crisp and brown. We love to serve these clams with a green salad and garlic French bread.

My choice of wine to accompany this dish:
CALIFORNIA RIESLING, CHABLIS,
PINOT CHARDONNAY OR SEMILLON

TUNA CHO-CHO-SAN brings delicate Oriental flavor and color to a luncheon or supper menu. To make 6 to 8 servings: Drain and slice water chestnuts (5-oz. can). Drain liquid from 4-oz. can sliced mushrooms into measuring cup; add enough California Chablis or other white dinner wine to bring to 1 cup level. (Will take about ⅔ cup wine.) Cook ¼ cup **each** finely chopped green onions and celery in ⅓ cup butter, until crisp-tender but not brown. Blend in ⅔ cup sifted flour, 1 teaspoon **each** seasoned salt and soy sauce, and ¼ teaspoon grated lemon rind. Slowly stir in 2 cups thin cream. Cook, stirring, until mixture starts to thicken; stir in wine-mushroom liquid. Bring to boil, stirring now and then; add water chestnuts, mushrooms and chunk-style tuna (9½-oz. can). Heat slowly a few more minutes. If desired, add 2 tablespoons **each** chopped pimiento and parsley. Spoon into baked patty shells, toast cups, or serve over toast, cornbread or rice, with the same wine accompanying.

SAUCES

Including Basic Bastes and Marinades

The suave, sumptuous flavor imparted to meats, poultry, game or fish by a good sauce or baste plays a major role in our most pleasurable dinner memories. Wine is often essential to the blending of a memorable sauce, since it is, after all (in terms of kitchen use), a liquid seasoning as basic as salt, pepper and herbs. Many main dishes reach new heights in taste when merely basted with California wine alone. But for those who enjoy trying special individual approaches, here are some favorite recipes from experienced cooks. (See also the marinating ideas on Page 90.)

UNIVERSAL B.B.Q. WINE BASTE

(2⅔ cups)

N. C. Mirassou, Mirassou Vineyards, San Jose

This sauce can be used on any kind of meat, fowl or fish that is barbecued. Leftover sauce can be frozen and used at a future date. Let thaw one day before using.

- ¾ cup California red or white dinner wine, or brandy
- ½ cup California wine vinegar
- ½ cup olive oil
- 1 cup finely chopped chives
- 1 cup finely chopped parsley
- 1½ teaspoons crushed or finely chopped garlic
- 1 tablespoon salt
- 1 tablespoon pepper
- 1 tablespoon monosodium glutamate

A day ahead, combine all ingredients in a glass or ceramic dish; let stand at room temperature. Baste meat, poultry or fish on one side 1 hour before barbecuing. Place basted side down on grill; while first side cooks, brush sauce on unbasted side.

My choice of wine to accompany the meal:
CALIFORNIA RED OR WHITE DINNER WINE
(CALIFORNIA CHAMPAGNE WITH HORS D'OEUVRE)

CUCAMONGA SPAGHETTI SAUCE

(2 quarts)

Mrs. John B. Ellena, Regina Grape Products Co., Etiwanda

- 4 medium-size onions, chopped
- ½ cup margarine, or
- ¼ cup oil and ¼ cup butter
- 3 cloves garlic, finely chopped
- ½ cup chopped parsley
- 1 cup chopped celery tops
- 1 green pepper, finely chopped
- 1 (4-oz.) can mushrooms, chopped
- 1 teaspoon rosemary
- 1 teaspoon basil
- ½ teaspoon pepper
- 2 teaspoons salt
- 2 lbs. ground beef
- 1 (1-lb. 4-oz.) can solid-pack tomatoes
- 1 (6-oz.) can tomato paste
- 1 cup California Zinfandel, Burgundy or other red dinner wine

Sauté onions in margarine until tender and golden. Add garlic; sauté about 2 minutes. Add parsley, celery tops, green pepper, mushrooms and seasonings; sauté well, stirring often. Brown meat in Dutch oven or heavy skillet, stirring until crumbly and no redness remains. Add sautéed vegetables; mix well. Add tomatoes, tomato paste and wine, stirring until well mixed. Bring to boiling; lower heat; simmer 3 hours, then serve on spaghetti.

My choice of wine to accompany this dish:
CALIFORNIA ZINFANDEL

NOTE: A hearty, aromatic flavor-blend, perfected by the wine and the patient slow cooking. Appetizing spaghetti sauces with individuality are also made by Mrs. Frank J. Pilone of Cucamonga Vineyard Co., Cucamonga, and Mrs. Dale R. Anderson of Di Giorgio Wine Co., Di Giorgio. Mrs. Pilone includes white wine and Italian sausage (or ground pork sausage), as well as ground beef, in hers. Mrs. Anderson prefers red wine in the sauce, and diced bacon.

MY FAVORITE SPAGHETTI SAUCE

(1½ qts.)

Mrs. Albert J. Puccinelli, Puccinelli Vineyards, San Mateo

        1 lb. ground beef
        1 (1-lb. 4-oz.) can tomato puree
     3¾ cups water
        1 cup California Sherry
      ¼ teaspoon *each*: oregano,
            thyme and marjoram
      ½ cup chopped parsley
      ¼ cup instant minced onion
        1 (6-oz.) can mushrooms
        1 tablespoon salt
      ½ teaspoon pepper

Sauté ground beef, stirring until brown and crumbly. Add remaining ingredients, mixing well. Simmer, covered, over low heat 4 to 6 hours. May be used with spaghetti, noodles, tagliarini, lasagna or risotto. (If used with lasagna or risotto, layer the pasta and sauce until dish is full; cover with grated cheese; bake until cheese is melted and dish heated through.)

NOTE: A thick rich sauce, with extra flavors brought out by the long slow simmering. With any of the dishes mentioned, a California red, Rosé or "vino" type would be delightful.

EASY ALL-PURPOSE WINE SAUCE

(About ⅔ cup)

Mrs. Dale R. Anderson, Di Giorgio Wine Co., Di Giorgio

This all-around barbecue sauce and marinade was a favorite recipe of our neighbor in Kerman, Mrs. Louise Fike, who was fond of cookouts. We have enjoyed it many times. It can be used for roasts, steaks, fowl or salmon.

      ¼ cup oil
      ¼ cup California Sherry
        2 tablespoons soy sauce
        1 teaspoon Worcestershire sauce
        1 teaspoon garlic powder
            Freshly ground pepper

Combine all ingredients. Marinate roast 24 to 48 hours; steaks 4 hours; poultry or salmon 2 hours. Use remaining marinade to baste while cooking.

NOTE: A simple, always-good combination. Serve your favorite California dinner wine with the meal, according to the dish.

NO-MIX BARBECUE SAUCE

(Any amount)

J. B. Cella, II, Cella Wineries, Fresno

This sauce is the simplest one I know. It involves no mixing, but merely a trip to your store for a bottle of your favorite California Dry Vermouth. This can be used to baste all forms of fowl, steaks and hamburger. In this you have the wine flavor of the Vermouth and the herbs that are blended into the Vermouth.

NOTE: Smart cooks are discovering that both Dry and Sweet California Vermouth can do much for cooking, and deserve more experimenting. At the table, serve whichever wine you prefer with the particular finished dish.

EVEN APPLESAUCE can gain in interest from a touch of wine. Next time you slice a pound of peeled cooking apples into the pan, add a few teaspoons sugar, to taste; 1 large onion, chopped; salt and pepper; and 2 tablespoons California Cream Sherry. Cover; simmer gently (stirring now and then) until tender. Serve with any pork dish, duck or goose. A bottle of chilled California white dinner wine on the table makes the dinner unforgettable.

BASIC WINE SAUCE

(2½ cups)

Brother Timothy, Mont La Salle Vineyards, Napa

Crush 2 cloves garlic in 2 tablespoons salt. Add 1 cup California dinner wine (Chablis for fish, **or** Claret for red meats, pork or game); ¼ cup lemon juice, 1¼ cups olive oil, 1 teaspoon freshly ground black pepper and 1 teaspoon crushed or powdered herb seasoning (thyme for fish, **or** oregano for red meats, pork or game). Use as marinade and also for basting.

NOTE: As versatile as it is flavorful. With dinner, serve the same wine as used in the sauce.

GINGER-VERMOUTH MARINADE

(1⅔ cups)

Mrs. W. W. Owen, California Grape Products Corp., Delano

    1 teaspoon tarragon
    1 tablespoon ground or grated fresh ginger
    ½ cup California Dry Vermouth
    1½ cups California Sauterne, Chablis
        or other white dinner wine
    1 tablespoon lemon juice
    1 tablespoon monosodium glutamate
    1 teaspoon salt

Combine all ingredients; pour over a cut-up chicken. Marinate several hours, turning occasionally. Bake or broil as desired, basting with remaining marinade.

NOTE: *A tantalizing flavor. Either white or Rosé would be fine served with chicken marinated in this manner.*

A FLAVORSOME MEAT LOAF SAUCE is recommended by Mrs. Myron S. Nightingale of Roma Wine Co., Fresno. Mrs. Nightingale mixes California Claret or other dry red dinner wine with brown sugar, canned whole cranberry sauce and ground cloves, spreading most of this mixture over the meat loaf. A small amount is reserved and blended with cornstarch and pan drippings, to be served as sauce at the table. The same red wine or a California Rosé would be ideal as accompaniment.

BARBECUED POULTRY PLEASER

(1½ cups)

Mrs. Keith V. Nylander, Di Giorgio Wine Co., Di Giorgio

    ¼ cup oil or melted butter or
        margarine
    ¾ cup California Sauterne, Chablis
        or other white dinner wine
    1 clove garlic, finely minced
    1 large onion, grated
    1 teaspoon salt
    1 teaspoon celery salt
    ¼ teaspoon black pepper
    ¼ teaspoon dried thyme
    ⅛ teaspoon dried tarragon
    1 tablespoon chopped parsley

Mix all ingredients together thoroughly. Let stand overnight. Marinate chicken or turkey in sauce several hours before broiling or barbecuing. Baste with remaining marinade during cooking. Chilled artichokes that have been cooked in boiling water with salt, garlic, white wine vinegar and tarragon go beautifully with chicken or turkey barbecued with this sauce. The menu could also include a pilaf, tossed green salad, garlic bread, and dessert combining fresh fruit with orange sherbet and California Champagne float.

My choice of wine to accompany this dish:
CALIFORNIA WHITE DINNER WINE

NOTE: *The "float" of Champagne, as topping for the fruit-and-sherbet dessert, deserves to be poured at the table, in front of guests. It's a colorful and dramatic touch, adding flair to the dinner.*

WILD DUCK BARBECUE SAUCE

(About 3 cups)

J. W. Fleming, Lockeford Winery, Lodi

This sauce is also very good with spareribs or any other barbecued pork.

    1 cup California brandy (or, ½ cup
        brandy and ½ cup California Sherry)
    1 cup soy sauce
    1 cup honey
    1 tablespoon salt

Combine all ingredients, heating slightly to blend well. Marinate ducks in sauce for 3 or 4 hours, depending on size. Cook in Chinese oven or on motor-driven spit in barbecue with hood, for about 1½ hours or until tender (legs will move easily from body). Baste occasionally during cooking.

NOTE: *A wonderfully rich glaze and flavor. If the dish is wild duck, a California red or Rosé dinner wine might be especially enjoyable; if domestic duck or pork, Rosé or white. Another interesting wild duck marinade is made by Mrs. W. W. Owen of Calif. Grape Products Corp., Delano. She uses dry white wine and ground mace in her recipe, and prefers this type of wine served with the wild duck. (See also note at bottom of Page 66, on red wine with wild duck.)*

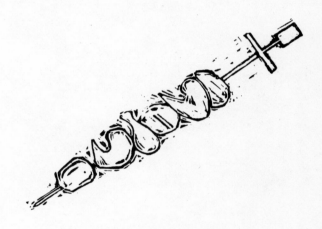

TURKEY BARBECUE SAUCE

(1½ cups)

Leonard P. LeBlanc, California Growers Wineries, Cutler

    1 cup California Sherry
    ¼ cup olive oil
    2 tablespoons butter or margarine
    1 medium onion, very finely minced
    1 clove garlic, crushed
    1½ teaspoons salt
    ¼ teaspoon paprika
    1 teaspoon fines herbs
    1 teaspoon minced parsley
    Freshly ground pepper

Combine all ingredients; simmer 15 minutes. Use to baste turkey barbecued on a spit, basting often.

NOTE: *Unusually appealing. With the turkey, serve your usual preference: California red, white or Rosé dinner wine.*

CLASSIC CUMBERLAND SAUCE

(About 1 cup)

Karl C. Krupp, Wine Advisory Board, Los Angeles

This sauce is traditional with wild or domestic duck, goose, cold turkey or chicken, or hot or cold ham.

- ⅓ cup red currant jelly
- ¼ cup California Port
- ¼ cup orange juice
- 2 tablespoons lemon juice
- 2 teaspoons dry mustard
- 1 teaspoon paprika
- ½ teaspoon ground ginger
- 1 teaspoon cornstarch
- 2 tablespoons grated orange rind

Stir jelly over low heat until melted. Blend remaining ingredients; add to jelly. Bring to boiling; reduce heat and simmer, stirring constantly, for 5 minutes. Let stand an hour or longer before serving, preferably with hot roast goose.

My choice of wine to accompany this dish:
CALIFORNIA CLARET OR ZINFANDEL

SHERRIED RAISIN SAUCE

(About 2 cups)

Mrs. Jake Rheingans, Sanger Winery Association, Sanger

This may be served on baked ham, corned pork or tongue.

- ¾ cup seedless raisins
- 1½ cups water
- ½ cup brown sugar (packed)
- 1½ tablespoons cornstarch
- ¼ teaspoon cloves
- ½ teaspoon salt
- 1 tablespoon butter or margarine
- ½ cup California Sherry

Rinse raisins and drain. Add raisins to water; simmer 10 minutes. Mix together brown sugar, cornstarch, cloves and salt; stir into raisins. Cook, stirring constantly, until clear and thickened. Blend in butter and Sherry; heat thoroughly.

NOTE: *A chilled California Rosé would be perfect with any of the dishes suggested with this spicy sauce.*

SPARERIBS BARBECUE SAUCE

(For 5 or 6 lbs. spareribs)

S. Martinelli, S. Martinelli & Co., Watsonville

- 1 cup California red or white dinner wine
- ¼ cup catsup
- 1 teaspoon brown sugar
- 1 teaspoon Worcestershire sauce
- 1 teaspoon salt
- ¼ teaspoon dry mustard
- ¼ teaspoon dry celery seed
- ¼ cup chopped onion
- Dash pepper

Combine wine, catsup and seasonings; mix well. Baste spareribs frequently with sauce during the barbecuing.

My choice of wine to accompany this dish:
CALIFORNIA DRY RED OR WHITE DINNER WINE

NOTE: *Mrs. Jake Rheingans of Sanger Winery Assn., Sanger, barbecues spareribs with a sauce that includes molasses and California Sherry. This would be tops with any pork. Crushed pineapple and Port are among the sparerib sauce secrets of Marvin B. Jones, Gibson Wine Co., Elk Grove.*

STEAK SAUCE BORDELAISE

(4 servings)

Mrs. A. D. Webb, U. of Calif. Dept. of Viticulture & Enology

There are two schools of thought about this classic sauce in Bordeaux—one prefers garlic, while the other prefers shallots. In any case, enough is used that the flavor is unmistakable.

- 3 tablespoons chopped garlic or shallots
- 1 cup California Burgundy, Claret or other red dinner wine
- ½ cup pan drippings from steaks

Gently simmer garlic or shallots in wine until volume is reduced by one half. Set aside. After steaks are broiled, stir the rich brown pan drippings into sauce. Spoon warm sauce over steaks just before serving. Accompany steaks with green salad and French bread, with cheese and fresh fruit for dessert.

My choice of wine to accompany this dish:
CALIFORNIA CABERNET OR ZINFANDEL

NOTE: *For another traditional steak sauce, the Marchand de Vin or Wine Merchant sauce, see recipe for PAPER-THIN STEAKS on Page 41.*

LEMON-CHABLIS FISH SAUCE

(1¼ cups)

Mrs. Walter Richert, Richert & Sons, Morgan Hill

    2 lemons
    1 tablespoon cornstarch
    1 cup California Chablis or other
      white dinner wine
    ¼ teaspoon salt
    1½ tablespoons butter or margarine

Remove peel from 1 lemon; slice lemon very thinly. Squeeze juice from second lemon. Make a smooth paste of cornstarch, wine and salt. Melt butter in small saucepan; add paste; cook, stirring constantly, until mixture is clear and slightly thickened. Add lemon juice and slices; heat a few minutes longer. Serve over baked, broiled or poached fish.

NOTE: Most people would like a California Rhine, Chablis or Sauterne with the fish served with the sauce.

UNCOOKED WINE HOLLANDAISE

(About 1½ cups)

Otto E. Meyer, Paul Masson Vineyards, Saratoga

    4 egg yolks
    ½ teaspoon salt
      Dash cayenne pepper or Tabasco sauce
    1 cup melted butter or margarine
    ¼ cup California Riesling or other
      dry white dinner wine
    1 tablespoon lemon juice

Beat egg yolks until very thick and light yellow (takes about 8 to 10 minutes). Blend in salt and cayenne or Tabasco, beating well. Add butter, a tablespoon at a time, beating well after each addition, until 6 tablespoons have been added. Combine wine and lemon juice; beat in very slowly, alternating with remaining butter. Spoon over hot cooked asparagus or broccoli. **(Do not heat sauce, however.)** Store leftover sauce in refrigerator. It will solidify upon storing. You can use it later as is, or let it soften at room temperature to its original airy texture.

NOTE: A vegetable with a sauce as luxurious as this would befit the most festive dinner — accompanied by California Champagne.

QUICK ROSÉ-CHEESE SAUCE

(About 1⅓ cups)

Helen Junker, Wine Advisory Board, San Francisco

This is a fast, easy sauce to serve over a hot cooked vegetable, such as asparagus, broccoli or cauliflower.

    ½ lb. process American cheese
    ½ cup California Rosé
    3 or 4 drops Tabasco sauce

Cut cheese into chunks; place all ingredients in top of double boiler over hot (not boiling) water. Heat, stirring now and then, until blended and smooth. We enjoy this vegetable and sauce with a steak dinner.

My choice of wine to accompany this dish:
    CALIFORNIA ROSÉ OR BURGUNDY

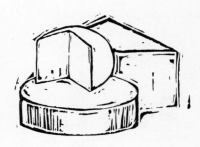

CHEESE, EGGS, PASTA & RICE

It has been widely noted that wine and cheese have an ancient affinity. Both typify man's quest for a more enduring and portable form for perishable foods. The transmuting of grapes into wine, and milk into cheese, were two of the brighter beacons in civilization's history. They proved to the old wandering tribes that Nature's own wonders (of wine fermentation and milk curding) could be controlled and improved upon by man. Not trivially, wine and cheese also bestowed upon the world a superlative companionship of taste: no two food products have ever done more for each other. Today's cooks still find the combination an irresistible one.

MACARONI & CHEESE WITH WINE

(About 6 servings)

Mrs. Ted Yamada, American Society of Enologists, Anaheim

- 2 cups uncooked macaroni
- 2 tablespoons soft butter or margarine
- 1½ cups cubed sharp Cheddar cheese
- ½ teaspoon salt
- ½ teaspoon dry mustard
- 2 eggs, beaten
- 1½ cups rich milk or thin cream
- ½ cup California Sauterne or other white dinner wine
- 2 or 3 tablespoons chopped canned green chiles
- ½ cup stale bread crumbs mixed with 2 tablespoons melted butter or margarine

Combine all ingredients except crumbs; mix well. Place in buttered 1½-qt. baking dish. Sprinkle with buttered crumbs. Bake, covered, in moderate oven (350°) for 40 to 50 minutes. Let stand 5 to 10 minutes before serving, to thicken liquid in casserole.

NOTE: Quickly made, and especially pleasing with a well-chilled California Rosé served on the side. Another easy idea for macaroni is offered by Mrs. Clifton Chappell of Thomas Vineyards, Cucamonga. She suggests substituting California Sauterne for all or part of the milk in your favorite recipe for macaroni and cheese—a "delightful variation for a standard recipe."

EGGS ARE LUSCIOUS when poached or fried very gently in California Sherry. Sprinkle with Parmesan cheese and serve on hot buttered melba toast. A glass of chilled Chablis is ideal on the side.

BAKED SPAGHETTI UKIAH

(6 servings)

Mrs. John Parducci, Parducci Wine Cellars, Inc., Ukiah

This dish may be made the day before and refrigerated. It is also excellent for freezing. If frozen, allow 6 hours in refrigerator for thawing before baking.

- 1½ lbs. ground beef
- 1 medium-size onion, minced
- 1 clove garlic, mashed or finely chopped
- ¼ cup oil
- 3 (8-oz.) cans tomato sauce
- 1 cup California Burgundy, Claret or other red dinner wine
- 1 teaspoon dried Italian or mixed herbs
- ½ teaspoon dried parsley (optional)
- 1 tablespoon sugar
- ½ teaspoon salt
- ¼ teaspoon pepper
- ½ lb. spaghetti, broken in 2" lengths
- 1½ cups grated American cheese

Sauté meat, onion and garlic in heated oil. Add tomato sauce, wine, herbs, parsley, sugar, salt and pepper. Simmer, covered, 1 hour, stirring occasionally. Cook spaghetti according to package directions; drain. Add spaghetti and ½ cup cheese to sauce. Turn into 3-qt. casserole; sprinkle with remaining 1 cup cheese. (If made ahead, do not sprinkle cheese on top until ready to bake.) Cover; bake in a moderately slow oven (325°) for 45 minutes. Uncover; bake 30 minutes longer.

NOTE: A meaty, full-flavored dish, that would be at its best with California Burgundy or Claret on the table.

LIVERMORE SPAGHETTI

(6 servings)

Mrs. Don Rudolph, Cresta Blanca Wine Co., Livermore

- ½ lb. ground pork
- ½ lb. ground lamb
- 1 lb. ground beef
- 5 medium onions, finely chopped
- 4 cloves garlic, finely chopped
- 1 cup grated Parmesan cheese
- 1 cup California Burgundy or other red dinner wine
- 1 cup fine dry bread crumbs
- ½ teaspoon Tabasco sauce
- 1 tablespoon Worcestershire sauce
- 2 eggs, beaten
- 2 tablespoons chili powder
- 1 (1-lb. 4-oz.) can tomatoes
- 1 (10½-oz.) can tomato soup
- 2 (8-oz.) cans tomato sauce
- 2 (4-oz.) cans mushrooms
- 2 tablespoons sugar
- 1 teaspoon garlic powder
- 1 tablespoon oregano
- Salt and pepper
- ¼ cup California Sherry

Combine pork, lamb, beef, 2 onions (chopped), garlic, cheese, wine, bread crumbs, Tabasco sauce, Worcestershire sauce, eggs and 1 tablespoon chili powder; mix well. Form into balls; arrange in baking pan. Bake in a moderate oven (350°) until brown, turning once or twice. Meanwhile, combine other ingredients and remaining 3 onions (chopped) and 1 tablespoon chili powder, in large saucepan. Cook 1½ hours, or until thick. Enrich sauce with drippings from meat balls, if desired. Combine meat balls with sauce; serve with spaghetti. Also on menu: green peas, tossed green salad and French bread browned with garlic and butter.

My choice of wine to accompany this dish:
CALIFORNIA BURGUNDY OR CLARET

SAVORY BARBECUE RICE

(5 or 6 servings)

Marjorie Lumm, Wine Institute, San Francisco

- ⅓ cup finely-chopped green pepper
- ½ cup sliced green onion
- ¾ cup regular rice, uncooked
- 3 tablespoons butter or margarine
- 1½ teaspoons salt
- 1 (1-lb.) can tomatoes
- ½ cup California Sauterne or other white dinner wine
- 1 cup cubed Cheddar cheese

Sauté green pepper, onions and rice in butter over moderate heat until rice is slightly browned and vegetables soft. Add salt, tomatoes and wine. Cook, covered, over low heat until rice is tender and liquid absorbed (about 25 minutes). Stir in cubed cheese; remove from heat and let stand, covered, a few minutes until cheese softens and melts slightly.

NOTE: This dish could help enliven any barbecue menu, with a favorite red, white or Rosé dinner wine poured for guests.

RISOTTO ALLA CUCAMONGA

(4 to 6 servings)

Mrs. John B. Ellena, Regina Grape Products Co., Etiwanda

- 1 medium-size onion, finely chopped
- ½ cup butter or margarine
- 1 cup regular rice, uncooked
- 1 (10½-oz.) can beef consommé
- ¾ cup water
- ¼ cup California Sherry
- 1 cup grated Parmesan cheese

Sauté onion in ¼ cup butter until tender and golden. Add rice; sauté until yellow. Stir in consommé, water and Sherry. Bring to boiling; lower heat; simmer, covered, 25 minutes or until all liquid is absorbed. Add remaining ¼ cup butter and cheese; mix gently but well. This is delicious with broiled or fried chicken. Or, it can be served as a meat substitute, with green vegetable and crisp green salad.

My choice of wine to accompany this dish:
CALIFORNIA WHITE WINE, CHILLED

NOTE: The Sherry makes this different from the traditional risottos cooked with dinner wines. A most appealing flavor.

NEXT TIME you make a pilaf or other rice dish, try adding a few raisins (first steamed over hot water, or soaked in a little wine, to soften) shortly before serving. It adds exotic flavor and a new color accent.

RISOTTO MILANESE

(6 servings)

Mrs. Eugene Morosoli, Wine Advisory Board, San Francisco

- ½ cup butter or margarine
- 1 large onion, chopped
- 1½ cups long-grain rice, uncooked
- ⅓ cup California Chablis or other white dinner wine
- 4¼ cups boiling hot chicken broth (canned or bouillon-cube broth may be used)
- ¼ teaspoon powdered saffron
- Salt and pepper
- ¼ cup chopped dried or button mushrooms
- 1 cup grated Parmesan or Swiss cheese

Melt butter in heavy skillet; sauté onion until soft. Add rice, stirring constantly, until rice begins to brown. Add wine and 2 cups of the boiling chicken broth; bring to rapid boiling. Stir in saffron, salt, pepper and mushrooms. Keep mixture boiling, stirring frequently; add remaining hot chicken broth as needed until all used up (takes about 25 minutes). When all the liquid is absorbed and rice is tender, stir in cheese.

My choice of wine to accompany this dish:
A VERY COLD CALIFORNIA WHITE DINNER WINE

WINE CHEESE FONDUE

(4 servings)

Mrs. Walter S. Richert, Richert & Sons, Morgan Hill

This recipe is of authentic Swiss origin. I have all of the ingredients ready ahead of time. After an evening of cards, a chafing dish is placed on the table and the fondue is cooked before all eyes. Each person is provided with a plate, fork, napkin and WINE glass. The same WINE used in cooking is served. This recipe is also useful for wine tasting parties, omitting the garlic and nutmeg.

    1 clove garlic
    2 cups California Riesling, Chablis
      or other white dinner wine
    1 lb. Swiss cheese, shredded
    3 tablespoons flour
    ½ teaspoon salt
    ⅛ teaspoon pepper
      Dash nutmeg
    3 tablespoons California brandy
      (optional)
    1 loaf French bread, cut in bite-size
      pieces with crust

Rub cooking utensil with garlic or force garlic through press. Pour in wine. Place over very low heat until air bubbles rise to surface. **(DO NOT BOIL!)** Coat cheese with flour. Stir wine, adding cheese by handfuls; completely melt each handful before adding the next. Keep stirring until mixture starts bubbling lightly. Add salt, pepper and nutmeg. Stir in brandy; place on table heating element. Guests should spear a piece of bread with a fork, dunk in fondue with a stirring motion, and eat heartily.

My choice of wine to accompany this dish:
CALIFORNIA RIESLING OR CHABLIS

NOTE: *The flavor of the grape comes through most agreeably in this fondue. Mrs. Richert's omission of garlic and nutmeg when serving it at a wine tasting party stems from a customary practice at this very specialized type of gathering. The practice is to avoid any highly seasoned food accompaniments. Where many wines are to be tasted, with their subtle flavor distinctions studied minutely, it is best to serve only the blandest of cheese complements. This saves the taste buds for the business at hand: the appreciation of good wines.*

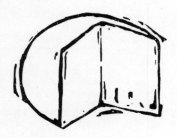

ANOTHER SWISS FONDUE VERSION (called American style), for a dinner or late supper dish, is used by Mrs. Rose Marie Pangborn, of the U. C. Dept. of Food Science and Technology, Davis. Mrs. Pangborn adds a little sharp Cheddar cheese to the Swiss cheese which dominates the recipe, plus extra nutmeg. She too prefers California Riesling (Johannisberg or Grey) served with hers.

CALIFORNIA RAREBIT

(4 or 5 servings)

Doris Paulsen, Wine Institute, San Francisco

For brunch, lunch, supper or snack, this is hard to beat.

    1 (10½-oz.) can cream of celery
      soup, undiluted
    ¼ cup California Sauterne or other
      white dinner wine
    ½ teaspoon mustard
    ½ teaspoon Worcestershire sauce
    1½ cups grated sharp Cheddar cheese
    1 egg, lightly beaten

In a saucepan, blend together soup, wine, mustard and Worcestershire sauce; heat thoroughly. Add cheese, stirring over low heat until melted. Slowly stir in lightly beaten egg; cook 2 or 3 minutes longer, stirring constantly, over very low heat until thickened. Serve at once over crisp toast or crackers.

My choice of wine to accompany this dish:
CALIFORNIA SAUTERNE OR ROSÉ

HOPPIN' JOHN

(4 servings)

Mrs. J. C. Russell, Almaden Vineyards, Los Gatos

This is a meal in itself, an old South Carolina dish.

    1 cup long-grain rice, uncooked
    2 teaspoons bacon fat
    2 onions
    1 cup broth (bouillon cube
      may be used)
    ½ teaspoon savory or fines herbs
    6 red pepper pods (optional)
    1 tablespoon butter
      Salt
    3 tablespoons California Burgundy or
      other red dinner wine
    2 (1-lb.) cans black-eyed peas

Cook rice according to package directions until tender and liquid is absorbed; stir in bacon fat. Simmer onions in broth until liquid evaporates. Combine rice with onions and remaining ingredients; heat through.

My choice of wine to accompany this dish:
A CALIFORNIA RED DINNER WINE

CHEESE SOUFFLÉ CHABLIS

(4 or 5 servings)

Kenneth E. Vogt, Wine Advisory Board, Milwaukee

Cheese and wine traditionally go together. This recipe adds showmanship when you have dinner guests.

        3 tablespoons butter or margarine
        3 tablespoons flour
        1 teaspoon salt
        ¼ teaspoon dry mustard
        ½ cup milk
        ½ cup California Chablis or other
            white dinner wine
            Dash Tabasco sauce
        1 cup grated sharp Cheddar cheese
        4 eggs, separated

Melt butter; blend in flour, salt and mustard. Stir in milk and wine (mixture may curdle a little but will smooth out on cooking). Cook and stir until mixture boils and thickens. Add Tabasco sauce and cheese; stir over low heat until cheese melts. Remove from heat. Beat egg yolks lightly; stir into cooked mixture. Beat whites until stiff; fold into mixture. Turn into 2-qt. baking dish. Set in pan of hot water. Bake in slow oven (300°) for 1 hour. Serve at once from same baking dish.

My choice of wine to accompany this dish:
ANY CHILLED CALIFORNIA WHITE DINNER WINE

SHERRIED SHRIMP RAREBIT

(6 to 8 servings)

Ralph H. Winters, Wine Advisory Board, New York City

This is a simple recipe that I worked up myself to use on television appearances. It is easy to remember and, best of all, very tasty.

        1 lb. aged Cheddar cheese,
            grated or diced
        1 (10-oz.) can frozen cream of
            shrimp soup, thawed
        ¼ cup California Cream Sherry

Combine cheese and soup in top of double boiler; heat over hot water, stirring, until cheese melts and is blended. Just before serving, stir in Sherry. Serve over toast points as a main course, or, in a chafing dish as a hot dip for potato chips.

NOTE: *As a supper dish, this might be accompanied by a chilled California Rosé. As a cocktail hour dip, it would be perfect with Sherry or Dry Vermouth on-the-rocks.*

SCRAMBLED EGGS SAUTERNE

(About 4 servings)

Mrs. Myron Nightingale, Roma Wine Company, Fresno

        6 eggs
        ½ teaspoon salt
        2 tablespoons cream
        ¼ cup California Sauterne, Chablis
            or other white dinner wine
        ⅛ teaspoon dried dill, rosemary
            or basil
        2 tablespoons butter or margarine
        ¼ cup coarsely crumbled blue cheese
        1 tablespoon chopped chives,
            parsley or pimiento

Beat eggs slightly. Stir in salt, cream, wine and seasoning. Melt butter in medium-size skillet; coat bottom and sides of pan. When hot enough to make drop of water sizzle, pour in egg mixture; reduce heat. Cook slowly, gently lifting eggs from bottom and sides with a spoon as mixture sets, so liquid can flow to bottom. (Do not overstir.) Add cheese and chives while eggs are still creamy. Cook to desired moistness. Serve at once, for a late breakfast or luncheon.

My choice of wine to accompany this dish:
THE SAME CALIFORNIA SAUTERNE

SHERRIED EGGS

(2 to 4 servings)

Sylvia Elwood Preiss, Llords & Elwood Wine Cellars, Fremont

        3 egg yolks
        1 cup cream
            Salt and pepper
        4 hard-cooked eggs, quartered
        ½ cup California Dry Sherry

Beat yolks in cream; season with salt and pepper. Cook over hot water in top of double boiler until thick. Add quartered eggs. When ready to serve, stir in Dry Sherry. Serve in hot ramekins.

NOTE: *This would be good for a Sunday brunch or late supper. A chilled white dinner wine or Rosé would be particularly pleasant as beverage.*

BAKED EGGS IN SPINACH NESTS gather compliments at Sunday suppers. To serve 6 generously: First make a cheese sauce. (Melt 3 tablespoons butter, stir in same amount flour, add 1 cup milk; cook, stirring constantly, until mixture boils and thickens. Stir in 1 cup shredded process Cheddar cheese, stirring until melted. Now add ¼ cup California Sherry to sauce, plus ½ teaspoon Worcestershire sauce, ¼ teaspoon prepared mustard, salt and pepper to taste.) Place 2 cups cooked or canned spinach (well-drained and chopped) in 6 oiled individual casseroles; depress each center to form a nest. Break an egg into each. Spoon some of cheese sauce over each egg; dust with paprika. Bake in moderately hot oven (375°) about 15 minutes, or until eggs are set. Serve with chilled California Rose.

VEGETABLES

Far too often, alas, the great taste potential of vegetables has been overlooked. Dull, waterlogged and soggy, or overcooked—these sad traits have exiled many an innocent vegetable dish from the family table, denounced as "rabbit food" or worse. But crisp-tender green vegetables or creamy-rich root vegetables, buttery and hot, and sauced or seasoned with California wine, are another matter. Wine cookery here is notably rewarding because of the welcome variations it brings. Vegetables take on a new distinction, a brightness of flavor. They become, at last, fully as enjoyable as the main dish itself—in perfect harmony with the good dinner wine on the table.

MODESTO POTATOES

(4 servings)

Lyman M. Cash, E. & J. Gallo Winery, Modesto

    3 tablespoons butter or olive oil
    1 tablespoon flour
    4 medium-size potatoes,
       peeled and sliced
    1 medium-size onion, sliced
    1 clove garlic, minced
       Salt and pepper
    ⅓ cup California Sauterne or other
       white dinner wine
    ⅓ cup chicken or beef broth
       (canned or bouillon-cube
       broth may be used)
    ½ teaspoon minced thyme or marjoram
    1 tablespoon minced parsley

Melt butter or heat oil in heavy skillet; mix in flour; brown quickly. Add potatoes, onion, garlic, salt and pepper. Fry, turning often, until slightly brown. Add wine, broth and thyme; cover tightly. Simmer until potatoes are tender and liquid is absorbed. Add parsley; mix well. Serve with a baked fish dinner (fillet of rock cod, fillet of sole, bass or salmon).

My choice of wine to accompany this dish:
CALIFORNIA SAUTERNE

NOTE: *Exceptionally good with any menu calling for potatoes. Shows what wine can do to make vegetables more interesting.*

FESTIVAL SWEET POTATOES

(6 servings)

Roy Petersen, Foote, Cone & Belding, San Francisco

    3 large sweet potatoes or yams
    6 slices canned pineapple
    4 tablespoons butter or margarine
    ½ cup brown sugar
    ½ cup California Sherry

Boil sweet potatoes in their skins 20 to 30 minutes, or until tender. Peel; cut lengthwise in halves. Arrange pineapple in single layer in shallow baking dish. Top each pineapple slice with a potato half, cut side down. Heat butter or margarine, sugar and Sherry together until sugar is dissolved; pour over potatoes and pineapple. Bake in moderately hot oven (375°) 30 minutes, basting often with syrup in pan. Serve with the festive holiday turkey or a baked ham dinner anytime.

My choice of wine to accompany this menu:
CALIFORNIA RED, WHITE OR ROSÉ DINNER WINE

DON'S FAVORITE BEANS

(3 or 4 servings)

Mrs. Don W. McColly, Wine Institute, San Francisco

These are easy and very good. Green beans are a favorite in our household, because both Don and I grew up on farms and enjoyed them fresh from the field. These days, we still like the old-fashioned bacon and onion flavors in the frozen wine-cooked beans.

    1 (9-oz.) pkg. frozen French-cut
        green beans
    1 teaspoon instant minced onion
    ½ teaspoon seasoned salt
      Dash or two seasoned pepper
    1 strip crisp cooked bacon
    ¼ cup California Riesling, Chablis
        or other white dinner wine
    3 tablespoons butter or margarine

Place frozen beans in saucepan. Sprinkle on onion, salt and pepper; crumble on bacon. Pour wine over all; cover closely. Cook over moderately high heat 6 to 10 minutes or just until beans are crisp-tender. Add butter, stir to blend and serve at once. (For those who like more liquid, another tablespoon or two of wine may be stirred in along with the butter.) We prefer these with leg of lamb, salad of butter lettuce and mandarin oranges, and a frozen lemon dessert with brownies.

Our choice of wine to accompany this menu:
CALIFORNIA RED, WHITE OR ROSÉ DINNER WINE

VINTNER'S BEANS

(10 to 12 servings)

Mrs. David Ficklin, Ficklin Vineyards, Madera

We use this dish traditionally for summertime outdoor suppers. It can be baked ahead and reheated easily. Excellent for pot-luck or buffet suppers as well as barbecues.

    1 lb. navy beans
    ½ lb. salt pork, thinly sliced
    1 medium-size onion, chopped
    ½ teaspoon dry mustard
    1 tablespoon salt
    ½ cup brown sugar (packed)
    1½ cups California Port
    1 cup strong hot coffee

Soak beans in cold water overnight. Place salt pork, onion and drained beans into bean pot or heavy casserole. Add mustard, salt, sugar, 1 cup Port and enough water to barely cover. Bake in slow oven (275°) for about 4 hours; add a little more water during last half hour, if necessary. Add remaining ½ cup Port and cup of strong hot coffee. Continue baking 1½ to 2 hours longer.

My choice of wine to accompany this dish:
CALIFORNIA CLARET

WINE-GLAZED CARROTS

(About 4 servings)

Brother Gregory, Mont La Salle Vineyards, Napa

Peel enough carrots for about 4 servings, and slice lengthwise, very thin. Parboil in salted water until just tender, still a little crisp. Drain and saute in 1 tablespoon butter until lightly browned. Add 2 tablespoons California Light Muscat and simmer until wine has evaporated.

NOTE: A delightful new flavor; would win compliments from guests. Try serving this dish with roast chicken or barbecued duck, and a chilled California Rhine or Sauterne.

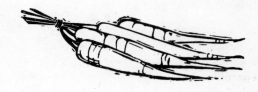

CARROTS IN SHERRY

(6 to 8 servings)

Mrs. Lewis A. Stern, E. & J. Gallo Winery, Modesto

    2 lbs. carrots, scraped and quartered
    ¼ cup butter or margarine
    1 teaspoon salt
    ⅛ teaspoon pepper
    ¼ teaspoon sugar
    ½ cup California Sherry
      Minced parsley

Sauté carrots in melted butter, turning until well coated. Sprinkle with salt, pepper and sugar. Add Sherry; simmer gently about 5 minutes. Add water just to cover; simmer, covered, 15 to 25 minutes or until tender. (Small young carrots take only about 15 minutes.) Remove cover; cook over medium heat until most of liquid has evaporated. Sprinkle with parsley. These go well with baked ham with pineapple; boiled potatoes with parsley-butter sauce; coleslaw; and chilled fruits with cookies for dessert.

My choice of wine to accompany this menu:
CALIFORNIA ROSÉ, CHABLIS OR SAUTERNE

CARROTS ALSO take to California Sauterne. Add 4 cups shredded carrots and 1 chopped onion to 2 tablespoons butter that you have melted in saucepan. Salt and pepper to taste, then add ½ cup Sauterne. Cover; cook 10 minutes, or just until tender. Or, can be baked in casserole in moderate oven (350°) about 25 minutes. Makes 4 servings. A nice change with a roast beef or leg of lamb, and California Rosé as beverage.

CALIFORNIA FRIED TOMATOES

(6 servings)

E. L. (Ted) Barr, Western Grape Products, Kingsburg

        6 medium-size firm tomatoes
     ¼ cup sifted flour
        1 teaspoon garlic salt
     ½ teaspoon rosemary or thyme
     ¼ cup butter or margarine
        2 teaspoons brown sugar
     ⅔ cup California Burgundy or
            other red dinner wine

Core tomatoes; remove skin if desired. Cut each tomato in half. Combine flour, salt and rosemary (or thyme). Dredge tomatoes in seasoned flour. Sauté on both sides over moderate heat in melted butter. Add sugar and wine; continue cooking until tomatoes are tender, about 5 minutes. Serve with any remaining liquid. Fine with wild game or steaks or any hearty dinner.

NOTE: *The same Burgundy or other red dinner wine would be enjoyable with such a menu.*

BROILED SHERRIED TOMATOES

(1 or 2 halves per serving)

Robert D. Rossi, Jr., United Vintners, Inc., San Francisco

        Medium large firm tomatoes
        California Sherry
        Salt
        Pepper
        Dried dill
        Mayonnaise
        Grated American cheese

Cut tomatoes in halves, crosswise. Pierce with fork and sprinkle with Sherry. Season with salt, pepper and dill. Broil 5 to 7 minutes or until heated through. Combine equal amounts of mayonnaise and cheese; put a spoonful on each tomato half. Return to broiler and brown lightly. Excellent with barbecued meats or chicken.

NOTE: *Try a chilled California Rosé with the menu: a sure pleaser.*

CAULIFLOWER SANTA ROSA

(5 or 6 servings)

Elmo Martini, Martini & Prati Wines, Inc., Santa Rosa

        1 large head cauliflower
     ¼ cup butter or margarine
     ¼ cup flour
        1 cup rich milk
     ½ cup California Rhine, Sauterne or
            other white dinner wine
     ½ cup water
     ½ cup shredded, blanched almonds
            Salt and pepper
     ¼ cup grated Cheddar cheese

Trim and wash cauliflower; separate into flowerets. Drop into boiling, salted water; cook 10 to 15 minutes, or just until tender when pierced with a fork. Meanwhile, prepare sauce. Melt butter and stir in flour. Add milk, wine and water; cook, stirring constantly, until mixture is thickened and smooth. Add almonds, salt and pepper. Drain cauliflower carefully; place in greased baking dish. Pour over sauce and sprinkle with grated cheese. Bake in moderately hot oven (375°) for 20 minutes.

NOTE: *Deserves a good steak or roast beef, with California Claret or Rosé served with the dinner.*

RED CABBAGE ETIWANDA

(6 to 10 servings)

Mrs. John B. Ellena, Regina Grape Products Co., Etiwanda

        1 medium head red cabbage
        5 cooking apples
        2 tablespoons sugar
        3 tablespoons California red
            wine vinegar
        1 tablespoon butter
     1¼ teaspoons salt
     ¼ teaspoon pepper
     ¼ cup California Burgundy, Claret
            or other red dinner wine

Shred cabbage finely; core and cut apples in small pieces. Combine with sugar, vinegar, butter, salt and pepper in saucepan. Cook slowly, covered, 45 minutes to 1 hour or until soft, stirring occasionally. Add wine last 10 minutes of cooking. This is delicious with roast pork.

My choice of wine to accompany this menu:
WELL-CHILLED CALIFORNIA WHITE DINNER WINE
SUCH AS FRENCH COLOMBARD OR RIESLING

NOTE: *Cabbage cooked with wine is also a favorite of Mrs. Don McColly, Wine Institute, San Francisco; Mrs. H. L. Archinal of Mt. Tivy Winery, Reedley; and Mrs. L. J. Berg of Mont La Salle Vineyards, Napa.*

AN EXOTIC CHINESE EFFECT can be given canned sauerkraut, using California wine. Cook the kraut only 3 or 4 minutes, covered; drain. Pour a little medium Sauterne over, and add small fillets of fresh white-meat fish on top of kraut. Sprinkle with dill and caraway seed. Cover tightly and simmer, to steam fish until done (5 to 15 minutes, depending on thickness of fillets). Just before serving, mix **very** lightly; fish should not take on sauerkraut flavor. This unusual and subtle recipe is from a wine industry supplier noted for his cooking.

CREAMED SHERRY SPINACH

(6 servings)

Joseph J. Franzia, Franzia Brothers Winery, Ripon

 1 (12-oz.) pkg. frozen chopped spinach
 ¼ cup butter or margarine
 ¼ cup flour
 ¾ cup canned condensed
     cream of mushroom soup
 ¼ cup California Sherry
 ½ cup grated process Cheddar cheese
 ½ cup (firmly packed) soft bread crumbs
 3 eggs, slightly beaten
 1 teaspoon grated onion
 ¼ teaspoon nutmeg
     Salt
     Pepper

Cook spinach according to package directions; drain well. Melt butter, stir in flour, add soup and wine. Cook, stirring, until mixture boils and thickens. Add cheese; stir over low heat until melted. Remove from heat. Add spinach and other ingredients. Turn into 6 well-greased custard cups. Set in shallow pan of hot water. Bake in moderate oven (350°) about 45 minutes, or until firm. Remove from oven; let stand 5 minutes or so before unmolding, to unmold easily.

NOTE: Even spinach-haters enjoy this recipe. Attractive and good for any kind of dinner menu, with California red or white dinner wine alongside.

BROCCOLI IN SHERRY-ALMOND SAUCE is an interesting new treatment. Cook broccoli in usual manner until tender. Meanwhile, make your own white sauce, or use canned type if you prefer. Heat, stirring. Blend California Sherry to desired consistency into thickened white sauce, and cook only a minute longer. Pour sauce over hot drained broccoli and sprinkle with chopped or slivered almonds.

GLAZED CELERY SAN JOAQUIN

(4 to 6 servings)

Lawrence Quaccia, Guild Wine Co., Lodi

 4 cups 1" pieces of celery
 ½ cup chicken broth
 2 teaspoons cornstarch
 ¼ cup California Sauterne or
     other white dinner wine
     Salt
     Slivered toasted almonds (optional)

Combine celery and chicken broth in saucepan; cook, covered, about 15 minutes, or until tender but still crisp. Stir cornstarch into wine; add to celery. Cook over low heat until mixture boils and thickens. Add salt. Serve hot. May be sprinkled with toasted slivered almonds, if desired.

NOTE: This is an elegant treatment, suited to the most festive dinner menu, and served with any California dinner wine or Champagne.

GLORIFIED ZUCCHINI

(6 to 8 servings)

Mrs. Leo Demostene, Soda Rock Winery, Healdsburg

This same mixture may also be stirred into French-cut green beans, baked the same way.

 4 or 5 medium zucchini, sliced 1" thick
     Salt
 1 large onion, chopped
 2 tablespoons butter or margarine
 2 tablespoons flour
 ½ cup California Sauterne, Chablis or
     other white dinner wine
 1 (10½-oz.) can cream of mushroom soup
     Grated cheese

Parboil zucchini slices in boiling salted water. Drain; place in single layer in buttered (9 x 11") baking dish. In saucepan, brown onion in butter; stir in flour. Add wine and soup; mix well. Pour over zucchini; sprinkle with grated cheese. Bake in moderate oven (350°) for 30 to 40 minutes. This is very good with any menu.

NOTE: And your favorite California dinner wine (red, white or Rosé) accompanying.

SPRING SQUASH IN WINE

(8 to 10 servings)

Mrs. Ernest A. Wente, Wente Bros., Livermore

 2 tablespoons butter
 2 tablespoons olive oil
 1 medium onion, minced
 2 large stalks celery, thinly sliced
 1 lb. yellow crookneck squash,
     diced in ½" cubes
 1 lb. scalloped or summer squash,
     thinly sliced
 1 lb. zucchini, thinly sliced
 ½ cup California Sauterne, Chablis
     or other white dinner wine
 ¼ teaspoon basil, crumbled
 ½ teaspoon salt
 ⅛ teaspoon pepper
     Nutmeg

Heat butter and oil in large saucepan. Sauté onion, celery and squashes until onion is clear. Add wine and seasonings; cover; simmer about 20 minutes or until tender. Season with additional butter before serving, if desired.

NOTE: Cheerful in color, with a fresh cheerful flavor. Would combine well with spring lamb chops or leg of lamb, served with California Rosé.

SHERRIED WINTER SQUASH (acorn squash) with pineapple is delightful. Cut squash into small squares and cook until tender in salted water. Drain; remove rind. Place squash in shallow baking dish and top with drained crushed pineapple and brown sugar. Drizzle with California Sherry and dot with butter. Bake in moderate oven (350°) about a half hour. Good with baked ham, served with chilled California Rosé.

SHERRIED CORN LUCULLUS

(6 to 8 servings)

Mrs. Edmund A. Rossi, Jr., Italian Swiss Colony, Asti

>   2 (10-oz.) pkgs. frozen
>   whole-kernel corn
>   ¼ cup butter, melted
>   ¼ cup water
>   Salt
>   Pepper
>   ¼ cup cream
>   ¼ cup California Sherry

Cook corn in melted butter and water about 4 minutes, stirring constantly. Add seasonings; stir in cream and Sherry. Heat thoroughly, stirring, and serve at once. Particularly good with a steak dinner.

NOTE: With a hearty California Claret or Burgundy on the table!

JERUSALEM ARTICHOKES

(4 servings)

Mrs. Herbert Cerwin, Cerwin Vineyards, Sonoma

As Jerusalem artichokes are a root vegetable, belonging to the sunflower family, they usually take the place of potatoes. They are highly regarded by many trying to diet, as they are not starchy.

>   1 small onion, chopped
>   2 tablespoons oil
>   1 pound Jerusalem artichokes,
>   pared and sliced
>   2 cups California Riesling or
>   other white dinner wine
>   Garlic salt
>   Pepper
>   Salt
>   Nutmeg
>   2 tablespoons finely-chopped
>   parsley
>   Parmesan cheese (optional)

Sauté onion in oil until clear. Add sliced artichokes and wine. Cover and simmer just until tender, about 25 to 30 minutes. Season to taste with garlic salt, pepper, salt and a dash of nutmeg. Just before serving, sprinkle with chopped parsley. You may like to add a sprinkling of Parmesan cheese. A garnish of a few sprigs of watercress, mint or tarragon is nice. This dish seems to go best with beef and a mixed green salad.

My choice of wine to accompany this menu:
CALIFORNIA CLARET, CABERNET OR ZINFANDEL
(OR RIESLING IF A WHITE IS PREFERRED)

BACCHANALIAN BRUSSELS SPROUTS

(3 or 4 servings)

Jessica McLachlin Greengard, Public Relations, Wines & Food

>   1 lb. fresh or 1 (10-oz.) pkg.
>   frozen Brussels sprouts
>   California Chablis or other
>   white dinner wine
>   ¾ cup white seedless grapes
>   Butter
>   Salt and pepper

Cook Brussels sprouts, using wine for all or part of cooking liquid. Drain; add grapes. Season with butter, salt and pepper. Heat through. This vegetable is especially good with wild duck, venison or turkey.

NOTE: Really delicious, a magic touch for sprouts. A velvety California Burgundy would be just right with the types of menus indicated.

GREEN PEAS GOURMET

(5 or 6 servings)

Robert D. Rossi, Jr., United Vintners, Inc., San Francisco

>   2 cups shelled fresh peas
>   (about 2 lbs.)
>   1 cup thinly sliced celery
>   1 teaspoon seasoned salt
>   1 cup chicken broth
>   ¼ cup California Sauterne
>   or other white dinner wine
>   3 tablespoons butter or margarine
>   Pepper
>   2 or 3 teaspoons cornstarch (optional)

Combine peas, celery, salt and broth in saucepan. Cover and cook gently until peas are tender. Stir in wine, butter, pepper and additional salt to taste. Thicken liquid with cornstarch mixed with a little water, if desired. Serve in sauce dishes with the richly flavored sauce.

NOTE: An epicurean treatment. Choose the dinner wine according to the main dish on the menu—usually red wine for red meats, white wine for white meats. Rosé or Champagne with anything.

BEETS BURGUNDIAN

(6 to 8 servings)

Mrs. J. H. M. Elwood, Llords & Elwood Wine Cellars, Fremont

>   Freshly cooked beets
>   2 tablespoons butter or margarine
>   1 tablespoon flour
>   ½ to 1 cup California Burgundy
>   or other red dinner wine
>   1 teaspoon sugar
>   Grating of nutmeg
>   Pinch cloves
>   Salt and pepper

Peel beets; grate enough to make 3 cups. Melt butter in saucepan; stir in flour. Stir in ½ cup wine. Add beets, sugar and seasonings. Simmer over low heat until tender. Add more wine during cooking, if needed.

NOTE: Serve them with a steak, buttery baked potatoes, hearts of lettuce with oil and wine vinegar dressing, and the same California red wine for a dinner-winner. The classic dish, Harvard Beets Burgundy, is similar in flavor but includes wine vinegar in the preparation.

LEEKS COUNTRY STYLE

(6 servings)

Mrs. A. D. Webb, U. of Calif. Dept. of Viticulture & Enology

This recipe was collected during a visit to Bordeaux. It's especially good with lunches including cold meat cuts, French bread and the more flavorful white wines. However, the dish is flavorful enough to be accompanied by either red or white wine.

- 2 bunches leeks
- ¼ cup butter or margarine
- 3 tablespoons flour
- ½ cup California Chardonnay, Chablis or other white dinner wine
- ¾ teaspoon salt
- ⅛ teaspoon pepper
- 4 egg yolks, lightly beaten
- ½ cup grated Swiss cheese
  Bread crumbs

Cut leeks in ¾" lengths, including part of green tops. Cook until tender in about 1¼ cups water; drain, saving cooking water. Melt butter in small saucepan; stir in flour. Add wine and 1 cup of the cooking liquid; cook, stirring constantly, until thickened. Season with salt and pepper. Add beaten egg yolks very gradually, stirring constantly. Add cheese, stirring until melted. Place leeks in casserole; cover with cheese sauce; dust lightly with bread crumbs. Bake in a moderate oven (350°) for 15 minutes. Serve as vegetable with entrée.

LEEKS ARE ALWAYS a refreshing change as a vegetable dish. Another cooking method, extremely simple, is to poach them in California Sauterne (or other white) and melted butter. First slit the leeks in half, lengthwise, keeping part of the green tops. Wash carefully, so that the halves hold their shape. Lay them in loaf pan, barely covering with wine and butter. Cover tightly with foil; simmer until tender. Dust with paprika and serve hot with any meat dish and your favorite California dinner wine. (The leftover cooked leeks may be refrigerated, to enrich a salad the next day.)

COMPANY ONIONS

(About 4 servings)

Mrs. Stanley Strud, California Wine Association, Lodi

- 1 (1-lb.) can small whole onions, drained
- ⅔ cup light cream
- 2 teaspoons cornstarch
- 2 tablespoons butter or margarine
  Dash of mace or nutmeg
- ¼ cup California Sherry
- ¼ cup fine dry bread crumbs

Place drained onions in shallow baking dish. Combine cream and cornstarch; cook and stir until thickened. Add 1 tablespoon butter, mace and Sherry; pour over onions. Melt remaining butter; blend with crumbs. Sprinkle over onions. Bake in moderate oven (350°) about 20 minutes, until well-heated and lightly browned. Serve with steak, roast or chops, with any favorite California dinner wine—red, white or Rosé.

SPRING ASPARAGUS ROSÉ

(About 2¼ cups sauce)

Alice Nelson, Wine Institute, San Francisco

This is an easy main dish for a luncheon or light supper.

- 1 lb. process American cheese
- ¾ cup California Rosé
- ½ teaspoon mustard
- 1 tablespoon instant minced onion
  Hot cooked asparagus
  Toast or toasted hamburger buns

Cut cheese into medium-size pieces. Place in top of double boiler; add wine, mustard and onion. Cook over hot water, stirring frequently, until cheese melts and mixture is smooth. Arrange hot buttered asparagus stalks on lightly buttered toast or buns. Spoon cheese sauce over each serving. Good accompanied by sliced tomatoes marinated in oil and wine vinegar, and any favorite dessert.

My choice of wine to accompany this dish:
THE SAME CALIFORNIA ROSÉ, CHILLED

MUSHROOMS BOURGUIGNON

(4 to 6 servings)

Mrs. Ernest C. Haas, East-Side Winery, Lodi

- ⅓ cup butter or margarine
- 2 small green onions, chopped
- 1 clove garlic, crushed
- 1 lb. fresh mushrooms, sliced
- 1 cup California Burgundy or other red dinner wine
  Freshly ground black pepper
- ½ teaspoon salt
- 2 tablespoons chopped fresh parsley

Melt butter in saucepan; add chopped onion, garlic and mushrooms. Sauté until tender, then add other ingredients. Simmer until wine is reduced by half. (Mushrooms will be quite dark.) Serve as accompaniment to broiled steak.

NOTE: *With a California Claret or Burgundy on the table, this would make dreamy dining.*

A 200-YEAR-OLD English recipe for a "fricassee of mushrooms" calls for 1 cup of Champagne or white wine, ½ cup or less of beef broth, butter mixed with flour, onions, herbs and mace. Simmer fresh mushrooms in this for 15 minutes. Just before serving, add mixed egg yolks and cream, and heat briefly. Squeeze some orange or lemon juice over the top and serve. We don't know the type of beverage wine preferred by the creator of this delectable dish, but a California white dinner wine would have been perfect with it. And not too far-fetched, either —the first wine grapes were planted in California in 1769.

MUSHROOMS NEWBURG

(6 servings)

Mrs. Emil M. Mrak, University of California, Davis

This makes a good Friday lunch dish on toast.

1 lb. fresh mushrooms
¼ cup melted butter or margarine
½ cup California Dry Sherry
3 cups Cream Sauce (see below)
½ cup blanched almonds, slivered

Wash mushrooms; drain. Simmer 10 minutes in small amount of salted water; drain. Slice; toss with melted butter. Stir Sherry into Cream Sauce. Pour layer of sauce in a 1½-qt. casserole; add layer of mushrooms; top with almonds. Repeat layers, ending with a layer of white sauce and sprinkling of almonds. Bake in moderate oven (350°) for 20 minutes.

CREAM SAUCE: Melt 6 tablespoons butter or margarine in saucepan; stir in 6 tablespoons flour. (DO NOT LET BROWN.) Add 1½ cups chicken broth, 1 cup light cream and ½ cup California Chablis or other white dinner wine; cook, stirring constantly, until thickened. Season with 1 teaspoon salt, ½ teaspoon monosodium glutamate and dash of pepper.

NOTE: Mrs. Mrak makes her own chicken broth, adding sliced onion and various herbs to the simmering chicken bones. However, canned chicken broth or bouillon-cube broth may be used instead, in making the rich Cream Sauce. The same California white dinner wine would be a delightful accompaniment. The dish would be equally good for a Sunday night supper.

BAKED MUSHROOMS CONTRA COSTA

(6 servings)

Judy Hibel, Wine Advisory Board, San Francisco

These are delicious and not at all difficult. They may accompany a very special chicken dinner, with chilled California Chablis on the table. Or, they're equally good as a hot appetizer, served at cocktail time with Dry Sherry.

12 large mushrooms
Lemon juice
2 tablespoons butter
2 tablespoons Swiss cheese, grated
¼ cup bread crumbs
2 tablespoons minced parsley
½ clove garlic, minced
1 tablespoon minced onion
Salt and pepper
2 to 4 tablespoons California Sherry

Wash mushrooms; remove stems, leaving caps intact. Sprinkle few drops lemon juice on each cap; set aside. Prepare stuffing as follows: Mince stems very fine; sauté in butter. Meanwhile, combine cheese, bread crumbs, parsley, garlic, onion, salt and pepper in a bowl. Add sautéed mushroom stems; mix thoroughly. Add enough Sherry to moisten mixture. Pile stuffing into mushroom caps; sprinkle with additional bread crumbs and dot with butter. Bake in moderate oven (350°) for 15 minutes. Serve piping hot!

SALADS & DRESSINGS

A crisp, zestful salad can be made doubly enjoyable by an artfully seasoned dressing. The greatest chefs and best home cooks know this calls for *wine* vinegar— aristocrat of vinegars, the oldest known to man. Wine vinegar adds the desirable lively tang without the harshness. Its smooth mild character and beguiling bouquet make all the difference in the fresh taste of any salad. When your recipe also includes a touch of wine, as well as fine California wine vinegar, you explore a whole new world of varied flavors.

BEAN SALAD ESCALON

(10 to 12 servings)

Mrs. Joseph Roullard, Petri Wineries, Escalon

This recipe has been used on a number of occasions at the winery, and is very popular.

- 1 (1-lb.) can cut green beans
- 1 (1-lb.) can red kidney beans
- 1 (1-lb.) can garbanzo beans
- 1 (8-oz.) can pitted ripe olives (optional)
- 1 red onion, thinly sliced
- ½ cup minced green pepper
- ½ cup oil
- ⅓ cup California red wine vinegar
- ¼ cup California Burgundy, Claret or other red dinner wine
- ½ cup granulated sugar
- ¼ teaspoon basil, or
  ¼ teaspoon mixed salad herbs
- ¼ teaspoon garlic powder

Drain beans and olives; combine with onion and green pepper. Combine remaining ingredients; pour over bean mixture. Cover; refrigerate several hours or overnight. Good with menu including prime rib roast with horseradish sauce, rice pilaf, platter of fresh raw vegetables (carrots, green onions, tomatoes, etc.), garlic bread and an apple pie dessert.

My choice of wine to accompany this dish:
CALIFORNIA SPARKLING BURGUNDY OR
BURGUNDY OR PINOT NOIR

POTATO SALAD SAUTERNE adds the touch of elegance to a picnic—with no muss or fuss. Simply marinate the boiled potatoes in California Sauterne while they are still hot, then follow up with your usual potato salad recipe. Pack a thermos jug of chilled Sauterne or Rose along with the salad, cold cuts and French bread, and you'll picnic with a flair.

PACIFIC CRAB SALAD

(6 to 8 servings)

Al Pirrone, F. Pirrone & Sons, Inc., Salida

This is a meal in itself, good on a warm day.

- 1 cup chili sauce
- 1 tablespoon prepared horseradish
- 1 to 2 tablespoons fresh lemon juice
- ⅛ teaspoon garlic powder, or 1 small clove garlic, crushed
- 1½ teaspoons instant minced onion, or 2 tablespoons chopped green onion
- ⅛ teaspoon dried dill
- ½ cup California Sauterne or Rose
- 1 lb. fresh crabmeat
  Crisp romaine lettuce or other greens
  Hard-cooked egg slices
  Ripe olives

Combine chili sauce, horseradish, lemon juice, garlic, onion, dill and wine; refrigerate several hours. Add half of crab to sauce. Arrange crisp lettuce on serving plates; top with remaining crabmeat. Spoon on crab cocktail sauce (or serve in individual lemon cups). Garnish with egg slices and olives; serve very cold.

My choice of wine to accompany this dish:
CHILLED CALIFORNIA GREY RIESLING

NOTE: *For a creamy or Louis-type dressing, add ½ cup mayonnaise or sour cream.*

ANOTHER LUSCIOUS LOUIS dressing uses California Sherry, with commendable results. (It keeps well in the refrigerator, too.) To make about 1½ cups: Combine 1 cup mayonnaise, ½ cup chili sauce, 3 tablespoons medium Sherry, ½ teaspoon Worcestershire sauce, salt and pepper. Chill well, and enjoy on any seafood or lettuce salad.

OLD-FASHIONED HOT POTATO SALAD

(4 servings)

Jim Morse, Beringer Bros., Inc., St. Helena

This is a delicious old-time salad, and an easy way to serve potatoes when you're serving a cold meat plate or frankfurters. It's especially good for buffet meals (if kept hot) or barbecues.

    4 medium-size potatoes
    4 slices bacon
    ¼ cup chopped onion
    1 teaspoon salt
        Pepper
    3 tablespons California wine vinegar
    2 tablespoons California Chablis
        or other white dinner wine
    2 teaspoons sugar
    2 hard-cooked eggs, chopped

Boil potatoes in skins until tender; peel and dice, keeping hot. Fry bacon until crisp; drain and crumble. Measure ¼ cup bacon fat and return to skillet. Saute onions lightly in measured fat. Add salt, pepper, vinegar, wine and sugar. Heat; pour over hot potatoes. Add chopped eggs; mix lightly to blend the dressing through salad. Serve immediately, while hot.

NOTE: This would make almost any meat or poultry menu a distinguished one — served with any favorite dinner wine, red, white or Rosé.

SPINACH SALAD & DRESSING

(8 servings)

Phil Hiaring, Wine Institute, San Francisco

    ⅔ cup salad oil
    ¼ cup California wine vinegar
    2 tablespoons California Chablis or
        other white dinner wine
    2 teaspoons soy sauce
    1 teaspoon sugar
    1 teaspoon dry mustard
    ¼ to 1 teaspoon curry powder
    ½ teaspoon salt
    ½ teaspoon garlic salt
    1 teaspoon freshly ground pepper
    2 bunches (about 4 qts.) young spinach
    1 pound bacon
    2 hard-cooked eggs, coarsely grated

Combine oil, wine vinegar, wine, soy sauce, sugar and seasonings in a covered jar. Shake well; chill; Meanwhile, thoroughly wash the spinach; tear into pieces, removing stems. Dice bacon; fry until crisp. Mix the bacon and eggs with spinach. Shake dressing again; pour over spinach.

NOTE: This would be good with many types of meat or poultry menus. Choose the accompanying wine according to the main dish served. Most people usually like a red dinner wine with red meats, white with white meats; Rosé with anything.

RANCHER'S TURKEY SALAD

(4 servings)

Mrs. H. T. Woodworth, Allied Grape Growers, Lodi

For a luncheon or Sunday night supper, this could serve as the main course, with hot rolls and dessert. It's an excellent way to use leftover turkey or chicken.

    1½ cups diced cooked turkey or chicken
    1½ teaspoons instant minced onion, or
        2 tablespoons finely chopped raw onion
    ¼ cup California Sauterne or other
        white dinner wine
    1 tablespoon fresh lemon juice
    ½ teaspon salt
    1 cup sliced celery
    2 hard-cooked eggs, diced
    3 tablespoons salad oil
    2 tablespoons drained sweet pickle relish
    1 tablespoon mayonnaise
        Salt
        Shredded lettuce

Combine turkey, onion, wine, lemon juice and salt; let stand 1 hour or longer. Drain, saving marinade. Add celery and eggs to turkey. Combine marinade with oil, relish and mayonnaise; blend well. Pour over turkey mixture; mix lightly. Salt to taste. Serve over crisp shredded lettuce.

My choice of wine to accompany this dish:
CALIFORNIA DEMI-SEC CHAMPAGNE

PORT-CHERRY SALAD MOLDS

(6 to 8 servings)

Mrs. E. Jeff Barnette, Martini & Prati Wines, Inc., Santa Rosa

I live at Blossom Hill Ranch, a half mile from the winery. We grow three kinds of cherries and we always have many kinds of wine on hand. I try to use our ranch produce, and in this recipe I am combining it with good California wine. This salad is perfect with so many kinds of food that I always use the accompanying meat as guide to the type of wine to be served.

    1 cup cherry juice, or cherry juice
        and water to make 1 cup
    1 (3-oz.) pkg. cherry or
        orange-flavored gelatin
    1 cup California Port
    2 cups cooked pitted black cherries,
        drained, or 1 (1-lb.) can
        pitted black cherries, drained
    1 cup chopped nuts

Heat cherry juice to boiling. Add gelatin; stir until dissolved; cool. Add Port; chill until slightly thickened. Fold in cherries and nuts. Turn into individual molds or 1 large mold. Chill until firm. This is good with almost any menu. I sometimes make the salad in an open ring mold and fill the center with chicken salad. This with a hot bread makes a delicious lunch.

NOTE: With such a luncheon, a chilled California Sauterne or Rosé would be delightful. (Mrs. Barnette also says of this recipe that Muscatel may be substituted for Port, if Royal Anne cherries are preferred in making salad.)

SPRING SALAD BUFFET MOLDS

(6 servings)

Mrs. Stanley Strud, California Wine Association, Lodi

1 (3-oz.) pkg. lemon-flavored gelatin
1 cup hot water
¾ cup California Sauterne or other white dinner wine
3 tablespoons California wine vinegar
2 tablespoons sugar
Salt
1 (10-oz.) pkg. frozen mixed vegetables, cooked and drained
½ cup finely diced celery
2 tablespoons grated onion
2 tablespoons chopped parsley

Dissolve gelatin in hot water; add wine, wine vinegar, sugar and salt. Stir well; chill. When mixture begins to thicken, stir in other ingredients. Spoon into 6 individual molds that have been rinsed in cold water or lightly oiled. Chill until firm. Unmold on crisp salad greens; serve with mayonnaise flavored with prepared horseradish. Tomato or pickled beet slices make a nice garnish. This goes well with almost any type of meat or poultry; is attractive for buffet service, with favorite California dinner wine accompanying.

VINTAGE ASPIC

(5 or 6 servings)

Marjorie Lumm, Wine Institute, San Francisco

The most endearing feature of this salad is the fact that it improves with age. It's an excellent tomato aspic to serve as soon as it has set; but refrigerate it for one or two days (carefully covered, of course) and the flavor becomes spectacular.

1¼ cups tomato juice
⅛ teaspoon crushed basil
¼ teaspoon salt
1 (3-oz.) package lemon-flavored gelatin
¾ cup California Sauterne or other white dinner wine
3 tablespoons California wine vinegar
⅓ cup crumbled blue cheese

Heat the tomato juice, basil and salt to boiling; add gelatin and stir until dissolved. Remove from heat; blend in wine and wine vinegar. Chill until mixture begins to thicken; stir in crumbled cheese. Turn into individual oiled molds or small ring mold; chill until firm. Serve on crisp salad greens, with topping of sour cream sharpened with a little grated horseradish. I like this with beef or veal saute, wheat pilaf, buttered peas, and for dessert fresh strawberries in Champagne.

My choice of wine to accompany this menu:
A CALIFORNIA CLARET WITH BEEF, OR
DRY SAUTERNE WITH VEAL

CRANBERRY-PORT SALAD

(10 to 12 servings)

Mrs. Myron S. Nightingale, Roma Wine Company, Fresno

1 medium-size whole orange, coarsely ground
¾ cup California Port
1 (3-oz.) pkg. raspberry-flavored gelatin
1 (1-lb.) can whole cranberry sauce
1 cup coarsely chopped walnuts
1 cup sour cream

Combine ground whole orange (including peel and juice) with Port in small saucepan. Boil 1 minute. Remove from heat; add gelatin, stirring until dissolved. Add cranberry sauce and nuts. Pour into mold; chill until firm. Unmold; serve with sour cream for dressing.

NOTE: An ideal salad to go with cold sliced turkey, for a buffet supper or luncheon, with California Rosé as beverage. Another delicious molded cranberry salad is made by Mrs. Joseph S. Concannon, Jr., of Concannon Vineyard, Livermore. She uses Claret in hers, with lemon gelatin, chopped celery and crushed pineapple.

SALMON SAUTERNE MOLD delights the eye and appetite. Soften 1 envelope unflavored gelatin in ¼ cup cold water; dissolve in 1 cup hot chicken stock or broth. Add ½ cup California Sauterne or other white dinner wine, 2 tablespoons lemon juice, and grated onion, salt and pepper to taste. Chill until mixture starts to thicken, then fold in 1 (1-lb.) can salmon, drained and flaked. Pour into oiled 1-quart mold, fish-shaped if available. Unmold on crisp lettuce and serve with mayonnaise. Excellent for luncheon main dish.

MOLDED FRUIT MEDLEY

(10 to 12 servings)

Janet Laird, Wine Institute, San Francisco

1 (3-oz.) pkg. lime-flavored gelatin
1 cup hot water
½ cup California Sauterne, Chablis or other white dinner wine
¼ cup sugar
1 teaspoon lemon juice
¼ cup orange juice
1 tablespoon grated orange rind
1 cup whipping cream, whipped
2 medium-size avocados, diced
1 (1-lb.) can grapefruit sections, drained
1 (1-lb.) can Royal Anne cherries, drained
1 (8½-oz.) can crushed pineapple, drained
¼ cup sliced almonds (optional)

Dissolve gelatin in hot water. Stir in the wine, sugar, lemon juice, orange juice and rind. Fold in whipped cream. Fold in the remaining ingredients. Pour into individual molds or a 2-quart mold. Chill until firm. Unmold on crisp salad greens.

NOTE: This would be an attractive main-dish salad for a luncheon, with hot buttered rolls and chilled California Sauterne or Rosé accompanying.

TANGY BLUE CHEESE DRESSING

(5 cups)

Mrs. Frank Lico, San Martin Vineyards Company, San Martin

⅓ cup chopped green onions,
    including tops
2 cups mayonnaise
1 cup sour cream
⅓ cup California wine vinegar
2 tablespoons California Sauterne or
    other white dinner wine
2 tablespoons lemon juice
½ lb. blue cheese, crumbled
1 or 2 cloves garlic, mashed or crushed
½ cup chopped parsley
½ teaspoon salt
¼ teaspoon pepper

Combine all the ingredients; mix with electric beater. Good with barbecued steak, baked potato, green beans and apple pie for dessert.

My choice of wine to accompany this menu:
CALIFORNIA BURGUNDY OR CLARET

NOTE: *Flavorsome and easy. If stronger vinegar flavor is desired, just increase wine vinegar and slightly decrease amount of wine.*

DE LUXE PARMESAN DRESSING

(About 2 cups)

Jim Morse, Beringer Bros., Inc., St. Helena

1 cup salad oil
¼ cup California Rhine or
    other white dinner wine
½ cup California wine vinegar
½ cup grated Parmesan cheese
2 raw eggs
1 teaspoon salt
½ teaspoon *each:* onion salt,
    garlic salt, paprika and
    coarsely ground black pepper
¼ teaspoon Worcestershire sauce

Combine all in mixing bowl. Beat with rotary beater until well blended, or whirl in electric blender. If you do not plan to use the dressing immediately, store in covered jar in refrigerator, and beat well just before serving. Good on tossed green or mixed vegetable salad, with a hearty beef dinner.

NOTE: *And glasses of California Claret, Burgundy or Zinfandel.*

TUSH DRESSING

(About 1½ cups)

Mario Lanza, Wooden Valley Winery, Suisun

½ cup catsup
⅓ cup salad oil
¼ cup California wine vinegar
⅓ cup California Sauterne or
    other white dinner wine
2 tablespoons granulated sugar
½ teaspoon salt
½ teaspoon paprika
1½ teaspoons grated onion
1½ teaspoons pressed or grated garlic,
    or 1 whole clove garlic

Combine all ingredients. Mix well.

NOTE: *What Mr. Lanza really said was "Shake the devil out of it — now eat it." And that's easy to do; it's delicious, as well as simple to make. Good on mixed cold vegetables or lettuce, with lamb chops, Claret.*

POOR MAN'S SALAD DRESSING

(4 servings)

Bill Bagnani, American Industries Corp., Geyserville

½ cup California red wine vinegar
½ cup mayonnaise
½ cup catsup
2 tablespoons prepared mustard
2 to 4 tablespoons California Dry Sherry
    Salt and pepper
1 head lettuce

Let not the little woman throw out dregs of empty mayonnaise, catsup and mustard jars. Store in rear of refrigerator. Disregard the precise measurements above. When sufficient jars are available, rinse each jar with a little wine vinegar. Pour the rinsings into the mayonnaise jar with Sherry, salt and pepper. Shake real well till dressing is smooth, light pink in color and delightful to taste. Quarter lettuce head, pour over dressing and serve.

NOTE: *Mr. Bagnani's directions, above, are as lucid and flavorful as the California wine and wine vinegar used in recipe. A good, practical idea.*

RIESLING SALAD DRESSING

(1½ cups)

Brother Timothy, Mont La Salle Vineyards, Napa

This is an original recipe.

½ cup California Riesling, Rhine
    or other white dinner wine
¼ cup lemon juice
¾ cup salad oil
1 teaspoon salt
½ teaspoon freshly ground pepper
    Dash garlic salt

Combine all ingredients; mix well.

NOTE: *A simple, satisfying blend on crisp greens. Perfect with game hen menu suggested on Page 63 — with the same wine accompanying.*

AVOCADO DRESSING LIVERMORE

(1¾ cups)

Mrs. Charles Rezendes, Cresta Blanca Wine Co., Livermore

1 ripe medium-size avocado
¼ cup sour cream
½ teaspoon onion salt
¼ teaspoon Worcestershire sauce
    Dash Tabasco sauce
1 teaspoon lemon juice
½ cup blue cheese
¾ cup oil
¼ cup California white wine vinegar
¼ cup California Sauterne, Rhine
    or other white dinner wine

Remove seed and peel avocado; mash until smooth. Blend in sour cream, onion salt, Worcestershire sauce, Tabasco sauce and lemon juice. Mash cheese until fairly smooth; blend in oil, wine vinegar and wine. Combine with avocado mixture; chill. Serve over crisp lettuce wedges or toss with salad greens.

NOTE: *Smooth and creamy, pleasantly different. Particularly good with barbecued chicken and the same white wine, or a Rosé.*

DESSERTS

Never underestimate the most basic of all final menu courses: a glass of dessert wine by itself. A California Port, Muscatel or Cream Sherry, rich with only the natural grape-sweetness, crowns any dinner and needs no bolstering by prepared desserts. (Many prefer a bit of cheese as complement, an unsurpassed combination.) If family tradition calls for a special dessert, it can still be as simple and easy to serve as wine-topped fruit or ice cream or pudding. But for more festive occasions, wine of course adds immeasurably to the making of elaborate pies or cakes or flaming desserts. The extra preparation here is often part of the fun. Whatever your pattern, the helpful thing is to have wine on hand—then you're ready for anything.
These recipes suggest the many variations in desserts cooked and served with wine.

DELANO PEACH DELIGHT
(4 servings)

Harry Baccigaluppi, Calif. Grape Products Corp., Delano

This dessert caps any meal. Italian macaroons or amaretti served with the following will add a final touch of elegance.

    4 nectarine or Elberta peach halves
       Vanilla ice cream
    ½ cup California Muscatel, Port
       or Sherry
    4 maraschino cherries

Place a nectarine or peach half in bottom of each of 4 sherbet glasses. Cover with ice cream. Pour 2 tablespoons wine over each serving; top with a cherry.

NOTE: *Simple, but so good; another proof of the great ease of adding wine to make food even better. Any favorite dessert wine would be suitable accompanying, or to end the dinner.*

CHAMPAGNE DESSERTS need not be extravagant. Buy small bottles, to pour over drained fruits at the table. Or, pour the Champagne on the fruits from a large bottle, then serve the rest as beverage. If served promptly, the Champagne bubbles are retained in any uncooked dessert. Even in a cooked dessert dish, Champagne flavor remains.

PEACHES IN WINE
(Any amount)

Mrs. Herman Ehlers, East-Side Winery, Lodi

Slice as many fresh or frozen peaches as desired into a deep glass bowl, alternating layer of peaches and layer of sugar. When desired amount is ready, pour over California Haut Sauterne or other light sweet wine, until almost covered. Cover tightly; chill 3 hours or longer. (Wine keeps peaches from turning brown.) Serve as dessert or pre-dinner fruit cocktail, adding whatever fruit is in season—strawberries and bits of pineapple are very good.

NOTE: *If you freeze your own peach slices, Mrs. Ehlers suggests that you do not add the wine in advance, before freezing. Pour it over fruit later, while thawing. This is an exceptionally good dessert, and would be pleasant indeed with the same wine served on the side.*

PEACHES sprinkled with California Muscatel and chopped almonds are a great flavor-team.

HOT DESSERTS are especially welcome in cold weather. And they can be fast. Turn a can of peaches with half the syrup into a skillet or saucepan. Add a nip of California Port or Sherry and heat until piping hot. Great with cookies.

STUFFED PEACHES PIEMONTESE

(6 servings)

Mrs. Cesare Vai, Cucamonga Vineyard Co., Cucamonga

This is a wonderful dessert for barbecued suppers.

- 7 fresh peaches
- 2 egg yolks, beaten
- 2 teaspoons ground cocoa
- 6 to 8 macaroons or amaretti, dried and crumbled
- 3 or 4 ground peach nuts (from inside peach seed)
- 1 tablespoon melted butter
- 2 tablespoons California brandy or Sherry
- ½ cup California Sauterne, Chablis or other white dinner wine (optional)

Cut 6 of the peaches in half; remove pit; do not peel. Arrange face up in buttered shallow baking pan. Mash pulp of remaining peach; add egg yolks, cocoa, macaroon crumbs, ground peach nuts, melted butter and brandy or Sherry. Fill peach halves with mixture. Bake in moderately slow oven (325°) for 1 hour. Increase heat to 400° last 10 minutes to brown. Pour white dinner wine over peaches while baking if more sauce is desired. Serve hot or cold.

My choice of wine to accompany this dish:
A CHILLED CALIFORNIA SPARKLING MUSCAT OR MOSCATO SPUMANTE

NOTE: Mrs. Frank J. Pilone of the same winery makes another version of the same dessert, from an old family recipe that includes almond extract and vanilla instead of peach nuts. She prefers a sweet Champagne as accompaniment. Still another version, much simpler, is favored by Mrs. J. B. Cella, II, Cella Wineries, Fresno. Mrs. Cella fills canned peach halves with crushed macaroons mixed with brandy and peach syrup.

BAKED PEARS SAN GABRIEL

(6 servings)

Domenic E. Viotti, Jr., Viotti Winery, San Gabriel

This is a family dessert recipe, taught to me by my mother, Mrs. Virginia Viotti.

- 6 brown baking pears
- 18 whole cloves
- 2 cups California Port
- 1½ cups sugar
- 3 cinnamon sticks

Wash pears, leaving in stem. Insert 3 cloves in lower half of each pear. Place pears in shallow baking dish. Pour over wine; sprinkle over sugar. Break cinnamon sticks into wine. Bake, uncovered, in slow oven (300°) about 2 hours, or until pears are very tender. Baste frequently. Remove cloves just before serving. Serve hot or cold, spooning wine sauce over pears.

NOTE: Sour cream or vanilla ice cream would be good with the pears, and a glass of California Port. (In making the recipe, Burgundy may be substituted for Port. In this case, increase the sugar to 2 cups.)

EPICUREAN BAKED APPLES

(6 servings)

Mrs. Edmund A. Rossi, Jr., Italian Swiss Colony, Asti

- 6 baking apples
  Spices
  Butter
- ¾ cup California Muscatel or Port
  Sour cream (optional)

Bake apples in usual way, adding spices and/or butter as desired. Just before removing from oven, pour 2 tablespoons wine over each apple. Serve hot or cold. A spoonful of sour cream is wonderful on each apple, added at the very last.

NOTE: The same dessert wine would be good accompanying.

STRAWBERRIES AMERICO

(Any amount)

Joseph Ghianda, Ghianda's Winery, Oroville

Americo Ghianda, the founder of our winery, grew both Zinfandel grapes and navel oranges, and he concocted this simple dessert as he was very proud of his fruit. This dish is good following a rich dinner, or to start a meal.

Wash and hull the best strawberries you can buy; sprinkle with powdered or granulated sugar. Pile into sherbet glasses and pour about ¼ cup fresh orange juice over each glass of berries. Fill the rest of the glass with California Zinfandel or other red dinner wine. (If a sweeter wine is preferred, use Port.)

NOTE: Really good, with either the dry or sweet wine. Another who likes a California Burgundy to marinate sugared berries is Mrs. Joe Cooper of Wine Advisory Board, San Francisco. The same wine used on the berries would be fine for beverage accompaniment.

STRAWBERRIES IN CHAMPAGNE

(4 to 6 servings)

Louis A. Benoist, Almaden Vineyards, Los Gatos

Stem a quart of large strawberries. (Do not wash; rinse with California white dinner wine.) Sprinkle with California brandy; chill. Before serving, sprinkle with sugar. At the table, pour California Brut Champagne over the berries; serve at once.

My choice of wine to accompany this dish:
THE SAME CALIFORNIA BRUT CHAMPAGNE

NOTE: An excellent treatment. And rinsing the berries in white wine is a good idea; water often makes them watery in flavor. (Many cooks avoid washing fresh mushrooms in water, for the same reason.) This is a popular dessert among California winemaking families, with variations. Mrs. Stanley Strud of California Wine Association, Lodi, marinates her strawberries in Champagne for 1 or 2 hours. Mrs. Alvin Ehrhardt of United Vintners, Inc., Lodi, uses frozen strawberries and adds frozen pineapple chunks. She removes fruit still frosted from packages, pours Champagne over fruit in serving bowl, stirs gently until frost is thawed, then serves immediately while the Champagne is still bubbling. An easy, refreshing dessert after a festive dinner.

WINE TASTER'S BANANAS

(4 servings)

W. W. Owen, California Grape Products Corp., Delano

- 4 bananas
- 2 tablespoons melted butter
- 1/3 cup California Muscatel
- 2 tablespoons brown sugar
- 1/8 teaspoon ground cloves
  Pinch of salt
- 4 tablespoons lemon juice

Arrange 4 peeled bananas in shallow pan. Combine all other ingredients and pour over bananas. Bake under broiler, basting frequently, until fruit is delicate brown.

NOTE: A new twist on an old favorite. The same dessert wine served on the side would be a flavorful dinner finale.

SHERRIED ORANGES

(Any amount)

Mrs. Louis P. Martini, Louis M. Martini Winery, St. Helena

This is an easy light dessert after a rich meal. The dish is especially good with plain pound cake.

Place drained, canned mandarin orange sections in individual serving dishes. Pour a little California Cream Sherry over each serving. (If the Cream Sherry is quite heavy, use 1 part Dry Sherry to 2 parts Cream Sherry.) Let stand in refrigerator 2 to 3 hours before serving. If desired, top with whipped cream.

My choice of wine to accompany this dish:
CALIFORNIA CREAM SHERRY

NOTE: Delectable. Sour cream could also be used. Another nice combination is diced oranges with grapes, in California Light Muscat, as recommended by Brother Gregory of Mont La Salle Vineyards, Napa.

SHERRIED GRAPEFRUIT

(2 servings)

Otto Gramlow, Beaulieu Vineyard, Rutherford

Cut grapefruit in half and section. Pour in just enough California Sherry to be level with tops of sections. Sugar to taste and serve chilled. Or, cover each Sherried grapefruit half with 2 tablespoons brown sugar and dot with 1/2 teaspoon butter. Place under broiler until lightly browned; serve hot. Hot or cold, Sherried Grapefruit is fine for first or final course at luncheon or dinner.

NOTE: If served at the end of a meal, accompany the grapefruit with a glass of California Cream Sherry or other dessert wine.

CANNED FRUITS become something special when wine is added. Try a little California Sherry over canned kadota figs.

GRAPEFRUIT ALASKA

(3 servings)

Kenneth B. Fry, Calif. State Fair & Exposition, Sacramento

This is a good dessert to serve after a rather heavy dinner, as it is not actually what you would call a "rich" dessert. The tartness of the grapefruit serves to give it the lightness one seeks after a heavy meal.

- 3 large grapefruit
- 6 tablespoons California White Port
  or other dessert wine
- 3 small scoops vanilla ice cream
- 2 egg whites
- 1 teaspoon sugar
  Dash salt

Cut grapefruit across 1/3 from stem end. With a sharp knife, loosen each segment from membrane. Cut membrane loose from bottom of fruit; remove. In each cavity formed, place a scoop of ice cream; pour over 2 tablespoons wine. Beat egg whites until stiff but not dry; add salt and sugar. Top each fruit with 1/3 of the meringue. (Be sure edges are sealed with meringue, and top is well covered.) Bake in moderately hot oven (400°) for 3 to 4 minutes or until meringue is nicely browned. Serve immediately.

My choice of wine to accompany this dish:
CALIFORNIA DEMI-SEC OR SWEET CHAMPAGNE,
OR A SWEET ROSÉ

NOTE: This is not only delicious, but spectacular—a dessert to delight your guests. It's quite easy to make. Grapefruit may be prepared in advance, with the wine added, then stored in refrigerator, covered. When ready to add ice cream and meringue, first stir the grapefruit segments gently, to blend the wine flavor throughout.

SARATOGA FRUIT CUP

(6 to 8 servings)

Mrs. Otto E. Meyer, Paul Masson Vineyards, Saratoga

- 4 cups fresh fruit in season (apples, oranges, grapes, cherries, melon, etc.— peeled, pitted and sliced)
- 1/4 cup California brandy
- 1 cup California Riesling, Chablis or other white dinner wine
- 2 tablespoons orange flower water
- 1/4 cup sugar

Combine equal parts of several kinds of fruit in a glass or ceramic bowl. Sprinkle with liquids and sugar. Cover; refrigerate at least 4 hours.

NOTE: Equally refreshing and eye-appealing: a glass of California Champagne or a Rosé as accompaniment.

LISA FRUIT CUP

(6 servings)

Mrs. William Bonetti, Charles Krug Winery, St. Helena

This is an original recipe.

- 1 apple
- 1 pear
- 1 orange
- 1 banana
- ½ cup fresh strawberries
- 1 (buffet-size) can apricots, drained
- ¼ cup orange juice
- 1 tablespoon lemon juice
- ¼ cup sugar
- ¼ cup California Port

Grate apple and pear; dice remaining fruit. Combine in large bowl. Sprinkle with orange and lemon juice. Add sugar and Port; toss lightly. Keep at room temperature 2 hours, then chill.

NOTE: *Mrs. Bonetti says that some fruits could be substituted for the above, but that the apple and orange should never be omitted. This would be particularly appealing with a glass of California Port.*

SAUTERNE FRUIT COMPOTE

(6 servings)

Mrs. Herman L. Wente, Wente Bros., Livermore

This is a good dessert after a hearty meat course.

- 3 ripe peaches
- 6 apricots
- 1 cantaloupe
- ¼ cup orange juice
- 2 cups California Sweet Semillon, Haut Sauterne or other light sweet wine
- Maraschino cherries

Peel peaches; cut into thick slices. Cut apricots in half, removing pits. Trim rind from melon, remove seeds and cut meat into chunks or balls. Place fruits in shallow dish; pour over orange juice and wine. Marinate for at least 1 hour. (Keep it cool, but do not refrigerate.) Garnish with cherries at serving time. Accompany with very plain cake slices, cookies or lady fingers.

My choice of wine to accompany this dish:
CALIFORNIA SWEET SEMILLON OR SAUTERNE

FRUTTA AMABILE

(4 to 6 servings)

Mrs. Louis P. Martini, Louis M. Martini Winery, St. Helena

- 1 fresh ripe pineapple
- Sugar
- California Light Sparkling Muscat or Champagne
- Maraschino cherries

Split pineapple in half, lengthwise through fruit and green top. With a grapefruit knife, remove core; cut pineapple in chunks. (Save shells for serving.) Place pineapple chunks in glass bowl; add sugar to taste. Pour over wine; marinate for 2 to 3 hours. To serve, return fruit to shells, add a little more wine and garnish with cherries.

My choice of wine to accompany this dish:
CALIFORNIA LIGHT SPARKLING MUSCAT

WINE-SPICED PRUNES

(8 to 10 servings)

Myrtle F. Cuneo, Regina Grape Products Co., Etiwanda

These prunes make a good dessert served with cheese and crackers—but may also be served for breakfast, or as a salad, with cottage cheese.

- 1½ cups prunes
- 2 cups water
- 1 (3-inch) stick cinnamon
- ½ teaspoon allspice
- ¼ cup brown sugar
- ½ cup California Port

Combine prunes, water, cinnamon and allspice in saucepan; cook until tender, about 25 to 30 minutes. Stir in brown sugar and Port. Cover tightly and let stand until cold.

NOTE: *The prunes become even more plump and flavorful if they stand overnight before using. Would be especially good with a glass of the same Port alongside.*

HONEYED GREEN GRAPES

(4 servings)

Mrs. Robert Weaver, U. of Calif. Dept. Viticulture & Enology

This is good after any heavy dinner requiring a light, refreshing dessert.

- 1 lb. Thompson seedless grapes (about 2½ cups)
- OR 2 buffet-size cans seedless grapes
- 1 teaspoon lemon juice
- ¼ cup honey
- 2 tablespoons California Sherry or brandy
- ½ cup sour cream

Wash grapes; remove stems. Mix lemon juice, honey and Sherry or brandy; pour over grapes. Refrigerate overnight and serve in tall crystal sherbet glasses. Just before serving, top with sour cream.

NOTE: *Ideal after-dinner drink to follow this would be a Cream Sherry.*

PLUM FLUFF

(6 servings)

Mrs. Edmund Accomazzo, Cucamonga Winery, Cucamonga

This recipe is Polish in origin, but has been used in our family for years. It is satisfying but not filling — delicious after a heavy meal.

    1 cup California Burgundy, Claret
       or other red dinner wine
  1¼ cups sugar
    2 lbs. fresh plums
    4 egg whites
    ½ teaspoon vanilla

Combine wine and 1 cup sugar in a saucepan; bring to boil, stirring until sugar is dissolved. Add plums; cover and simmer 20 to 25 minutes, or until plums are soft. Beat whites until they form soft peaks; gradually beat in remaining ¼ cup sugar and vanilla until stiff and glossy. Pour hot plums and juice into baking dish or 6 individual casseroles. Spread meringue over fruit. Bake in moderately hot oven (375°) about 12 minutes. Serve hot.

NOTE: *A fruity-flavored Port could follow this, for after-dinner sipping.*

RHINE FARM LEMON CREAM

(8 to 10 servings)

Mrs. Otto Dresel, Rhine Farm Vineyards, Sonoma

(This recipe was contributed with Mrs. Dresel's permission by Mrs. Frank H. Bartholomew of Buena Vista Vineyards, Sonoma, who writes:)

This pudding is light as air—perfect climax to a heavy dinner. The Dresel Champagne family of Germany planted the great Rhine Farm Vineyards in Sonoma, which were ended by Prohibition. But laws could not abolish good living among the vineyards of Sonoma. Of enduring fame are the Dresel recipes, of which this is one. (Before 1890, leaf gelatin was used, if available; or you boiled meat bones and skimmed off the gelatin. Then came Mr. Knox.) Garnish this with a lemon leaf and blossom, if a lemon tree grows in your garden.

    5 eggs, separated
    1 cup plus 2 tablespoons granulated sugar
      Juice and grated peel of 1 lemon
    1 envelope plain gelatin
    ¼ cup cold water
    ¾ cup California White Riesling (Johannisberger)
      or other white dinner wine, heated

Combine egg yolks, sugar, lemon juice and grated peel; beat 10 minutes. Soften gelatin in cold water; dissolve in hot wine. Add slowly to egg mixture. Beat egg whites until stiff; fold into gelatin mixture. Chill; serve mounded high in parfait or sherbet glasses.

My choice of wine to accompany this dish:
CALIFORNIA WHITE RIESLING (JOHANNISBERGER)

PUDDING-IN-A-HURRY

(6 servings)

Mrs. Fred Perelli-Minetti, A. Perelli-Minetti & Sons, Delano

    1 (3¼-oz.) pkg. vanilla pudding mix
  1½ cups milk
    1 teaspoon shredded orange rind
    ¼ teaspoon salt
    ¼ cup California Sherry
    ½ cup whipping cream
    1 box fresh strawberries **or**
      2 large bananas

Make pudding mix as directed on package, but using only 1½ cups milk. Add salt, orange rind. Remove from heat; stir in Sherry; cool. Beat cream until stiff; fold into cooled pudding. Wash and hull berries (or peel and slice bananas). Divide fruit in 6 dessert dishes; top each serving with pudding. Garnish with extra whipped cream and fruit, if desired.

NOTE: *This is a light, fresh dessert to which the wine contributes a very subtle richness. A glass of California Cream Sherry on the side would be highly suitable.*

PORT OF NAPA GELATIN

(8 servings)

Brother Timothy, Mont La Salle Vineyards, Napa

    2 envelopes unflavored gelatin
  1¼ cups water
    ¼ cup lemon juice
    1 cup sugar
    1 cup orange juice
    1 cup California Port
      Red food coloring (optional)
      Whipped or sour cream
      Seedless grapes

Soften gelatin in ½ cup cold water; add ¾ cup boiling water; stir until gelatin dissolves. Add lemon juice, sugar, orange juice and Port. If desired, add a few drops of red food coloring to intensify the color. Pour gelatin into large wine glasses (or other serving dishes); chill until firm. Served topped with whipped cream and a seedless grape.

NOTE: *A glass of Port or a Light Muscat would be pleasurable accompanying this dessert.*

ROSÉ STRAWBERRY CREAM

(6 servings)

Viola Moehrle, Wine Advisory Board, San Francisco

    1 (8½-oz.) can crushed pineapple
      California Rosé wine
    1 (3-oz.) package strawberry gelatin
      Few grains of salt
    1 pint vanilla ice cream

Drain pineapple thoroughly. Add wine to pineapple juice to make 1 cup liquid; heat to boiling. Combine liquid with gelatin and salt, stirring until dissolved. Blend in ice cream. Chill until slightly thickened; fold in pineapple. Spoon into individual serving dishes; chill until firm. Serve topped with whipped cream.

My choice of wine to accompany this dish:
A SEMI-SWEET CALIFORNIA ROSÉ

SHERRIED CARAMEL CUSTARD

(6 servings)

Paul Huber, E. & J. Gallo Winery, Fresno

- 3 eggs
- 1/3 cup sugar
- 1/4 teaspoon salt
- 1 1/3 cups evaporated milk
- 1 cup water
- 6 tablespoons California Sherry
- Caramel Sauce (see below)

Beat eggs lightly; stir in sugar, salt, milk and water, stirring until sugar is dissolved. Blend in Sherry. Pour into custard cups; set in pan of hot water. Bake in moderate oven (350°) about 1 hour, or until barely set. Cool. Turn out in dessert dishes and top with Caramel Sauce.

CARAMEL SAUCE: In saucepan, mix 1 tablespoon cornstarch, 1/3 cup brown sugar and dash of salt. Gradually add 2/3 cup California Sherry and 1/3 cup cold water, stirring until mixture is smooth. Stir over low heat until sauce boils and thickens; continue cooking another minute or two until it is clear. Remove from heat and add 2 tablespoons butter or margarine. Cool. Pour over custards and top with 1/2 cup toasted coconut. (This makes about 1 cup of sauce.)

NOTE: *Would be perfection followed by a glass of California Cream Sherry as after-dinner drink.*

CHAMPAGNE JELLY

(8 servings)

Kenneth B. Fry, Calif. State Fair & Exposition, Sacramento

- 2 envelopes plain gelatin
- 1/2 cup California strawberry wine
- 1/2 cup granulated sugar
- Dash salt
- 2 cups hot water
- 1 1/2 cups California Champagne, chilled
- Whipped cream
- Maraschino cherries or strawberries

Soften gelatin in strawberry wine. Add sugar, salt and hot water; stir until gelatin and sugar dissolves. Chill until mixture begins to thicken. Whip Champagne quickly into slightly thickened gelatin; pour into parfait glasses. Chill until firm. Top with whipped cream and a maraschino cherry or fresh strawberry before serving.

NOTE: *Some of the Champagne bubbles are retained in this airy dessert, if Champagne is whipped into thickening gelatin as directed. An attractive climax to a festive dinner, with Haut Sauterne or Champagne accompanying.*

BRANDY PUDDING SELMA

(12 servings)

Mrs. Walter Staley, Western Grape Products, Kingsburg

We enjoy this for Christmas or other holiday meals. Top of pudding can be decorated with candied fruit, if desired.

- 1 1/2 cups chopped pitted dates
- 1 teaspoon soda
- 1/3 cup California Sherry
- 2/3 cup boiling water
- 1/4 cup butter or margarine
- 1 cup sugar,
- 1 egg, beaten
- 1 1/4 cups sifted all-purpose flour
- 1/4 teaspoon baking powder
- Dash of salt
- 1 cup chopped nuts
- Brandy Sauce (see below)

Combine dates and soda; pour over Sherry and boiling water; let stand. Meanwhile, cream butter and sugar; beat in egg. Sift together flour, baking powder and salt; add to creamed mixture. Add date mixture and nuts. Pour into a buttered 8 x 12" pan; bake in slow oven (300°) for 1 hour. Pour Brandy Sauce over hot pudding. Serve with whipped cream.

BRANDY SAUCE: Combine 2 cups sugar, 1 cup water and dash of salt in a saucepan; bring to boil; cook 5 minutes. Add 1 teaspoon butter or margarine, 1 teaspoon vanilla and 1/4 cup California brandy.

NOTE: *A glass of California Muscatel, Port or Cream Sherry would be appropriate with this festive, rich-looking dessert.*

FOOD FOR THE GODS

(6 to 8 servings)

Mrs. Kurt G. Opper, Paul Masson Vineyards, Saratoga

- 2 cups California Riesling, Chablis or other white dinner wine
- 3/4 cup sugar
- 1 teaspoon vanilla
- 6 eggs, separated
- 2 tablespoons cornstarch
- 1/4 teaspoon salt
- 24 macaroons or vanilla wafers
- 2 tablespoons powdered sugar

Combine wine, sugar, vanilla, egg yolks, cornstarch and salt in a saucepan; bring to boiling, stirring constantly; remove from heat. Cover bottom and sides of a 8 1/2" square casserole with macaroons or vanilla wafers. Beat egg whites until stiff; fold half into cooked mixture; pour over cookies. Sweeten other half of egg whites with powdered sugar; spread evenly over mixture in casserole. Bake in moderate oven (350°) about 15 minutes, or until meringue is lightly browned. Remove from oven; cool.

NOTE: *Rich, yet exquisitely light and fluffy. A glass of Haut Sauterne or Champagne would be a fitting accompaniment.*

ZABAGLIONE CLASSIC

(4 servings)

Mrs. August Sebastiani, Samuele Sebastiani, Sonoma

This is a very old Italian dessert, good after a heavy dinner or any lunch. It is especially nice because it can be made on the spur of the moment.

    3   egg yolks
    ½   cup sugar
    ¼   cup California Sherry
        Grated rind and juice of 1 lemon

Measure ingredients into top of double boiler; place over boiling water. Beat constantly with a rotary beater until mixture thickens and mounds like whipped cream. Remove from heat. Serve hot or chilled in tall parfait glasses by itself, or as a topping for sponge cake or canned fruit.

My choice of wine to accompany this dish:
CALIFORNIA CHAMPAGNE

NOTE: *Mrs. Bruno T. Bisceglia of Bisceglia Bros. Wine Co., Fresno, recommends spooning Zabaglione as a sauce over Sherry-soaked sponge cake, or similar plain cake. This is one of the most popular desserts among California winemaking families.*

EASY ZABAGLIONE

(8 servings)

Mrs. Albert J. Puccinelli, Puccinelli Vineyards, San Mateo

    3½ cups cold milk
    2   (4 ½-oz.) pkgs. instant
        vanilla pudding mix
    ½   cup cold California Sherry

Measure milk into a bowl; add pudding mix. Beat slowly with rotary beater 1 minute. Add Sherry; beat ½ minute longer. Pour into serving dishes. Top with whipped cream, as a pudding dessert.

NOTE: *This version of Zabaglione could also be used as a cake sauce. Sherry or Champagne would be a welcome flavor-mate.*

WARM THE BRANDY very slightly in a double boiler before you ignite it, when you want to serve a flaming dessert. To keep the flame burning longer, set a lump of sugar on top of the dessert, and pour the warmed brandy over all. Touch your match to the sugar.

APPLE CHARLOTTE FLAMBÉ

(10 to 12 servings)

Dr. J. F. Guymon, U. of Calif. Dept. of Viticulture & Enology

This is especially recommended for a Thanksgiving dinner dessert—or for any fall or wintertime party when good apples are available. It is very easy to flame, and is as tasty as it is spectacular.

    3   lbs. apples
    2   cups granulated sugar
    2   tablespoons California Sherry
    ¼   cup butter or margarine
    ⅓   cup California brandy
    1½   to 2 cups fine dry bread crumbs

Pare apples, halve and seed; slice thinly. Place slices in a bowl; add about ⅓ cup sugar and Sherry. Cover; let stand 2 to 3 hours, turning occasionally with a large spoon. In buttered shallow baking dish, place layer of apples; sprinkle with part of the bread crumbs and remaining sugar; dot with butter. Repeat layers until dish is filled (should be closely packed). Place dish in shallow pan of hot water; bake in moderate oven (350°) for 1½ hours. Remove and place dish on tray or platter. Pour over brandy which has been sweetened and warmed. Set aflame and serve. Top servings with sweetened whipped cream flavored with vanilla and brandy.

My choice of wine to accompany this dish:
A FRUITY-FLAVORED CALIFORNIA MUSCATEL
OR HAUT (SWEET) SAUTERNE

ROYAL WINE TORTE

(10 to 12 servings)

Mrs. Edmund Accomazzo, Cucamonga Winery, Cucamonga

This dessert is of Hungarian origin. It may also be made with a red dinner wine, such as Burgundy.

    ¾   cup California Rhine, Chablis
         or other white dinner wine
    ¾   cup sugar
    1   teaspoon fine dry bread crumbs
    1½   cups very finely chopped walnuts
    1   (6-oz.) pkg. semi-sweet
         chocolate pieces
    6   eggs, separated

Combine wine, sugar, crumbs, nuts and chocolate pieces in a saucepan. Cook over low heat, stirring constantly, until chocolate is melted and mixture thickens, about 15 minutes. Cool to lukewarm. Beat egg whites until stiff, but not dry. With same beater, beat yolks until light. Stir yolks into cooled chocolate mixture; fold in whites. Spread this batter in a well-buttered, lightly floured 9 x 12″ loaf pan. Bake in moderately slow oven (325°) for 50 to 60 minutes. Cool in pan; serve cut in squares. Top with whipped cream or vanilla ice cream, and sprinkle with chopped nuts, if desired.

My choice of wine to accompany this dish:
CALIFORNIA CHAMPAGNE OR CHABLIS

THIRSTY TORTE

(8 servings)

Mrs. Herman Ehlers, East-Side Winery, Lodi

4 eggs, separated
¾ cup sugar
1 cup sifted all-purpose flour
1 teaspoon baking powder
½ teaspoon salt
⅓ cup melted butter
1 teaspoon vanilla
  Wine Sauce (see below)

Beat egg whites to soft peaks; gradually add ¼ cup sugar, beating until stiff. Beat yolks with remaining ½ cup sugar until thick and lemon colored; fold into meringue. Sift dry ingredients together; fold into eggs. Gently fold in melted butter and vanilla. Pour into 2-qt. casserole. Bake in moderately hot oven (375°) for 30 minutes or until done. When done, poke holes all over cake with a fork or a skewer; spoon over Wine Sauce. Sprinkle with coconut or chopped nuts. Top with whipped cream or ice cream.

WINE SAUCE: Combine 2 cups sugar and 2 cups water in a saucepan; bring to boil; cook until soft ball forms in cold water. Add ½ cup California Sherry.

NOTE: *Tantalizing with a glass of Cream Sherry, as dessert or mid-afternoon refreshment.*

CREAMY REFRIGERATOR CAKE

(12 servings)

Mrs. Charles M. Crawford, E. & J. Gallo Winery, Modesto

This is a good dessert for company dinners, as it is made the day before and easy to serve, although very elegant. Since it is rather rich, we prefer to serve it after a fairly plain meal, such as roast beef or lamb, with rice or potatoes and tossed green salad.

24 macaroons
½ cup sugar
1 tablespoon plain gelatin
¼ teaspoon salt
¼ teaspoon nutmeg
1 cup milk
3 eggs, separated
½ cup California Dry Sherry
1 cup whipping cream

Butter an 8" or 9" cakepan; line with macaroons. Crumble remaining macaroons and make bottom crust (filling in any holes). Save some crumbled macaroons for top. Mix together sugar, gelatin, salt and nutmeg in top of double boiler; cook until thickened. Cool slightly; stir in Sherry. Chill. Beat egg whites until stiff. Whip cream and fold it and egg whites into gelatin mixture. Decorate top with remaining macaroon crumbs. This cake is better after standing overnight in the refrigerator.

My choice of wine to accompany this menu:
CALIFORNIA ROSÉ OR BURGUNDY

NOTE: *A luscious cake, that could also shine as a mid-afternoon or late-evening refreshment, with glasses of Cream Sherry.*

PORT-PINEAPPLE FRUIT CAKE

(2 loaves or 1 large tube pan)

Mrs. E. Sonnikson, Sonoma County Co-Op Winery, Windsor

Make this cake before Thanksgiving, and it will be nicely mellowed by Christmas.

2 cups (1 pkg., 16-oz. size) mixed candied fruits
2 cups seedless raisins
1 cup chopped dates
1 cup chopped walnuts
1 (No. 2) can crushed pineapple, drained
1 cup California Port
¾ cup shortening
1 cup brown sugar, firmly packed
¼ teaspoon cinnamon
¼ teaspoon nutmeg
¼ teaspoon cloves
4 eggs, well beaten
2½ cups sifted all-purpose flour
1 teaspoon baking powder
1½ teaspoons baking soda
1 teaspoon salt

In large bowl, mix together candied fruits, raisins, dates, nuts and pineapple. Pour Port over fruits; set aside, stirring occasionally. Meanwhile, cream shortening, brown sugar and spices until light and fluffy; blend in beaten eggs. Sift dry ingredients together; add to creamed mixture. Stir in fruit and wine mixture, mixing well. Grease and flour 2 (9x5x3") loaf pans or 1 large tube pan. If 2 pans are used, divide batter equally or pour into large pan. Bake in slow oven (300°) for 2 hours or until wooden cocktail pick inserted in center comes out clean. Remove from pans; cool thoroughly. Wrap in cloth moistened with brandy, then in heavy waxed paper or foil. Store in covered container or in cool place for at least 1 week before cutting.

My choice of wine to accompany this dish:
CALIFORNIA SHERRY

QUICK EASY WINE CAKE

(16 to 20 servings)

Mrs. W. H. Lubsen, Wine Advisory Board, Washington, D.C.

The flavor here can be varied in successive bakings, by using Dry, Medium or Cream Sherry. The cake has a light, spongy, pound-cake texture.

1 (1-lb. 3-oz.) pkg. yellow cake mix
1 (3¾-oz.) pkg. vanilla instant pudding mix
4 eggs
¾ cup oil
¾ cup California Sherry
1 teaspoon nutmeg

Combine all ingredients. Mix with electric beater about 5 minutes at medium speed. Pour batter into greased angel food cake pan. Bake in moderate oven (350°) about 45 minutes or until done. Cool in pan about 5 minutes before turning out on rack. Sprinkle with powdered sugar.

My choice of wine to accompany this dish:
A CALIFORNIA SHERRY

ALMOND SHERRY COOKIES

(About 3 doz.)

Joseph Ghianda, Ghianda's Winery, Oroville

- ½ cup butter or margarine
- ⅓ cup granulated sugar
- 2 egg yolks, unbeaten
- 1 cup almonds, coarsely ground
- ½ teaspoon grated lemon rind
- ¼ teaspoon vanilla
- ¼ cup California Sherry
- 1 cup sifted all-purpose flour
- ⅛ teaspoon salt

Cream butter; add sugar gradually. Add egg yolks; beat until light and fluffy. Add ½ cup almonds, lemon rind and vanilla. Stir in Sherry alternately with flour and salt, sifted together. Drop by tablespoon onto remaining almonds sprinkled on waxed paper. Toss dough until coated with nuts. Quickly shape into balls, about 1" in diameter. Place on lightly greased baking sheet. Place on upper rack of moderate hot oven (400°); bake 12 to 15 minutes, or until delicately browned.

My choice of wine to accompany this dish:
CALIFORNIA SHERRY

NOTE: *These are not sweet cookies, and could be served with any wine at any time, as a refreshment. A similar cookie is made by Mrs. Leo Demostene of Soda Rock Winery, Healdsburg, who uses anise extract instead of the vanilla.*

APRICOT-WINE COOKIES

(About 9 dozen)

Mrs. Laura M. Quaschnick, Bear Creek Vineyard Assn., Lodi

- 1 cup butter or margarine
- 1 cup sugar
- 1 cup brown sugar
- 2 eggs
- 2 teaspoons vanilla
- 3½ cups sifted cake flour
- 2 teaspoons baking powder
- ½ teaspoon salt
- Apricot-Wine Filling (see below)

Cream butter and sugars. Beat eggs with vanilla until light. Sift dry ingredients; add to creamed mixture alternately with eggs. Chill dough. Divide dough in half; roll out each half on lightly floured board to oblong shape (14 x 10 x ¼"). Spread each half with Apricot-Wine Filling; roll like a jelly roll. Wrap in waxed paper; chill several hours or freeze. Slice about ¼" thick with thin-bladed sharp knife. Place on greased baking sheet; bake in hot oven (400°) for about 8 minutes.

APRICOT-WINE FILLING: Combine 1 (7-oz.) pkg. dried apricots, chopped, ¾ cup sugar, juice of 1 lemon and ¾ cup California Muscatel in a saucepan. Let stand 1 hour to soften. Bring to boiling; cook, stirring constantly, until mixture thickens. Cool. Add 1 cup chopped walnuts and, if necessary, a little additional Muscatel to bring to spreading consistency.

NOTE: *A very good cookie; would be worth freezing a batch, to have on hand. California Muscatel would be the ideal beverage.*

MENDOCINO NUT DROPS

(About 4 doz.)

Mrs. John Parducci, Parducci Wine Cellars, Inc., Ukiah

This is our favorite cookie.

- 1½ cups butter or margarine
- 1¾ cups sifted powdered sugar
- ¼ teaspoon salt
- 3⅓ cups sifted flour
- ½ cup California Dry Sherry
- 1 cup finely chopped walnuts

Cream butter thoroughly. Gradually add sugar, beating until well blended. Mix in salt. Add flour alternately with Sherry, mixing well. Stir in nuts. Drop by small teaspoonfuls on greased baking sheet. Bake in moderate oven (350°) for 20 to 25 minutes.

NOTE: *Delicious with any light sweet wine or dessert wine, for dessert or an afternoon refreshment.*

QUICK CAKE DESSERT: Sprinkle slices of leftover sponge or pound cake with Port, Muscatel or Cream Sherry. Or, pile pieces of angel food cake in sherbet glasses; moisten with any of these wines and top with whipped or ice cream.

THIN some raspberry, strawberry, boysenberry or cranberry jelly or jam with California Port. Heat and serve over pound or angel food cake. It's terrific, and so easy.

SHERRY BALLS

(About 60 balls, 1" size)

Mrs. Albert J. Puccinelli, Puccinelli Vineyards, San Mateo

- 2 (7¼-oz.) pkgs. vanilla wafers, finely crushed
- ½ cup honey
- ¾ cup California Sherry
- 4 cups finely ground walnuts
- Granulated sugar

Combine wafer crumbs, honey, Sherry and walnuts; mix well. Shape into round balls (about 1" in diameter); roll in sugar. Store in metal can or cookie jar. Flavor improves with age.

NOTE: *With these on hand, unexpected guests would be no problem. A good mid-afternoon or evening refreshment with glasses of California Cream Sherry or other dessert wine. Raymond H. Mettler of Bear Creek Vineyard Association, Lodi, makes a similar delicacy, Brandy Balls, mixing 2½ cups vanilla cookie crumbs, 1 cup sifted powdered sugar, 2 tablespoons cocoa, ¼ cup California brandy, 1 cup walnut meats (chopped fine) and 3 tablespoons corn syrup. He recommends similar procedure and storing.*

PORT-DATE PINWHEELS

(3 to 5 doz.)

Mrs. Laura M. Quaschnick, Bear Creek Vineyard Assn., Lodi

Actually any basic ice box cookie recipe will do here for the cookies themselves. Using the Port-Date filling is my own experiment.

- ½ cup butter or margarine
- ½ cup granulated sugar
- ½ cup brown sugar (packed)
- 1 egg, beaten
- ½ teaspoon vanilla
- 2 cups sifted all-purpose flour
- ½ teaspoon soda
- 1 teaspoon salt
- Port-Date Filling (see below)

Cream butter and sugars thoroughly. Add egg and vanilla; mix well. Sift dry ingredients together; add to creamed mixture; mix well. Chill dough. Divide dough in half; roll out one half into rectangle ¼" thick. Spread with ½ chilled Port-Date Filling; roll up like a jelly roll. Repeat with remaining half of dough. Wrap rolls in waxed paper; chill several hours. Slice ¼" thick; place on greased cookie sheet. Bake in moderately hot oven (400°) for 8 minutes.

PORT-DATE FILLING. Combine 1 lb. chopped pitted dates, ½ cup sugar and ½ cup California Port in saucepan. Bring to boiling; cook, stirring constantly, until mixture thickens slightly. Cool. Add ½ cup chopped walnuts just before ready to spread on dough. If mixture seems too thick to spread easily, thin with little additional Port.

NOTE: A delightful cookie, served either with ice cream, as a dessert, or with glasses of California Port as an anytime refreshment.

BABS' BABA

(10 servings)

Mrs. D. C. Turrentine, Wine Advisory Board, San Francisco

- 1 (1-lb. 1-oz.) pkg. pound cake mix
- ⅓ cup California Sherry
- ⅓ cup orange juice
- ½ cup sugar
- ½ teaspoon grated orange rind

Following package directions, bake pound cake. While baking, combine other ingredients in small saucepan. Bring to boil, lower heat and simmer about 10 minutes; cool. Cool baked cake in pan until lukewarm; gently poke holes all over top surface, inserting fork tines as far as possible. Carefully spoon orange syrup over cake top. Slice; serve warm or cold, plain or topped with whipped cream.

NOTE: Delicious, interesting and quick. A glass of California Cream Sherry would be good either on the side or following the dinner.

DESSERT WINE DUMPLINGS

(10 to 12 servings)

Mrs. Kurt G. Opper, Paul Masson Vineyards, Saratoga

- 3 eggs, separated
- 3 tablespoons cornstarch, or flour or fine dry bread crumbs
- 3 tablespoons sugar
- Shortening
- 3 cups California Haut Sauterne or other light sweet wine

Beat egg yolks until thick and lemon colored; add cornstarch, flour or crumbs and sugar. Beat whites until stiff; fold into yolk mixture. Heat kettle of shortening to just below boiling. Drop egg mixture a teaspoonful at a time into hot shortening; cook 1 or 2 minutes. Remove dumplings to a bowl. Sweeten wine to taste, if desired; heat and pour over dumplings. Serve hot.

NOTE: Light and delicate. An unusual dessert that would harmonize beautifully with a glass of Haut Sauterne, Sweet Semillon or Champagne.

DAVIS DATE BARS

(About 16 bars)

Mrs. Klayton Nelson, U. of Cal. Dept. Viticulture & Enology

- 1 cup dates, finely cut
- 1 cup granulated sugar
- ½ cup California Sherry
- ¼ cup water
- 1 tablespoon lemon juice
- 1 teaspoon lemon rind
- 1 cup chopped nuts
- 1 cup brown sugar
- ¼ teaspoon salt
- 1 teaspoon baking soda
- 1¾ cup uncooked quick-cooking rolled oats
- 1½ cups flour
- ½ cup butter or margarine

Combine dates, sugar, Sherry and water in saucepan. Bring to boil; reduce heat and simmer, stirring frequently, until mixture is quite thick. Remove from heat; add lemon juice, rind and nuts. Cool. Meanwhile, mix dry ingredients. Work in butter to make a crumbly mixture. Spread half or crumbs in greased 8" pan; pat down firmly. Spread cooled date mixture evenly over crumbs; top with remaining crumb mixture, patting down firmly. Bake in moderate oven (350°) for 30 minutes. Cool in pan; cut into small squares.

My choice of wine to accompany this dish:
CALIFORNIA MUSCATEL OR PORT

SHERRY CREAM PIE

(8 servings)

Mrs. Lewis A. Stern, E. & J. Gallo Winery, Modesto

This is really a company dessert, and gets lots of oh's-and-ah's from guests who love good eating.

    1½   cups fine graham cracker or
         zwieback crumbs
    1¼   cups sugar
    ½   cup butter or margarine, melted
    6   egg yolks
    ½   teaspoon salt
    1   envelope unflavored gelatin
    ½   cup cold water
    2   cups whipping cream
    ½   cup California Sherry
         Finely sliced almonds

Combine crumbs, ¼ cup of sugar and melted butter. Press into a buttered 9″ pie plate; chill 20 minutes. Meanwhile, beat egg yolks until light; stir in remaining cup of sugar and salt. Soften gelatin in cold water; dissolve over boiling water in top of double boiler. Pour gelatin over egg mixture, stirring constantly. Whip cream until stiff; fold into egg mixture. Stir in Sherry. Cool mixture until it begins to thicken; pour into pie shell. Chill until firm. Sprinkle with almonds.

NOTE: *Rich, high and handsome. Mrs. John Parducci of Parducci Wine Cellars, Inc., Ukiah, makes a similar Sherry Cream Pie, using chocolate cookie crumbs in the crust. She recommends the dish as a bridge dessert. A Cream Sherry would be good sipping after such a pie.*

FROZEN BRANDY PIE

(1 pie, 9″ size)

Mrs. J. F. Guymon, U. of Calif. Dept. Viticulture & Enology

Guests always comment on the flavor surprise here, since this Bisquit Tortoni dessert looks like cheesecake.

    20   graham cracker squares, finely crushed
    3   tablespoons brown sugar
    ⅓   cup soft butter or margarine
    1   cup whipping cream
    ½   cup sifted powdered sugar
    2   tablespoons *each* California Sherry
         and brandy; *or,* ¼ cup brandy
    4   egg yolks

Combine graham cracker crumbs, brown sugar and soft butter; mix thoroughly. Press firmly into 9″ pie pan, reserving about 2 tablespoons crumbs for topping. Chill. Meanwhile, whip cream until stiff; blend in powdered sugar, Sherry and/or brandy (at low speed, if mixer is used). Beat egg yolks until light-colored and thick; fold into cream mixture. Pour filling into chilled crust; top with reserved crumbs. Freeze. Serve frozen.

My choice of wine to accompany this dish:
CALIFORNIA CREAM SHERRY

SHERRIED FRESH PEACH PIE

(1 pie, 9″ size)

Sandra Hancock, Wine Institute, San Francisco

    4½   cups sliced fresh peaches
    ¾   cup sugar
    ¼   teaspoon salt
    3   tablespoons flour
    ¼   cup California Sherry
    2   tablespoons butter or margarine
         Pastry for double 9″ pie crust

Thoroughly wash and slice fresh peaches. Combine sugar, salt and flour; sprinkle over peaches in saucepan. Add Sherry and butter and heat just to boiling. Turn into pastry-lined pie pan. Cover with top pastry, sealing edges together well. Cut a few slits in the top. Bake in hot oven (400°) 35 to 40 minutes, until pastry is golden.

My choice of wine to accompany this dish:
CALIFORNIA CREAM SHERRY

VALLEY MINCE PIE

(Any amount)

Evins Naman, Wine Institute, Fresno

This idea couldn't be any simpler, but it makes all the difference in that festive holiday pie. Follow the pie directions given on the mincemeat package, adding 1 or 2 tablespoons of California Muscatel or Sherry for each cup of mincemeat used. I guarantee your guests will enjoy it.

My choice of wine to accompany this dish:
CALIFORNIA MUSCATEL OR CREAM SHERRY

VINEYARD HOLIDAY PIE

(6 servings)

Mrs. James Concannon, Concannon Vineyards, Livermore

    2   cups canned pumpkin
    1   (15-oz.) can (1⅓ cups)
         sweetened condensed milk
    1   egg
    ½   teaspoon salt
    ½   teaspoon cinnamon
    ¼   teaspoon ginger
    ¼   teaspoon nutmeg
    ½   cup California Sherry
    ½   cup hot water
    1   (9″) unbaked pastry shell

Combine pumpkin, condensed milk, egg, salt, spices, Sherry and water in a large bowl. Beat or stir vigorously until well blended. Pour into unbaked pastry shell. Bake in moderately hot oven (375°) for 50 to 55 minutes. Cool. Serve topped with sweetened whipped cream.

NOTE: *It is important to use the sweetened condensed milk in this recipe, NOT evaporated milk. The pie is delicious for any festive occasion. Follow it with a glass of Cream Sherry as after-dinner beverage.*

TANGY LEMON-RAISIN PIE

(6 servings)

Mrs. James E. Roberts, Bakersfield

1½ cups sugar
¼ cup flour
1 egg
⅛ teaspoon salt
3 tablespoons lemon juice
1½ teaspoons grated lemon peel
1 cup water
1 cup California Sherry
1 cup raisins
1 (9") unbaked pie crust

Mix sugar, flour and egg. Add all other filling ingredients and cook over hot water in top of double boiler for 15 minutes, stirring constantly. Cool. Pour into unbaked pie crust. Bake in hot oven (450°) for 10 minutes. Reduce heat to moderate (350°); bake 20 minutes longer.

NOTE: *Wonderfully rich; would be good with sour cream topping. Port, Cream Sherry or any other dessert wine could follow for after-dinner enjoyment.*

RAISINS added to desserts are easily softened or "plumped" first, by soaking for a couple of hours in a little Port or Muscatel or other dessert wine. This also adds to the flavor.

SOFTEN Cheddar cheese spread with California Sherry, to top apple pie. (Or use some Sherry in the apple filling.) Serve **with** Cream Sherry on the side: a perfect dessert.

SEAFOAM PUDDING SAUCE

(2 cups)

Mrs. Fred Snyde, Woodbridge Vineyard Association, Lodi

½ cup soft butter or margarine
1 cup brown sugar (firmly packed)
1 egg, well beaten
Few grains salt
¼ to ½ cup California Sherry

Cream butter and sugar thoroughly until fluffy. Add egg and salt; beat well. Just before serving, gradually beat in Sherry. Place over hot water in top of double boiler; heat, beating constantly, until soft but not syrupy (about 1 minute or so).

NOTE: *A light, thin, foamy sauce, different and most enjoyable. Serve a glass of California Cream Sherry as the after-dinner drink.*

ANOTHER TOPPING is suggested by Brother Gregory of Mont La Salle Vineyards, Napa, who likes a Light Muscat poured over vanilla ice cream. And Kenneth Knapp of Selma Winery, Selma, recommends adding 2 tablespoons California Sherry or Muscatel per pint to your favorite recipe for homemade vanilla ice cream, or the prepared mix.

PORT WINE SUNDAE SAUCE

(4 or 5 servings)

Dan C. Turrentine, Wine Advisory Board, San Francisco

A panel of 48 wine men tried this sauce on vanilla ice cream. It was rated excellent by 34, good by 11, and fair by 3.

¼ cup sugar
1 tablespoon cornstarch
1 cup California Port
1 teaspoon lemon juice
2 teaspoons grated orange rind

Mix sugar, cornstarch. Add to Port in saucepan and cook, stirring frequently, until thickened and clear, 5 to 10 minutes. Add lemon juice and orange rind. Chill. Pour over vanilla ice cream or pineapple sherbet. More or less sugar may be used, according to taste. For an especially fruity, delightfully different flavor, use Muscatel in sauce instead of Port.

My choice of wine to follow this dish, with demitasse:
THE SAME WINE TYPE USED IN THE SAUCE

NOTE: *See also PORT VOLCANO recipe, listed below, for an even easier topping: Port alone. Muscatel is good the same way, simply poured over ice cream by itself. Another who prefers a cooked Port sauce similar to the above is Mrs. Myron Nightingale of Roma Wine Company, Fresno. Her recipe includes butter and nutmeg instead of the lemon juice and grated orange rind; she recommends her sauce especially for puddings or custards.*

PORT VOLCANO

(1 serving)

Dick Davis, Wine Advisory Board, San Francisco

This is good any time, any place—a simple answer to anyone who fears wine cookery is involved or time-consuming. In a wine glass (any wine glass), make a mountain of vanilla ice cream. Spoon out a crater in the ice cream mountain. Into the crater pour deep red California Port. The striking color of the Port overflowing onto the white ice cream makes a beautiful dish. Quick and delicious.

My choice of wine to accompany this dish:
CALIFORNIA RUBY PORT

NECTAR FOR FRUITS

(1½ cups)

Myrtle F. Cuneo, Regina Grape Products Co., Etiwanda

This syrup for fruits makes a very light and refreshing dessert.

> ¾ cup honey
> 1 tablespoon grated lemon peel
> 2 tablespoons lemon juice
> 2 tablespoons orange juice
> ⅓ to ½ cup California Sherry

Combine all ingredients in small saucepan. Cook, stirring constantly, over low heat for 5 minutes. Remove from heat; cool slightly; pour over fruit. (Any variety of fresh fruit, cut in serving or bite-size pieces, may be used. If grapes are used, cut in half to absorb syrup.) Allow fruit to marinate in syrup several hours before serving. Garnish with fresh mint leaves for color and flavor, if desired.

NOTE: *A sip of Sherry or any other favorite dessert wine would be a pleasing accompaniment.*

GALA DESSERT TOPPING

(About 1½ cups)

Mrs. Leonard Maullin, Paul Masson Vineyards, Saratoga

This topping will keep several days, refrigerated and covered. It is delicious on fresh or canned fruits or cake slices, and unique on chocolate or coffee ice cream.

> 8 to 10 coconut macaroons (dry type)
> 1 tablespoon brown sugar
> ½ cup California Cream Sherry
> 1 cup sour cream
> 3 tablespoons chopped roasted almonds

Crumble dry macaroons into very small pieces; add sugar and Sherry. Let stand 30 minutes. Add sour cream and nuts; blend thoroughly. Chill at least 2 hours before serving as a topping for one of the desserts indicated.

NOTE: *Choose the accompanying wine according to the dessert. If the topping is served on fruit or plain cake, a sweet dessert wine would please guests.*

IT'S EASY TO COOK WITH WINE

QUICK TIPS FOR BEGINNING COOKS

If you keep wine on hand just for cooking, remember that once the bottle is opened, some wines have a storage time limit, just as milk does. For storage tips, see Pages 92-93.

Even the busiest cook can turn out a delicious dinner in no time and with little effort. Stir up a package of instant vanilla pudding using ¼ cup California Sherry for part of the liquid. Add a pinch of salt and a bit of grated lemon or orange rind.

Whether you're frying meat or fish, a little California white dinner wine (such as Sauterne or Chablis) stirred into the pan drippings makes a quick, easy sauce. The rest of the bottle of wine does double duty **with** dinner.

For best-ever spaghetti, cook your favorite kind as you like it, soft or firm. Heat canned spaghetti sauce with a bit of California Claret and a pinch of rosemary or oregano. Combine sauce and spaghetti with plenty of Cheddar or Parmesan cheese—and serve with glasses of the same red dinner wine.

Easiest way to enhance grilled poultry, lamb or fish is with a simple wine-butter baste. Combine equal parts butter and California Rosé, or a white dinner wine such as Sauterne or Rhine. Add squeeze of lime and pinch of your favorite herb. Heat in small pan, and brush often over meat while cooking.

Beef stew tastes extra good zipped up with California Claret, a bouillon cube or two, and a pinch of curry or herbs to your liking. Use your favorite canned stew as base; add about ½ cup red dinner wine. If gravy is a trifle thin, stir in a little cornstarch mixed with water. A tablespoon of butter or bacon drippings does wonders for the flavor.

Every wine type known can be—and is—used for cooking. Wines labeled as "cooking wines" are wines with a little salt added. If you are using one of these, you may want to reduce the amount of salt called for in the recipe.

Almost any fresh fruit or melon will be delicious as a salad or appetizer if it is molded in gelatin flavored with white dinner wine. Substitute ½ cup of California Chablis or Sauterne for ½ cup of the water. To make the jellied base as refreshing as the fruits themselves, allow a few sprigs of fresh mint to simmer in the hot water used to dissolve the gelatin. Lemon juice will add piquancy, too.

Improvise with canned soups for a hearty chowder. Start with creamed soup such as mushroom, chicken, shrimp or celery. Add canned mushrooms, shrimp or other seafoods. Then flavor with California Sherry, 1 to 2 tablespoons per cup of chowder.

To give added flavor and texture to less expensive cuts of meat (pot roasts, stews, etc.), before cooking marinate them overnight in California dinner wine (either red or white) to cover. Turn meat occasionally. Add seasonings as desired: salt, whole peppercorns or ground pepper, onion and garlic, bay leaves and other herbs, cloves and other spices, etc. When you're ready to cook the meat, strain this marinade, if necessary, and use some of it as all or part of the liquid in cooking the meat. You'll be well rewarded with extra flavor and a new tenderness in the finished dish.

Chicken that is to be broiled or barbecued is especially good if marinated in white dinner wine for several hours before cooking.

Smoked Sausages, browned quickly, then poached in California Sauterne, are delicious fare any meal of the day. Thicken the rich pan liquid slightly with a little cornstarch in water, and spoon over sausages and eggs.

WINE SERVING

Wine is one of the easiest things to serve at a dinner—far less complicated than carving a roast, for example. Simply set your wine glasses to the right of the water glasses, as shown below. Put the bottle on the table, or near at hand, so guests may be invited to help themselves. In this case, the wine is usually passed as soon as the first course is begun.

First step in opening a bottle is to **cut** the foil or cellulose band just below the bottle lip, using a small sharp knife. This keeps the bottle neat-looking. Wipe the bottle mouth before inserting corkscrew, and again after cork is pulled.

A good corkscrew **is** important, and can make wine serving really simple. In shopping for a corkscrew, look for one with rounded worm-edges, as shown below. (A sharp-edged worm tends to tear or break the cork.) A good corkscrew will also have its point in line with the worm-spirals, and an **open** space down the center of the worm. (Several newer-type cork-pullers are now on the market which eject corks instantly by means of a harmless gas. These are fast, efficient, and spark conversation.)

Champagne service is a little different, of course—requiring no cork-puller but you. Untwist, loosen and remove the wire hood; the foil comes off with it. Hold your thumb on the cork meanwhile, so it won't pop out. Slant the bottle, pointed away from guests. Twist the cork gently, or work it from side to side if needed; hold onto it as it leaves the bottle. (It will still pop!) Have a glass handy to catch the first foam.

If you like to be a bit ceremonious, pour a little wine into your own glass first, as host or hostess. This old traditional custom allows the host to taste first, to assure that the wine is sound. It also gives him, not his guests, any cork bits in the bottle.

Another, more important custom is never to fill a dinner wine glass more than half or two-thirds full. Air space above the wine gathers aroma and bouquet, necessary to full enjoyment of the wine. It also lessens chance of spilling. This is why a **large** wine glass is preferable.

Give the bottle a slight twist before raising it from the glass. This catches drops on bottle-lip, avoiding drip. Or, use one of the dripless metal wine pourers; or, one of the foam-lined flower-wreaths around the bottle neck, to catch stray drops.

When do you need a wine cradle, or serving basket, as shown below? Hardly ever, unless you like wine accessories. A cradle merely helps you to handle a **very old, red wine** gently, to avoid stirring up any sediment in the bottom of the bottle. Another method is to decant or pour off an old red wine into another bottle or decanter, slowly, without shaking sediment.

When do you need an ice bucket? Again, hardly ever, unless you simply like the looks of one. A bucket **will** chill faster; but most people prefer the refrigerator. If you use a bucket, keep it handy to the dinner table, and wipe bottle with napkin before pouring. Never wrap napkin clear around bottle, hiding label. (For temperature tips, see Pages 92-93.)

A large bottle of **dinner wine or Champagne** ("fifth" size—see Page 8) will pour 6 servings, averaging 4 ounces or more. A gallon jug will give 32 servings this size. The sweeter **dessert and appetizer wines** are usually poured in smaller, 2½- to 4-ounce servings. In this case, a large bottle will provide as many as 10 servings, and a gallon jug as many as 50.

YOUR WINE DESERVES CARE

WINE is a living thing, and as such is subject to change. (For example, wine is the only beverage that can continue to improve after bottling.) After the bottle is opened, a few simple precautions will help to protect the wine's flavor, color, aroma and bouquet, so that it will give maximum pleasure.

DINNER WINES (such as Burgundy, Sauterne or Rosé), because of their low alcohol content, averaging about 12%, are perishable once they are exposed to air, as is milk. Once opened, such wines should be used within a few days, even though the bottle is recorked or recapped and stored in the refrigerator. Gallon dinner wines may be decanted, or transferred after opening to sterilized smaller bottles, if they are not to be used within a few days. (Fill to ¾" or 1" from the top, to allow for expansion, then recork or use a screw-cap bottle.) In many families, dinner wine left over from meals or entertaining is used later in the kitchen, for cooking.

AN OLD TRICK that helps keep dinner wines longer, if intended for cooking use, is to float a thin film of cooking oil on the wine's surface — just enough to seal off the wine from the air in the top of the bottle. (Or, pour wine for cooking into smaller bottles and cork tightly.)

SPARKLING Wines should of course be used immediately after opening, before their sparkle is lost. If you do have leftover Champagne, however, the same rules apply as above; it will still be good for a few days, even without the bubbles. If recorked and returned to a refrigerator within a few minutes after opening and serving a portion, the remainder of the bottle will probably have a fair amount of bubbles the next day.

DESSERT or Appetizer Wines (such as Port or Sherry), because of their higher alcoholic content, averaging about 20%, will keep up to several months opened, in partly-filled bottles. Store them in the refrigerator in very hot weather.

IF NATURAL sediment should appear in wine as a result of aging (more likely in a red dinner wine than in other types), stand the bottle upright for 1 or 2 hours before serving. Avoid shaking the bottle. This harmless sediment will then settle to the bottom, and the clear wine may be poured gently. Such wine may be decanted, or transferred from the original bottle to another clean bottle, if desired.

RED Dinner Wine is at its best an hour or so **after** opening the bottle. The flavor really comes up if the wine is opened this far in advance of dinner, to allow the wine to "breathe."

IT'S ALWAYS wise to store wines in a cool, relatively dry place, where temperature is fairly even, with no sudden changes or extremes. **Ideal** storage temperature is between 50° and 60°—with 70° considered the highest safe temperature for long-term storage. (If your

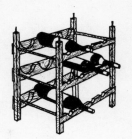

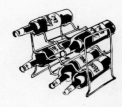

Any cupboard or closet can be converted easily to wine storage. For free booklet of do-it-yourself diagrams, "Little Wine Cellar All Your Own," write Wine Advisory Board, San Francisco 3, California.

Or, you may be able to find ready-made wine racks, of metal or wood, at a reasonable price in local stores. Most of these will fit inside a cupboard or closet.

cellar, closet or wine cupboard gets warmer than 70°, line it with insulating material such as wallboard. The important thing is to avoid extreme changes.)

THIS MEANS wine should not be stored near furnaces, hot water heaters, steam pipes or radiators. It should be kept out of sunlight. Since wall temperatures tend to change sharply, do not store wine right up against an outside wall.

CORKED wines should rest on their sides, if stored long, so that corks will stay moist and air-tight. If you leave corked bottles in their case, turn the case on its side. Screw-cap bottles may stand upright.

IF YOU have a wine cellar or closet, store Sparkling and White Dinner Wines in the lowest racks or bins, because it is cooler there; and Red Dinner Wines in the next section up. Dessert and Appetizer Wines may be stored on top, because they are the least affected by higher temperatures.

WHITE and Rosé Dinner Wines are generally chilled in the refrigerator 1 to 3 hours before serving, and Sparkling Wines 4 to 6 hours. Red Dinner Wines are best at **cool** room temperature. (Not above 70°—in very hot weather, you may want to put a Burgundy into the refrigerator for a while.) There is no rule for Dessert or Appetizer Wines, but the same general customs are preferred by most people: the whiter types like Sherry or Muscatel chilled, the red like Port at cool room temperature. Many persons prefer **all** wines chilled. Your own personal taste is the best guide.

WINE may be stored in the refrigerator, but some authorities feel it is best to use it within 1 or 2 weeks, to avoid slight impairment of flavor. Once it is chilled, however, do not store it again at room temperature. Never chill wine below 35°.

INDEX

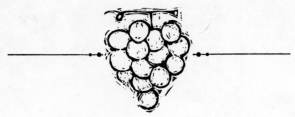